The Psychology of Poker

By

Alan N. Schoonmaker, Ph.D.

A product of Two Plus Two Publishing

www.twoplustwo.com

FIRST EDITION

FOURTH PRINTING
JANUARY 2005

Printing and Binding
Creel Printing Co.
Las Vegas, Nevada

Printed in the United States of America

The Psychology of Poker

For information contact: **Two Plus Two Publishing LLC**
600 West Sunset; Suite 103
Henderson, NV 89015
www.twoplustwo.com

ISBN: 1-880685-25-6

DEDICATED TO

***The players and staff at
Atlantic City's Taj and Trop,
my "research laboratories."
Thanks, I couldn't have written
it without your help.***

Table of Contents

Foreword
by Mason Malmuth

Two Plus Two Publishing has become recognized as having the best books in the poker/gambling field. But as the years have gone by, we have been criticized for not sufficiently addressing the psychological aspects of poker.

Of course, this isn't true. Many of the tactics that appear in our books are based on the psychology of your opponents. For example, against an opponent whose psychological make up causes him to bluff at a high rate, we would tell you to up your calling frequency. We might also suggest raising with marginal hands in multiway pots, to make sure that you do not get overcalled.

Thus, psychology plays an important role in this decision as it does in a large number of poker decisions. It is an important part of the game and should never be neglected.

There is however an area that until now our family of books have not addressed. It is your psychology and my psychology. Put in other words, it is what makes all of us "tick" and why we each tick a little bit differently.

When at the poker table have you ever wondered why some players seem extremely aggressive while others are passive? Why some are tight and others loose? Furthermore, have you ever wondered why some tactics seem to come naturally to you while other important tactics don't?

This text, written by Alan N. Schoonmaker, Ph. D. will answer many of these questions. It will attempt to explain why you are what you are at the poker table, and what drives your opponents to make the decisions they do. In addition, it suggests strategy adjustments to improve your results against different types of opponents, and it also suggests adjustments that you should make on a personal basis so that you will play better and enjoy the game even more.

In time, I believe that Schoonmaker's text will become recognized as one of *the* important poker books. It is meant to be read along with more strategic oriented books, especially David Sklansky's *The Theory of Poker*. Dr. Schoonmaker does not claim to be an expert on poker theory or strategy. In fact, he explicitly admits that he is a psychologist, not a strategy expert. Instead of providing advice on strategy, he refers you to the specific pages of our own or other author's books that provide strategic advice *you* need (which may be very different from what other readers need). Thus if you are one of the many beginning or intermediate poker players who can't quite get a "complete grip of things" at the poker table, then this book is for you.

About Alan Schoonmaker

Alan Schoonmaker earned his Ph.D. in industrial psychology at Berkeley. He taught and did research at UCLA, Carnegie-Mellon, and Belgium's Catholic University of Louvain. After running management development at Merrill Lynch, he worked as a consultant in twenty-nine countries on all six continents.

He has written or co-authored three research monographs and five books on industrial psychology. His work has been translated into French, German, Spanish, Swedish, Japanese, and Indonesian. A major theme of his work is understanding and adjusting to different kinds of people, which is also the theme of this book.

His attitude toward our game is unique for a poker writer:

> "I play only in smaller games because maximizing my profits is much less important to me than relaxing and learning about people. I became a psychologist because I enjoy people-watching, and a cardroom is a wonderful place to do it.
>
> "Players in small games are much more interesting than the more serious players. They are more varied, open, and relaxed. They laugh more, tell better stories, and never forget that the purpose of playing any game is to have fun.
>
> "As the stakes get higher, the players become more serious and homogeneous. Most of them study the same books, know the same odds, and try to use similar strategies. In the smaller games there are more rocks, more maniacs, more calling stations, more nerds, more 'Deluded Experts,' and more oddballs, which means I learn more and get better material for my writing.
>
> "Most poker writers focus on how the champions think and play, but hardly anything has been written about ordinary

players. I want to help them to understand themselves and the people in their games."

Acknowledgments

Many people helped me to write this book, and I am very grateful for their help.

Most of all, I am grateful to Mason Malmuth for being a tough, constructive editor, and David Sklansky for his helpful suggestions. I have worked with many good editors, but never with two renowned authorities.

John (Rich) Valleau, Billy ("Red") Hodgkiss, and Dave Adams read the entire book and made many valuable suggestions.

Countless players have made comments, suggestions, and criticisms that have shaped this book. I cannot acknowledge them individually — in fact, I don't even know many of their names — but I am extremely grateful.

Michael Carroll has always been there for me, encouraging, commenting, sometimes just listening.

Suzanne DeLaPointe is not a poker player, but she is a great writer, and her editorial suggestions helped me shape the book.

My sister, Sue Ann, did her usual, thorough job of correcting my spelling and grammar. I hate to think of what my work would look like without her help.

My brother, Brian, Doug Lind, and Jim Bogan read and commented on a related book, and their comments improved both books.

Many thanks to the editors of *Poker Digest* magazine for printing a series of articles on selecting and adjusting to different games.

I am also grateful to the editors at *Card Player* magazine for allowing me to reprint slightly different versions of three articles that they published: "The Right Stuff," "Our Deadly Sins," and "The Only Winning Style."

Finally, I need to thank Donna Harris for her meticulous proof reading, and Dave Clint of Creel Printing for his cover design and artwork throughout this book.

Introduction

General Discussion

On a good night, with the right cards, you can beat David Sklansky, Doyle Brunson, Mason Malmuth, or any other professional, but you can never beat yourself. You can be your own best friend or your own worst enemy, and you are probably both.

This book will show you how you beat yourself and tell you how to stop doing it. Many other poker books are about cards, general strategy, and money, and their advice is the same for everybody: "One size fits all." But we beat ourselves in different ways, and we each need to build on our individual strengths and overcome our personal weaknesses. We should also understand why a few players are long term winners, and how to identify and adjust to the many different types of poker players.

We can't do these things without taking a hard look at both ourselves and other players, but most poker players don't do it. Other games emphasize self-criticism and objective analysis. Football and basketball teams review game films to learn how they and other teams play, then revise their game plan for the next opponent. Bridge players conduct endless "post mortems," replaying hands again, and again, trying to improve their skills. Most poker players never even try to analyze their game.

Instead, we whine about our luck and tell "bad beat" stories. Most stories essentially say: "I played my hand well, but this idiot's stupidity, and my terrible luck cost me the pot." It's as if a football coach played the films of a losing game, not to learn how to win next time, but to prove they were unlucky to lose. Bad beat stories may make you feel better, but they do not help your game. In fact, they hurt you by telling other people how you play and excusing your bad results.

Winning poker players do the same thing as winning football coaches and bridge players. They objectively analyze how they and their opponents play, accept responsibility instead of putting all the blame on bad luck, work hard on their game, and ask their friends for critical comments.

This book will be your personal coach. It will help you to examine your play, learn how and why you play the way you do, then provides specific advice that fits *you.*

Most poker books are written by expert players and are geared towards tough games. They are fun to read, but may be irrelevant to you. You are not necessarily a great player, and you may never play against experts. You need a coach who analyzes the way you play, and tells *you* how to beat the people you normally play against.

Most poker writers could probably beat me, yet I'm a long term winner, while more skilled players — including some experts — are often broke. Why? Because I'm honest about my abilities and select games carefully, while they deny their limitations, and keep trying to beat better players or the wrong kinds of games.

I'm like your local tennis pro; he could not make it on the tournament circuit, but his coaching can do much more for your game than all the videos from Pete Sampras and the other greats.

It is fun to watch them stroke so perfectly, and we all enjoy learning about their strategies against each other, but it will not do much for your game. Your local pro will watch the way you play, then tell you how to improve both your strokes and your strategy. This book will do exactly the same thing for your poker.

It will ask you *lots* of questions, including some uncomfortable ones, about how and why you play. Then it will tell you exactly what you have to do differently. At times you will become frustrated, perhaps even angry, which is the reaction you might have to a good tennis coach.

You want him to say, "Nice shot," and he says, "You had to rush that shot because you were out of position." But his coaching will improve your anticipation so you stop rushing your shots.

Good coaches take your game apart, identify your strengths and weaknesses, and tell you how to develop a strategy that fits you. If you take this book seriously, and complete all the irritating questionnaires, it will do the same for you. Those questionnaires provide the foundation for extremely specific recommendations that apply directly to you

Overview of the Book

"Part One: The Right Stuff" asks two questions: "Do you have the 'right stuff?' " and "Why do you play poker?" Both chapters are quite short because they cover only the general principles. A detailed questionnaire in the appendix will tell you how much of the "Right Stuff" you have.

The book begins by discussing these subjects because you are the first player you have to beat. In a moment we will see that Stu Ungar, who some regarded as the world's greatest player, ended up a loser, probably because he never looked objectively at himself. If denial could destroy someone like him, it might be a good idea for you to take a hard look at yourself.[1]

If you don't want to analyze yourself, you can ignore the whole issue of self-analysis and read only the later sections on how to develop your skill, and the ability to adjust to other players. You will improve those skills, but you will not get many of the potential benefits. It's your decision.

"Part Two: The Right Skills" will test and improve two essential skills, reading hands and selecting games. The third skill, adjusting to different players, will be covered in Parts Three through Seven.

"Part Three: Styles and Ratings" describes a system for identifying and understanding your own and other players' styles.

---

[1] A little over a year after winning $1,000,000 in the $10,000 Championship at the World Series of Poker, Unger was found dead in his room at a run down Las Vegas motel.

Parts Four through Seven discuss the four major types of players, loose-aggressive, loose-passive, tight-passive, and tight-aggressive. Each part focuses on one type and has two chapters. The first one is about that style opponent, and it covers recognizing them quickly, strengths, weaknesses, reading their cards, playing against that type of player, and playing in that kind of game.

The second chapter is titled: "If You are a Loose-Aggressive (or other style) Player," and it covers accepting the consequences, understanding your motives, improving your play, selecting the right game, and getting your act together.

This consistent organization enables you to make quick comparisons between types on any subject. For example, how can you quickly spot a loose-passive player? What must you do differently to read the cards of a rock, calling station, or maniac? What should you do when a rock leaves the seat on your left and a maniac takes his place? (Change seats and your entire strategy.)

Other than the books that taught you how poker should be played (which is not my purpose) the two chapters on your own style may be the most valuable words you will ever read about poker, because they focus directly on you. You will learn how good players beat you, why you play the way you do, the effects of your style, the stylistic changes you should make, and the best types of games for you.

"Part Eight: Our Deadly Sins" describes the deadly sins that plague us all.

The *"Conclusion"* ties together our major themes, and suggests ways to continue to develop your game.

Most *"Appendices"* cover subjects that would interfere with the book's flow, such as a detailed questionnaire and whether you should try to make it as a full-time professional. You can ignore the appendices, read them when the text refers to them, or read them after finishing the book.

Appendix C, the "Quick Summaries" gives you a quick overview of the main points for each type of player. Refer to them whenever you need help. For example, if playing against a maniac bothers you, just look at that quick summary before you play to see how to keep calm and adjust your strategy. If you are, say, a tight-passive player, just look at that quick summary frequently to see what games to select and ways to improve your own style.

Appendix D, the *"Suggested Reading"* does not just list the titles of useful books: It and the text will tell you which books and even which pages to read for different kinds of help. The books or pages that would help one player would waste another's time, and they could actually harm a few people. For example, a beginner or loose player, who plays low limit, small ante games, should read, *Seven Card Stud: The Waiting Game*, but it would bore most experienced players and actually reinforce a rock's greatest weakness.

Who Needs Poker Psychology?

If Freud had played poker and ignored the odds and strategic principles, he would have gone broke. He was the greatest psychologist, but the odds and strategy come way ahead of psychology. To play winning poker, you *must* master and apply the odds and basic strategic concepts.

However, just applying them alone will not make you a winner, except at the lowest limits. (So many low limit players ignore the game's odds and basic precepts failing to realize that in most of these games you can win by just playing tightly and applying the basic strategic rules.) However, as you move up, the players get better and smarter, wiping out the edge you can get from mechanically applying a simple set of guidelines.[2]

In many games nearly everyone understands the basic odds and uses a reasonably sound strategy. In that case much of your

---

[2] Generally the better players participate in less hands. But the experts who populate the high limit stud tables actually reverse this trend due to the relatively large ante structure that many of these games exhibit.

winning edge can come *only* from psychology and the appropriate adjustments.

Roy Cooke spelled it out in *Card Player* magazine (June 27, 1997, p. 13). "Poker is a people game... If you want to be successful at the game, you need to be able to read people, get into their heads, think how they think, and make accurate decisions from the information."

David Sklansky has also said the same thing. In *The Theory of Poker,* he states:

> "What we mean by the psychology of poker is getting into your opponents' heads, analyzing how they think, figuring out what they think you think, and even determining what they think you think they think."

The problem is that nobody has told you *how* to do it. The experts provide useful tips and insights, but nobody has constructed any sort of system. They don't provide a system because they don't need or have one. They are *intuitive psychologists, not systematic ones.* They have a natural feel for players, an uncanny ability to understand what other people are thinking and doing. A lot of this comes from experience and the ability to replay a hand or many hands quickly in their minds. But if you are relatively new to poker you won't have much success duplicating their abilities.

In fact, some of them *don't know* how *they know.* It is just a gift, as natural to them as his miraculous moves were to Michael Jordan. When someone unexpectedly blocked him, he responded instantly: Switching hands, twisting his body, and shooting the ball a little higher with a little different spin. He could never tell you how he did it; it was just by feel or instinct.

Great poker players have that gift: They remember how you played a certain hand, or they see a look in your eye, or they sense something from the way you handle your chips, and they make exactly the right play. If you ask why they did it, they probably can't say. It just felt right.

Some authors don't realize that their advice is meaningless because their readers can't apply it. For example, Doyle Brunson wrote in *Super/System* (pages 430 ff):

> "Whenever I use the word 'feel'... I recall what happened... Even though I might not *consciously* do so... I recall that this same play came up (or something close to it) and this is what he did or somebody else did. So I get a feeling that he's bluffing or that I can make a play here and get the pot. But, actually my subconscious mind is reasoning it all out.
>
> "Stick to your **first** impression. Have the courage of your convictions."

If I had his "feel," I would do exactly what he does, but I don't have it, and neither do you. That sort of advice is as silly as telling a young basketball player that he should develop Michael Jordan's reflexes. Those reflexes are a gift that he will never have. He has to work with the abilities he has, just as you and I have to work within our own limitations.

After studying and teaching psychology for many years, I am still amazed by some people's intuition. Let me tell a personal story. I once worked with someone for months. After meeting him for two minutes, my wife said: "He's a crook; don't trust him." I later learned that I should have listened to her, but she never could tell me how she knew; she just did.

If we don't have that gift, nobody can teach it to us. We must rely on what we can develop: Careful observation and systematic logic. I can never make those amazing mental leaps, but *I can tell you how to be right much more often than you are now.*

Being right frequently is much more valuable than making great plays. Winning and losing do not depend upon making great plays, except at the highest levels. For us, the great plays we read about are the equivalent of slot machine jackpots: They get all the live ones' attention, but the casinos always end up ahead by having a little edge over thousands of bets.

The methods described here will give you a little edge here, and a little edge there, enabling you to make the right decisions more often than you do now. How much more often? It is hard to say, but if you choose your games more intelligently, it can mean the difference between winning and losing *immediately*, and, if you make just one more good bet, one more good raise, and save one bad call a night, it will mean thousands of dollars in no time, and you can do much better if you really try.

What's In It for You?

You will *play better*, winning more money or losing less than you do now. You should already know basic strategy. If not, buy the recommended books and start studying.[3] If you know the proper strategies, your problems are making sure you apply them, reading players, choosing the right game, and adjusting your strategy to fit different conditions, are the subjects we will emphasize here.

You will also *enjoy playing* more. Many poker authors act as if everyone plays poker just to make money, but that's nonsense. Poker is a game, and people play it for lots of reasons. We will examine these other motives and look for ways to be more successful *and* have more fun.

You will get these benefits because you will have a much better understanding of:

1. *Your own style*, skill, motives, strengths, and weaknesses.
2. *Other players'* styles, skills, motives, strengths, and weaknesses.

You will therefore be able to:

---

[3] This book will *not* provide instructions on strategy. That's the job of my colleagues at Two Plus Two and other poker writers. I will however, recommend specific pages of various books.

1. *Improve* your own style.
2. *Choose* the right games for you.
3. *Adjust* to different types of players and games.

You will also enjoy the stories. The experts tend to emphasize beating tough games and sometimes discuss great plays by great players. This book is about people like us.

Our Central Principles

This book is based upon eight central principles.

1. Your greatest enemy is denial. The entire gambling industry is based on it, and you can't beat poker without resisting it.
2. You should understand yourself more deeply. Why do you play the way you do? How does your style affect other players and your results?
3. You should focus primarily on the other players. What are they thinking and doing?
4. Playing styles are caused by and reveal people's desires and fears. Understanding why they play the way they do will help you adjust to them.
5. Poker requires betting correctly, not managing cards, and every significant decision directly involves the first four principles.
6. You should "think visibly," (make your assumptions and thought processes explicit). If you think visibly, you can improve your decisions.
7. One of the best ways to improve your results is to change your style.
8. You must constantly adjust to the players in *this* game and *this* pot.

Let's look at these principles in a little more detail.

Principle No. 1: Your greatest enemy is denial. Without denial, the gambling industry would collapse immediately. The casinos know the live ones haven't got a chance, but they keep kidding themselves. It is impossible to beat most casino games, and only a few people consistently beat poker.

Poker winners do *not* deny reality. In fact, they make their profits from *other people's* denial. Every time anybody plays weak cards, or chases hoping to catch a miracle card, or sits in a game with superior players, he is acting like a slot machine player, denying the reality that he is going to lose — perhaps not today, but certainly over the long term.

Most players also deny the truth about their own abilities and even their past results. In fact, they are in deeper denial than the slot machine players. Most casinos have pictures of average people who have won enormous jackpots, but an average poker player will *never* win serious money, and about 90 percent of all cardroom players are long term losers.

You certainly know lots of heavy losers who claim to be good players and insist that they are just unlucky. They may also forget about their total losses, remember and exaggerate their occasional wins, and pretend that they are "about even, maybe a little behind."

Although poker winners are usually realistic, nearly all of them occasionally act foolishly. We all know good players who are always broke because they cannot resist the temptation to play craps, or the horses, or to sit down in games they can't beat. Your way of denying reality is different from mine, but we all do it, and we all pay for it.

The first and most important step to becoming a consistent winner is to stop kidding yourself. If you continue to do so, your skill may let you win a few dollars, but you will still think and act like a loser.

Principle No. 2: You should try to understand yourself more deeply. The poker culture is usually superficial and simplistic, with occasional intense and complex moments. For example, many experts insist that the only or primary reason to play poker is to win money. They overemphasize making money because poker is their business, perhaps their sole income source.

But it is not necessarily your business. You enjoy winning money, but it is still a game, and you play it for lots of reasons: To make money, get some excitement, test your skills, pass time, socialize, and so on. If you say — as so many people do — that you play only for the money, you are denying reality.

Of course, you have the right to do so, but it will cost you. This book will discuss your other motives and show you how your motives and thoughts affect your play and choice of games. It will also help you to see how well you play and why you win in some games, but lose in others.

But knowledge alone is not enough. You must take the next step: *Accepting responsibility for your own results.*

Most losers reject this responsibility. It is part of their denial. That's why they tell bad beat stories. They essentially say, "I would have won if I just had normal luck." But we all have close to normal luck (over the long term), and blaming bad luck for your results *guarantees* that you will never improve.

Whenever I make this point and ask people how their own play could be improved, their reaction tells me whether they are winners or losers. Losers get mad at me for being unsympathetic, and they insist that *nobody* could win with their terrible luck. Winners take the question seriously and analyze the way they played.

Principle No. 3: You should focus primarily on the other players. Although you should analyze yourself, you should focus primarily on the other players. Every expert does it. In fact, a major difference between experts and the rest of us is that the *experts focus intently on the other players, while we focus on ourselves:* The cards in *our* hands, the cards *we* hope to catch, the money *we* have lost or won tonight, or even what we will have for lunch.

In fact, a fast way to evaluate new players is to look at their eyes: Weak players look at their cards or let their eyes wander around, strong players pay attention to the game and study the other players.

If you look carefully, many people will tell you how to beat them. You know that you should be more alert and observant, but you may not know what to look for or what various signals mean. This book will describe many important signals, tell you what they mean, and recommend ways to use them. Just knowing what to look for will help you to see signals you now overlook.

Of course, psychological signals are never 100 percent reliable, and — because poker is a game of deception — some of them are less reliable than usual. The better players are especially likely to send confusing signals, and just reading this book will cause some opponents to send — consciously or unconsciously — some confusing signals.

However, once you know what to look for, it becomes easier to shift your focus. A major goal is to help you to shift your focus to the important information you are now missing.

Principle No. 4: Playing styles are caused by and reveal people's desires and fears. Understanding their drives will help you to beat them. Countless experts have discussed ways to play against different types of players, but they ignore the question of *why* people play in certain ways. If you understand why someone is, say, loose-passive, you can do better against him. This book will help you to understand how and why people play the way they do.

You need to understand their real motives because exactly the same action by two different players means quite dissimilar things. For example, if Bill bets forcefully and loudly proclaims, "I raise," it suggests he has a good hand, while Charlotte is signaling a bluff, and Ed is saying indirectly: "I'm too mad to control myself." Obviously, your best reaction depends upon what they mean, and you can't know that unless you understand their desires and fears.

The key to this understanding is right in front of you. Everybody has a distinctive style, and it expresses and reveals the underlying drives. If you know *how* someone plays, you know a lot about *why* he plays, and vice versa.

By going beneath the surface and looking at these drives, you will make sense out of things that now confuse you. *Why* does an intelligent man like Joe make so many stupid plays? *Why* did you make that bet when you knew it was a mistake? *Why* does Bob go on tilt over little things, but Mary never gets upset? *Why* do you play in this game where you usually lose instead of that one where you usually win? You have asked this sort of question. Now you are going to get some answers.

I will not psychoanalyze you or anyone else. I will just help you to understand and take advantage of your own and other people's motives and fears.

Principle No. 5. Poker requires making bets, not managing cards, and most decisions involve the first four principles. The basic idea of poker could not be simpler. Over the long run we all get about the same number of strong and weak hands. *If you play your hands well, you win. If you do the opposite, you lose.* That's it. End of story.

The critical skill in poker is therefore betting correctly, while in most other games it is card management. Poker involves little more than betting, while in bridge, for example, you have to bid, select a suit, and decide when to play each card. Betting correctly not only allows you to win the maximum on your good hands, but it may also save you a pot that a weak player would lose.

Although the principles are simple, applying them is often difficult because, unlike some other games, *poker hands have relative rather than absolute value.* The critical skill is determining how good your hand is *compared to the other hands.* The great players can make uncanny reads.

For example, on page 34 of *The Biggest Game In Town,* Alvarez reported that Stu Ungar once "called a last bet of several hundred dollars ... holding only a pair of threes, then raked in the pot contemptuously before his opponent showed his down cards, knowing without a flicker of doubt that all the other man had in the hole 'was dreams.' "

Can I help you to make that sort of play? Hell, no, only a few players have this level of hand reading skill. Unless you have a natural gift, it requires much experience and hard work. I don't have that gift, and you probably don't have it either. If you did, you wouldn't be reading this book.

Since we don't have that gift, we need a system, which is exactly what this book provides. It will help you to make the right play more often, and that is what winning poker is all about. Great plays can turn you on, but they have little impact on your bottom line. In fact, some people lose money by being too creative. You have certainly played with "creative geniuses" who lose heavily because they make fancy plays that nobody understands. Then they get mad at the "idiots" who beat them by "being stupid" and at the tight-straight-forward players who just sit there, unimaginatively playing better hands.

Your long term profitability depends primarily upon *how often* you make the right play. You have to get a little edge here, and a little edge there to end up a winner. That is exactly what casinos do. The live ones get the thrill of the slot machine jackpots and keno prizes, but the casinos get their long term profits from having a little edge over many bets.

If you make enough negative expectation bets (ones with bad odds), you *must* lose, no matter how many great plays you make or how many of your hunches work out. If you make enough positive expectation bets, you *must* win, even if you never make a great play. That is what this book will hopefully do for you, give you a little extra edge again and again. Leave the great plays to the "creative geniuses" who would rather show off than win.

Principle No. 6. You should "think visibly." Make your thought processes visible to yourself by verbalizing exactly how you make decisions. An excellent bridge partner once told me:

> "As long as you can tell me *why* you made a bid or played a card, I will never get angry at you because I can straighten

> out your thinking. For example, if you tell me that you played the queen of clubs because you thought the king was on your left, I can review the bidding with you and show you why you should have realized it was on your right. But, if you just played the queen without thinking, I'll get mad."

It was some of the best advice I have ever gotten about card playing or anything else. By making my thought processes visible, I can improve them. Conversely, when I do not think visibly, I make the same mistakes again and again.

This process is the exact opposite of intuition. My dictionary defines "intuition" as "the process of coming to direct knowledge without reasoning or ... rational thought." By that definition nobody can teach intuition. You either have it or you don't.

In fact, intuition, feel, or whatever you wish to call it is not even done by the same part of the brain as logical thinking. The left side of your brain (often called your "left brain") controls logical thinking, while your "right brain" controls intuition, and related subjects such as musical and artistic abilities. Trying to train your right brain to think logically is essentially the same as trying to develop your artistic skills by teaching you the geometrical basis of painting. It just won't work.

Since I don't have intuition, I have studied the way I made good and bad decisions, and I can help you to do the same thing. If you see how you reached a decision, you can learn from your mistakes.

Visible thinking is *not* natural, but, as I will say repeatedly, *it is natural to lose.* Every tennis pro gets clients who try to follow their advice, but complain: "It doesn't feel natural." They often respond: "Of course, it doesn't feel natural. You're used to doing it wrong!"

To become a consistent winner you have to replace your natural impulses with visible thinking. Every winner, except the intuitive geniuses, plays that way. Let's listen as a professional "talks" to himself. The first decision is a simple one; the second is much more complicated.

1. (With a drawing hand and one card to go) "The odds against making my hand are 4-to-1. The pot offers odds of 3-to-1, and the bettor is all in so there will be no more bets. Thus I should fold."
2. (In a hold 'em hand on the flop) "Joe is a moderately tight player who never slow plays big hands. Before the flop he flat called the big blind in an early position; I called, and another player called behind me. The flop is

in three suits. The big blind checked, and Joe bet.

"If he had AA, KK, or AK, he would have raised before the flop. He therefore does not have trip aces or kings or aces and kings.

"He would not have called in an early position with 22 or A2, not even suited. He therefore does not have trip deuces or aces and deuces.

"With two callers behind him he would not bet a pair of kings with an ace on the board. He therefore has an ace, and he would not have called in that position without at least AJ unsuited or A5 suited.

"Since I have AJ, the only hand he could have that would beat me would be AQ, and I can beat most of his possible hands. (Note: Since I can account for two aces, there are 8 ways in which he can have AQ, either suited or unsuited. There are also two ways each that he can have ATs down through A5s for a total of 12 combinations.) Plus he probably would have raised coming in with AQ.

> "If I raise, I will probably knock the player out behind me plus get more money in the pot; and he might even fold.
> "I should raise."

Neither decision could be reached without preparation. For example, you cannot calculate the pot odds if you do not count the pot as bets are made, and every good player does it automatically. You cannot figure out Joe's hand in a few seconds unless you made a mental note that he was a tight player and had flat called in early position, and started thinking immediately about what kind of hand he might have. It is not easy or natural to think that way, but it will pay huge dividends.

Thinking visibly can help you with every aspect of the game, especially when and where you play. If you carefully select your games, you will do much better than more skilled players who are not selective. In fact, if you play reasonably well, the ability to choose the right games can have more impact on your bottom line than anything else you do.

You cannot select the right game without understanding your own style, how it affects other players, and which kind of game is best for you. Most people do not think carefully about that decision; they just take any empty seat, then move if they get bad cards or feel uncomfortable.

Even if they deliberately choose a certain kind of game, they often make a huge mistake. For example, lots of players love games with aggressive players, but can't beat them. You hear them complain all the time, but they never learn. They keep picking those games, losing their bankroll, complaining, building up a stake, and blowing it again.

Visible thinking also applies to so-called money management decisions. Most money management rules are silly superstitions such as "Quit while you are ahead, or when you have doubled your stake, or after you have lost three buy-ins."

Instead, these decisions should be based on a thoughtful analysis of the situation, covering questions such as: Do the others play better than I do? Is the style of the game favorable or unfavorable to me? How well am I playing? Will I enjoy playing with these people? Can I expect to win or lose?

If the answers are positive, you should play regardless of whether you are ahead or behind. If the answers are negative, get out, even if it means taking a nasty loss. It hurts to quit when you are losing badly, but it is a lot better than blowing your bankroll.

Some parts of this book may annoy and frustrate you because you are not used to thinking visibly. You may prefer to act more naturally and impulsively rather than to think visibly and accept responsibility for your decisions. It is much easier to blame bad luck or think in cliches, but, if you want to get the most from poker, it's the way to go.

Principle No. 7: One of the best ways to improve your results is to change your style. *If you play the wrong style, you are going to lose.* It is as simple as that. You can read the books, memorize the odds, even make an occasional brilliant play, but you will end up losing.

The word "style" refers to a consistent *pattern of habits.* Everybody's style contains two basic dimensions, tight-loose (*how many* hands you play) and passive/aggressive (*how much* you bet or raise on different kinds of hands). Many people confuse these dimensions, even though they are quite distinct.

They may, for example, describe two quite different games as loose because both have huge pots. In one game several people call one or occasionally two bets on every round, while in the other only two or three players raise and reraise. Both patterns produce huge pots, but the first is loose-passive, while the second emphasizes aggression.

It is quite easy to beat the first game, much tougher to beat the second one. In addition, the strategy that is optimal for one will not be optimal for the other (and may even cause you to lose).

To win consistently, you must *develop a tight-aggressive style.* In many situations, the key to winning is to decrease your losses on your losers while increasing your profits on your winners. Aggression also increases your chances to win many pots. And the best way to do these things is to become tighter and more selectively aggressive.

The tighter you are, the less you lose on your losers. The more selectively aggressive you are, the more you will tend to win on your winners and the more pots you will win. (However, on a few of your losers you will lose more.) When you merely call, you are responding to another player's initiative; he wants more money in the pot, and you are accommodating him. When you bet or raise, you are initiating the action because you want more money in the pot or you want your opponents to fold.

Aggressive play also produces more winning hands. If you call, you can win *only* by having the best hand. If you bet or raise, you can win in *three* ways:

1. By having the best hand,
2. By knocking out a better hand, and
3. By knocking out a hand that you have beaten now that would have drawn out on you.

The extra money you risk by betting or raising often dramatically increases your chances of winning the entire pot. (This important strategic concept comes up more in stud than hold 'em, but is nevertheless important in both games.)

Nearly all successful professionals are both *tight and selectively aggressive.* Some successful high limit seven stud players are slightly loose (and extremely aggressive). Their success comes from adjusting to the high ante structure of these games and their great reading skills. Most of us can succeed only if we are tight-aggressive. Fortunately, it is easy to become tighter and more aggressive. In fact, the rule for improving your style can be summarized in seven words: *Call less, but bet and raise more.*[4]

---

[4] By "call" I mean enter less pots. When you do in fact enter them however, you may be forced to call quite often due to pot size.

The tight-aggressive style is so unnatural that it can be seen in only a few places besides poker games. Rocks (tight-passive people) are everywhere; they hate risks, act cautiously, and rarely assert themselves. We see maniacs (loose-aggressive) all over the place, showing off, taking foolish risks, loving excitement and attention. The calling station (loose-passive) is just acting out the common desires to go along with other people's initiatives, to respond passively to everything, even when it hurts them.

But tightness and related qualities such as caution and control are not normally combined with aggressiveness. In fact, you will hardly ever see that combination outside of highly specialized occupations such as fighter pilots and police officers.

Because it is so unnatural, the tight-aggressive playing style rarely occurs without lots of work. All you need to become a maniac or calling station is the right personality and enough money to indulge yourself. To become a rock you need the right personality and some study of the odds and strategy. To become a tight-aggressive player takes the right personality, lots of study, and extreme discipline.

Tight-aggressive players are made, not born. Instead of just acting naturally, they have *worked* to hone their skills and develop the right attitudes and habits. You may not want to adopt such an unnatural style. If so, you resemble the tennis hackers who objected that hitting the ball properly "doesn't feel natural."

Good tennis, golf, and other sports require lots of unnatural actions. So does good poker. If you object to doing something unnatural, remember: *It is natural to lose.*

Most players lose precisely because they do what feels natural. They play too many hands, or check when they should bet, or do not raise unless they have a lock, or take lots of other "natural," but self-defeating actions. *If you want to win, you have to do the unnatural things that other winners do.*

Let's look at tennis lessons again. One of the unnatural things that good players do is keep their eyes focused on the ball until after the racket hits through it. It is much more natural to shift your focus at the last instant to where you want to hit it. I've taken lots of tennis lessons, and one coach kept nagging me: "Look at the ball! Look at the ball! Look at the ball!"

Finally, I got annoyed and said, "That's all you ever say. Why don't you tell me what else to do?" He gave me that look that teachers give to inept students and said, "Until you look at the ball, nothing else matters." Exactly the same principle applies to poker. Unless you play against very weak players, *until you play the right style, nothing else matters. You are going to lose.*

If that statement offends you, I apologize, but you probably knew it already. You may have denied it and wished that there was some way to win and still enjoy the pleasure you get from your current style, but you can't do it.

Denying that reality is the same as saying: "I want to lose weight, but still eat whatever I enjoy." The diet gurus pander to this denial with a new "miracle" every week, and they all follow the same depressing cycle. People get excited; their creators make a bundle; but they don't work, and the wishful thinkers switch to the next miracle. If you really want to lose weight, you have to change your eating habits. If you really want to win at poker, you have to change your playing style.

Your style at poker is probably the same as it is at work, home, and other places. You play the way you do because you are what you are. That is another reason to look more deeply at yourself.

We will soon describe the motives that cause people to use various styles. If you understand why you play a certain way, you can stop doing what comes naturally and develop a more effective style. You will not become an expert, but you will become much more successful and satisfied.

Principle No. 8: You must constantly adjust to these players and this pot. You must constantly adjust to the overall game, and you must immediately adjust to the players in this particular pot. This book will spend more time on these adjustments than on any other topic. It will describe the kinds of adjustments you should make in your own style, and the specific adjustments needed to play against every other type of player or game.

For example, for every major type of player and game you will be told where to sit, how to read their cards, what sorts of hands to play or fold, whether you should or should not try to check-raise and lots of other tips.

How to Use This Book

First, skim the whole book quickly to get an overall picture.

Then go through it much more slowly two or more times. *The first time focus on yourself; the second time focus on other people.* Separate these tasks because they conflict with each other: Improving your general style and strategy is quite distinct from adjusting them to beat specific players.

Focus on Yourself First

Even though this book emphasizes adjusting to other players, you are naturally most interested in that fascinating person — you. Read the chapters on the style closest to you at least twice, and refer frequently to the most relevant quick summary.

You may not like those chapters, but they could have an immense impact on you, and you will certainly be surprised by some points. You will see how others quickly identify your style, the strengths and weaknesses of that style, how good players adjust to you, and the results to expect. Pay particular attention to the advice on improving your play and selecting the best games. For many of you that advice can improve your results *immediately.*

Focus on Other Players Second

Concentrate on one style at a time, and focus on just one player you know well and will encounter soon. The best "target" is someone who has frequently beaten you. Make specific plans to beat him next time. Use the appropriate "Quick Summary" to improve your plans and help you during the game. If you focus on him and adjust your game, you may have a delightful surprise. You may even beat up somebody who has been taking your money for ages.

Once you have learned how to cope with him, apply the same principles to other players with the same general style.

Then shift to another style and take the same steps: Focus on one player until you can beat him, then apply the same strategy to similar players.

Then use the book as if it was a dictionary or encyclopedia. When you don't understand a particular player, or you are not sure whether you should play in a certain game, read the appropriate pages. The table of contents is quite detailed to help you find the help you need.

Final Remarks

You are not going to like some of this book. You, I, and almost everyone else want to deny unpleasant realities. However, the natural tendency to deny reality can become your friend instead of your enemy. If you resist it and face reality, you will beat the hordes who deny reality.

Virtually all poker players have a little denial in us. That part of us wants to pretend that only bad luck prevents us from having the results we "deserve." That's why we tell bad beat stories, play in games we can't beat, and complain about our luck.

But we can't afford that luxury. Ours is a brutally realistic game. If we play well and select the right games, we win, maybe not today, but certainly over the long term. If we play badly or select the wrong games, we lose, and we *deserve* to lose.

This book will tell you some unpleasant things you need to hear. It will open your eyes, make you a better player, and increase your earning potential.

If you have a comment or question, email me at alannschoonmaker@hotmail.com. I enjoy hearing from readers, especially when they disagree with me. It forces me to keep learning.

Good luck!

Part One

The Right Stuff

The Right Stuff

Introduction

Part One lays the foundation for the rest of the book by discussing two unusual topics, whether you have the "right stuff" and why you play poker. Most poker books have ignored both subjects because the entire poker culture is uninterested or actively opposed to looking at ourselves.

If you doubt me, just listen to cardroom conversations. You will almost never hear anyone talk about why they play poker (except for macho nonsense such as "I play only for the money"), nor do people discuss how their own drives and attitudes help or hurt them. It just isn't done.

Instead of looking at ourselves, we talk about specific hands, luck, or strategy. If we discuss psychology, the focus is on other people and the ways to beat them, not on ourselves. However, as Pogo once said, "We have met the enemy, and it is us." Or, as Roy Cooke put it: "Only in love do I see more self-denial, lack of honesty with oneself, and bad decisions based on emotion than at poker." (*The Cooke Collection*, p. 269)

We beat ourselves because we do not know ourselves. We repeat our mistakes because we do not perceive why we made them. We do not objectively assess our own strengths and weaknesses, nor do we understand how our own drives — including irrational ones — affect our entire approach to the game.

The next two chapters will begin the self-examination process that continues throughout the entire book. First, we will look at the attitudes and skills that separate the winners and losers. Then we will analyze why you play poker and why you have chosen your playing style.

Do You Have "The Right Stuff?"

Tom Wolfe coined that term for the intangible qualities that distinguished the astronauts from the other hot pilots. Anyone who flies the fastest jets has superb skills, but they had something extra.

Since nobody ever clearly defined it, they had to prove they had it by the most primitive test: *Survival*. If you passed one test, you proved you had it — until the next, and more demanding test, when you had to prove it all over again. If you had it, you kept going higher and higher, while the others proved they didn't have it by washing out of the program or being killed.

Survival is the ultimate test in our little world. We all know excellent players who *seem* to have the right stuff. They read cards like a magician and make miraculous plays, but they are often broke, while less gifted players are consistent winners. What's the difference?

The winners are willing to do whatever it takes to win, but the losers do what makes them comfortable and perhaps enjoy their time at the table too much. Their extreme commitment makes them winners, but you might not want them as a neighbor or brother-in-law.

Here are some characteristics that most winners possess.

Characteristic No. 1: Winners always *demand an edge.* That edge can come from a better hand, a good draw, favorable position, superior skill, greater concentration, or lots of other things. But without it, winners won't play. They will fold their cards, change seats, move to another table, or go home. (The one exception occurs when they will accept a situation without an edge for a short period of time for the sake of a greater long term edge.)

Characteristic No. 2: Winners are obsessed with winning. As Vince Lombardi put it, "Winning isn't everything; it's the only thing." Jack Straus added his version to our mythology when he said: "I'd bust my own grandmother if she played poker with me." Their obsession makes them do lots of unpleasant or unnatural things that others refuse to do. Perhaps the hardest and most important is to "put their egos in their pocket" because egotism can make fools of us all.

One of its most destructive effects is making us care more about what people think of us than what we actually accomplish. We take foolish chances, show off, or give away information to make ourselves look good, even when we know it reduces or wipes out our edge.

Characteristic No. 3: Winners have extreme self-control. Without self-control that obsession can become self-destructive. It can force you to take foolish chances, continue to play long after you have lost your edge, refuse to accept that your hand is beaten or that the game is too tough for you, and do many other stupid things.

Characteristic No. 4: Winners are brutally realistic. They don't kid themselves about their own cards, the other hands, the odds and risks of winning, their own skill, the ability of the other players, or anything else. It is often painful to accept reality, but — since they are obsessed and controlled — they pay the price.

Denial drives the entire gambling industry. Without it, the industry would collapse immediately. The players lose billions every month because they deny that it is impossible to beat craps, roulette, lotteries, etc. You can beat poker, but only if you are realistic about *everything*, especially yourself.

This book may irritate you by repeatedly asking, "Are you kidding yourself?" That question is needed because we all kid ourselves sometimes, and we always pay for it, sooner or later. Every time you play a hunch, or chase with a weak hand, or sit down in the wrong game, or try to get even when you are on tilt, you are kidding yourself and — over the long term — it must cost you lots of money.

Characteristic No. 5: Winners concentrate intently. They focus all of their attention on the game because they implicitly agree with the principle: "In an otherwise even contest, the man with the best concentration will usually win."

They study almost every card, bet, gesture, and word. They know who is winning and losing and how they play when they are ahead and behind. They often remember not only who made each bet, but *how* that bet was made. Were the chips piled neatly or thrown messily? Was the bet made quickly or slowly? What did he say? And how did he say it?

They concentrate even when they are out of the pot. Most of us, when we fold our cards, do what comes naturally: We check the baseball scores, make small talk, or just relax. But the winners keep working, picking up information they might miss while playing.

Characteristic No. 6: Winners think visibly. They verbalize their assumptions, observations, conclusions, and the way they reached them. They know why they have made a bet or chosen a game, and they never just yield to an impulse.

Characteristic No. 7: Winners admit mistakes quickly. Realistic, visible thinking, and control of their egos enables them to admit their mistakes. They may have loved the hand or the game, but — if they get new information such as an unexpected raise or signs that the table is tougher than they thought — they can fold their cards or leave the game.

Characteristic No. 8: Winners learn from their mistakes. Everybody makes mistakes, but winners rarely make the same one twice. Their obsessive need to win combines with their other qualities to help them learn from their mistakes.

Characteristic No. 9: Winners accept responsibility. They do not complain about bad beats, stupid plays, dealers' mistakes, losing streaks, or anything else. They don't complain because they accept the game as it is — with all its frustrations. Their acceptance of responsibility lets them focus on the only thing they can control: Their own decisions.

Characteristic No. 10: Winners depersonalize conflicts. Since winning is everything, and anger or a desire for revenge would reduce their edge, they don't let themselves get angry or try to get even. They are like lawyers who fight intensely in court, then enjoy lunch together. It's not a personal conflict; it's just the way the game is played.

Characteristic No. 11: Winners adjust to changes. They constantly monitor the game, explicitly decide how they should play *now*, then make whatever changes are needed. If, for example, the game tightens up, they become tighter, looser, more aggressive, or whatever they think will increase their edge.

Characteristic No. 12: Winners are selectively aggressive. Because they insist on always having the edge, they pick their spots. They wait until they have the right cards, the right position, the right opponents, or preferably all three, and then they attack as appropriate.

Of course, you can't be selectively aggressive unless you do all the things we've already discussed, *especially putting your ego into your pocket.* You must realistically assess your cards, your skill, and your opponents, then attack only when you have the edge.

Because he could not do those things, Nick "The Greek" was the second best example of the highly skilled loser. You have probably read of his heads-up confrontation with Johnny Moss, a much better player, and Nick's famous statement that being in action is more important than winning. That's why he died broke.

His gravestone should read: "Here lies a fool whose ego made him challenge a better player."

An even better example was Stu Ungar, perhaps the greatest no-limit tournament player of all time. He is the only three time winner of the World Series of Poker No Limit Hold 'em Championship. He was even better at gin, but he died broke in a crummy motel room.

Part of his problem was drug addiction — which is based on denial — but he was so hooked on action that he would gamble on *anything*. His enormous ego kept him from accepting his obvious limitations at other games. In fact, he often acted like an utter fool.

Even though none of us has remotely as much talent, he was a loser, but we can be winners. If we accept and work within our own limitations, and never, ever make a bet without an edge, success is virtually guaranteed.

That's what this book is all about, getting that edge. Stu Ungar and Nick "The Greek" ended up as losers because they denied reality. They had much more skill than we do, but they were blind to their own limits. They played games they couldn't beat, and it destroyed them.

You may kid yourself in the same sort of way. One of our major goals is to help you to be honest with yourself. You can start that process now by completing "The Right Stuff Questionnaire" in the Appendix. Or you can keep reading, do it later, or just ignore it.

Why Do You Play Poker?

If you asked that question, most people would reply, "To make money," but they would be kidding themselves. First, most of them lose, and any loser who claims to be trying to make money is obviously denying reality.

Second, we do hardly anything for just one reason. For example, most of us don't work just to make money; we also want other satisfactions such as making a contribution, being respected, keeping busy, and meeting people. If we *work* for more reasons than money, why would anyone claim that we *play a game* just for money?

Because poker is a macho game with a macho culture. The very purpose of the game is to take each other's money. Machismo is so important that some people who don't really care about winning pretend they play to win.

We humans are competitive creatures, and we compete at or in almost everything: Poker, golf, our cars, houses, and social positions, whatever. We play games because we are so competitive, and lots of us take them very seriously — even if no money is at stake. A popular poster says: "Tennis is not a matter of life or death. It's much more important than that."

Since the money we win or lose measures our success at poker, we naturally over-emphasize it. Lots of golfers play for money, but you will never hear one say, "I play to make money." They play for fun, and winning money is just a small part of the pleasure.

The myth that people play just or mostly for money is reinforced by many poker books. If their authors don't win, they don't eat. Since winning is so important to them, they commit the Egoistic Fallacy by assuming that their readers' have the same priorities. For example, the author of one common poker book states: "The only purpose in playing poker is to win money."

Nonsense! Many people want to win lots of pots, even if it means they lose money. The kick of winning all those pots is more important to them than the bottom line. Why else would they make so many loose plays? They know their looseness is very expensive, but the kick of winning many pots is more important to them than the money.

Poker is a *game,* not a business for most of us. We play games for all kinds of reasons, but mostly for pleasure. The dollars won and lost are essentially the same as strokes in golf, just a way to keep score.

It is competing, winning for its own sake, cutting strokes off their handicap that drives many people, not the money. In addition, *everybody* — even the most profit-oriented professional — has completely unrelated motives such as the desire for excitement, machismo challenges, socializing, and just having a pleasant time.

Anyone who says that people play to maximize their winnings is blind to what actually happens in many poker games. For example, many players deliberately turn away or tell others not to flash their cards; they don't want to win that way. Some players will not bet a lock when they are heads-up with a friend. And nearly everybody — including me — occasionally takes foolish risks such as playing weak hands, ignoring pot odds, and playing against superior players.

You cannot understand your own or any other player's motives until you realize that the *insistence that most people play to win is just flat wrong.* This position is identical to the economists' axiom that business people try to maximize their profits. Until very recently profit maximization was an article of faith, a foundation of their discipline. Nobody dared challenge it.

Finally, Prof. Simon, my former colleague at Carnegie-Mellon University, looked at what business people actually do. He wrote that the economists were wrong: Nearly all business people strive for satisfactory rather than maximum profits because trying to maximize would force them to do lots of things they don't want to do.

Traditional economists went ballistic. They ranted and raved and nearly screamed: "Heresy!" In an earlier century they would have burned him at the stake. The "fact" that business people tried to maximize profits was as obvious as the "fact" that the sun revolves around the earth.

But he won the argument, and he did it in exactly the same way that earlier scientists changed the way we regard the solar system: By producing undeniable evidence. For analyzing what business people really do he was awarded the Nobel Memorial Prize for Economics. It's hard to argue that a Nobel Laureate is out of his mind.

Simon's "satisficing" principle means that you, me, and nearly everybody else wants to win a satisfactory amount or avoid losing too much; we are not willing to do everything it takes to win the most possible money. We would have to treat poker like a job, and it's not a job to us. *It's a game*, and we should never forget that fact.

To understand your own motives you should ask a second question: *Why do you play the way you do?* Each style satisfies some needs and frustrates others. For example, calling stations and maniacs do not play to win (no matter what they say). Calling stations play to socialize and pass time, and maniacs are literally addicted to action.

Rating Your Own Motives

So stop kidding yourself about why you play poker. Ignore what other people say you should want and discover why you really play by completing the next little "questionnaire." This one is included in the text because it will take you only a few minutes to complete it, and you need these scores to get the full benefit of later chapters.

The procedure is quite simple: Just divide your total motivation (100%) into as many pieces as you think are correct. For example, if your only motive is to make money, and you treat it as just a job, assign 100 percentage points to "Make money."

If your primary motive is to make money, but you also enjoy socializing and meeting people, like to test yourself against competitive challenges, get a little kick from taking a risk, and want to pass time, you might rate "Make money" 40 percent, "socialize" 20 percent, "competitive challenge" 20 percent, "excitement or risk," 10 percent, and "pass time" 10 percent.

If you really don't care about making money, if the chips are just score keeping tokens, you might assign all your points to other categories.

If you have motives other than the ones listed, write them in the blank spaces and assign numbers to them.

Use pencil so you can make changes, and make sure that your numbers add to exactly 100 percent.

Table I: My Motives for Playing

Motive	Percent
Make money	______%
Socialize, meet people	______%
Relax	______%
Get excitement of risk	______%
Test self against competitive challenges	______%
Sense of accomplishment from winning	______%
Pass time	______%
Other (specify)	
____________	______%
____________	______%
____________	______%
Total (must be 100%)	______%

Dog-ear or put a paperclip on this page so that you can refer to it easily. And remember those numbers. You don't have to be too precise, but remember the general pattern. For example, you might remember that you estimated making money as much more important than competitive challenge, without worrying about the exact numbers.

Motives and Playing Styles

About two-thirds of this book focuses on players' styles, and there is a strong relationship between these styles and the players' motives. If you know *how* someone plays, you also know a good deal about *why* he plays (and vice versa). In addition, players with extreme styles are so dominated by their primary motives that they are rigid and predictable. They act in a certain way even when it is self-defeating.

For example, maniacs are so addicted to action that they cannot keep themselves from jacking it up, even when a little voice in them says, "Slow down." Calling stations have such a strong need to get along with others and such a strong aversion to acting aggressively that they just call, call, call, even when they know they should raise or fold. Rocks are so conservative and timid that they let aggressive players run over them.

However, many extreme players have selective memories or kid themselves about why they play the way they do. They essentially make excuses for yielding to their impulses. For example, maniacs tend to remember the times they had a huge win or pulled off an outrageous bluff, while ignoring their losses. Or they say silly things such as, "You have to be in to win."

Maniacs are usually extremely optimistic; they keep thinking they are going to get lucky. Rocks have the exact opposite attitude. They are pessimists who always fear the worst. If you asked a rock why he did not raise with a king high flush, he would not say, "Because I'm a wimp." He would probably say, "I thought he might have the ace."

We will focus on the extreme players because it is easier to see the pattern — in yourself or other people — but *all* loose-aggressive players have a strong need for action, and so on. In general, the more extreme a player's style is, the more his primary motives overwhelm his other drives — including the desire to win. Conversely, the more balanced a person's motives are, the more flexible, rational and effective he will be — at the poker table and everywhere else.

The relationship between styles, motives, and fears is especially important when you are trying to develop yourself as a player. If you do not understand why you play the way you do, you cannot overcome the inner forces that cause you to beat yourself.

As you read later chapters, ask yourself whether your ratings on motives are consistent with the way you play. Any inconsistencies suggest that something is wrong. For example, if you rated making money as your primary motive, but you lose regularly because you can't resist tough games, you should recognize and try to resolve this contradiction. Our goal is to find out what is really happening inside your head and at the table.

Motives and Trade-Offs

Consider *all* your motives. Most poker decisions will satisfy some motives at the expense of others. You have to *trade satisfactions,* and your trades should fit your real priorities. Let's take, for example, deciding which games to play. The games that are most profitable may frustrate your other motives.

Loose-passive games are the easiest to beat. If you want to maximize your profits, you should look for one. However, you might be bored because the game is too easy; it's like shooting fish in a barrel, great if you are starving, but a bore if you fish for fun. (Some players refer to playing in these games as "bottom feeding.")

This type of game can also be frustrating because you will have people draw out on you again and again. You will start out with the best hand, and they will make dumb plays to beat you.

For example, everybody has heard that classic bit of father to son advice: "Son, *never* draw to an inside straight."[5]

But loose players do it all the time (even when the pot odds are tiny), and they occasionally make the winning hand. You should be glad they do. If they *always* lost, they would soon stop throwing away their money for dumb draws. In fact, their beating you by drawing to an inside straight is the same as the live ones' putting money into a slot machine. If they never hit a jackpot, they would stop throwing away their money.

Do the casinos get mad at the jackpot winners? Hell no, they love them. They even put their pictures on the walls, billboards, and television. They want people to keep coming back, and, you should *want* the live ones to make an occasional inside straight. The more times they draw to them, the more money you will win over the long term. However, that fact may not make you feel one bit better right after you lose. If that frustration is truly more important to you than the increased profits, don't play in loose-passive games.

Exactly the same logic applies to countless other decisions. The most profitable style is tight-aggressive, but waiting for good cards may bore you and frustrate your need for action. Playing a loose-aggressive style is exciting, but expensive.

Nearly everybody unconsciously rejects the idea of trade-offs. We want it all. We want to win, to have excitement, action, and a generally good time. Unfortunately, we can't do it. There is no free lunch. The decision that satisfies one motive is going to frustrate others. You should therefore consider *all* your motives before acting. Make sure you know what you are giving up as well as what you are getting, then make the trades that fit your priorities. (Assuming, of course, that you are happy with your priorities.)

---

[5] Actually this advice is occasionally wrong, but we won't get into that now.

Part Two

The Right Skills

The Right Skills

Introduction

You cannot win at poker without understanding and applying the odds and basic strategies, and this book does *not* attempt to teach them. If you do not grasp those subjects, buy and study some of the books mentioned in the "Suggested Reading."

This part deals only with two critical skills, reading hands and choosing the right games. It does *not* try to teach the basic principles and techniques for either skill. Since I am a psychologist, not a strategy expert, other people — particularly my colleagues at Two Plus Two — can give you much better advice than I can. I will, however, refer you to the specific pages of various books that provide the best advice.

My goal here is to help you to understand and apply a few psychological concepts that affect these skills. First, this section will help you to understand how your own attitudes and habits cause you to misread hands or choose the wrong games. Second, it will help you to get "into the heads" of other players so that you can understand how their attitudes and habits cause them to play in certain ways and choose certain games. The ultimate goal is, of course, to help you to read hands more accurately and select the best games *for you* (which may not be the best ones for me).

The next two chapters just lay out the basic ideas. Later chapters will directly relate them to each type of player. For example, every chapter titled, "If you are a ... player" contains a section on selecting the right game.

Reading Hands

Reading hands is the premier skill, the one you must develop to be more than a mediocre player, and the one at which all great players excel. This chapter will cover four subjects.

1. How Well Do You Do It?
2. Improving Your Card Reading
3. Understanding Tells
4. Seeing Telegraphs

How Well Do You Do It?

Because poker hands have relative, not absolute value, you must first determine what the other players have, then take action. This distinction between thinking and acting means that there are two independent dimensions, one in your brain and one in your heart. Your brain determines your *skill* (how accurately you can read their hands), but your heart determines whether you have enough *confidence in your judgment* to act decisively.[6]

The best players are high on both. The worst players have very little ability to read cards, but lots of confidence in their own bad judgment.

The *Card Reading Grid* rates you on these two independent dimensions. The *first* number refers to *card reading skill* and the *second* to *confidence in your own judgment.*

---

[6] Heart (or courage) can be hard to come by since some plays which are profitable and necessary, only work occasionally.

Figure I: The Card Reading Grid

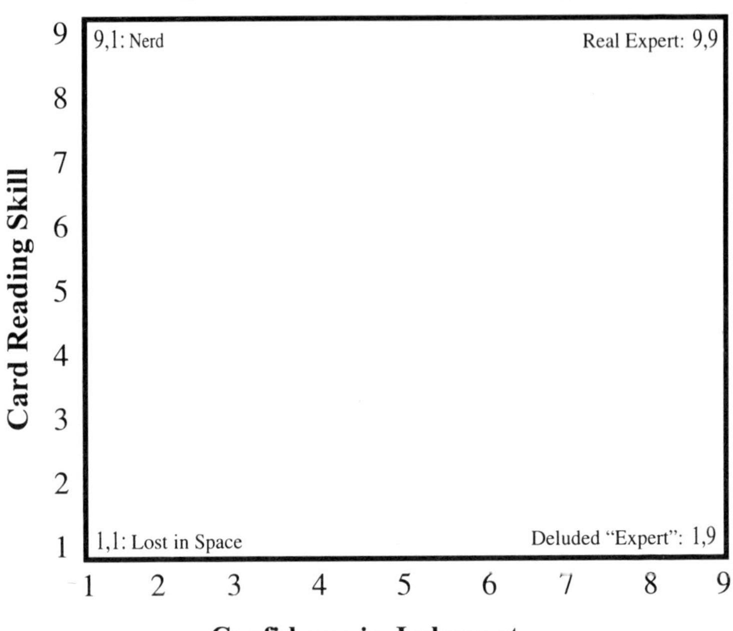

Let's look at the grid's four corners because they illustrate the pattern. These descriptions are caricatures. Nearly everyone is less extreme.

1,1 Lost in Space **(very little skill or confidence).** He does not know what is happening or why. He plays his own cards and does not really care what other people have. You've seen him raise on a straight because it is a good hand, even though somebody else obviously has a flush.

He might not even look at the board. When a refugee from a blackjack game sat down at the end of the table, a near-sighted player said he would not sit there because he could not see some players' cards. He replied: "I never look at other people's cards. It confuses me."

***1,9 The Deluded "Expert"* (extremely low skill, but extremely high confidence).** He can't read cards for beans, but he thinks he can. He is an amazing combination of ignorance, arrogance, and obnoxiousness.

You've met a few. They will give you a lecture on anything: Poker, politics, the economy, sports, whatever. Half of their facts are wrong, and they have no judgment at all, but it does not stop them. They often claim to win lots of money, but they're lying.

They lose a pot, then blame it on the other players' stupidity. Our "expert" made a brilliant play, but some ignorant peasant made a mistake that cost him the pot. The movie, "The Cincinnati Kid" had a deluded expert. He took lots of notes, did complicated calculations, then made losing bets. Was it his fault? "No," he insisted, pointing at the winner, "He shouldn't have called!"

Despite being very irritating, they are often welcome because they are losers. We tolerate their irritating personalities to get their money. Of course, that "confidence" is just a veneer covering up their insecurity. But we don't want to psychoanalyze them; we just want their money. In fact, beating them is not just good for our wallets; it's good for our psyche. We *love* to beat them.

***9,1 The Nerd* (extremely high skill, but no confidence).** He has great card reading skill, but is so unsure of himself that he gets little benefit from it. We have all heard him say: "I know I'm beaten, but I've got to call." or "I don't know why I didn't raise. I knew I had the best hand, but I was afraid that you might have four eights (or some other extremely unlikely hand)."

***9,9 The Real Expert* (extremely high skill and confidence).** He reads cards extremely well and has the confidence to make great moves. He folds good hands when he thinks he is beaten, but calls or raises with hands that most of us would fold. We rarely realize how good he is because he doesn't show his hands or talk about them. He knows he is good, but does not want us to know it.

5,5 The Average Player. The average player sees some signals, but misses lots of them, and he often misunderstands the ones he sees. Once in a while he makes a great or a terrible play, but most of his plays are merely routine. He calls with acceptable hands, raises with very good ones, and rarely does anything imaginative.

Take a hard look at yourself. None of these caricatures completely fits you, but you may see bits of yourself in them. We use the grid because it helps you to see how similar you are to those four caricatures. If you wish, take a few moments to rate yourself on both dimensions. Of course, you can just skip the ratings or do them later.

Start with your ability to "put people on hands." How well can you figure out what they have? This rating ignores what you do with that information. If, for example, you often correctly decide that you are beaten, but you call to make sure, give yourself a high rating for card reading skill (but not for "confidence in your judgment," the next dimension).

Circle the number that best describes you in Table I below. Compare yourself *only* to the players in your game, not to the champions or abstract standards such as how well you think you *should* read cards.

Table I: Card Reading Skill

1. I am an extremely poor card reader, one of the worst in my game.
2. I am a very poor card reader.
3. I am a poor card reader.
4. I am a little below average.
5. I am about average for my game.
6. I am a little above average.
7. I am a good card reader.
8. I am a very good card reader.
9. I am an extremely good card reader, one of the best in my game.

The next rating scale measures how willing you are to *act* on your card reading. It deals primarily with borderline situations, when it is not obvious what you should do. For example, do you call if you think there is a decent chance that someone is bluffing when you have a hand that can beat nothing but a bluff? Of course, for all of these decisions you have to consider the size of the pot; a difficult decision in a small pot may be a "no-brainer" when the pot is huge.

Confidence is the most difficult quality to rate, and you should probably regard the ratings you make now as quite tentative. As you get more information, you may want to change them. Circle the best number in Table II.

Table II: Confidence in My Judgment*

1. I have no confidence in my judgment. I focus on my own cards, betting the good ones, raising with the great ones, and folding the bad ones, without much regard for what I think other people have.
2. I have very little confidence in my judgment. If I have a good hand, I will call, even if I am almost sure I am beaten. I want to be sure.
3. I have a little confidence in my judgment. If I have a good hand, I will probably call, even if I think I am beaten.
4. I have a little less confidence than average. If I have a good hand, I may or may not call if I suspect I am beaten.
5. I have about average confidence.
6. I have a little more than average confidence in my judgment. I will fold a good hand if I am almost sure I am beaten.
7. I have considerable confidence in my judgment. I will fold a good hand if I think that I am probably beaten.
8. I have a great deal of confidence in my judgment. I will fold a very good hand if I think I am beaten.
9. I have extreme confidence in my own judgment. I will fold a very big hand if I think I am beaten, and I'll raise with a marginal hand if I think it is a winner.

* Points 6 through 9 are assuming that the pot is not very large. In large pots you should frequently call even if you feel that it is likely your hand is second best.

Write your grid score here, with the Card Reading Skill score first, and the Confidence in My Judgment score second

My Card Reading Grid scores are ___,___

Go to the "Card Reading Grid" graphic on page 42 and insert an "X" at the spot that matches your scores.

Then look at the description of the caricature in the closest corner. For example, if you scored "7" on skill, but "3" on confidence, the closest corner is "The Nerd." In what ways are you similar and different? Write down those similarities and differences. Then write what you intend to do about it.

My score is closest to the corner named ____________

I have the following similarities and differences from the __________.

Similarities

Differences

How do these similarities and differences affect your poker playing?

What are you going to do about it?

Dog-ear this page or put a paperclip on it. We will refer to it again.

Improving Your Skill

There are two ways to read cards: Observing betting patterns and picking up tells. This section discusses betting patterns; the next one focuses on tells.

Many experts have described the general techniques for understanding betting patterns. Buy and read their books. You can't be a good player without this skill, and you will soon win back whatever you spend. I particularly recommend Sklansky, *The Theory of Poker,* pp. 48-60, Sklansky and Malmuth, *Hold 'em Poker for Advanced Players: 21st Century Edition, pp 225-236* and 300-305, Sklansky, Malmuth, and Zee, *Seven Card Stud for Advanced Players: 21st Century Edition,* pp. 177-186 and 289-294, and Othmer, *Elements of Seven Card Stud,* pp. 163-170. Those books provide the foundation, and this section is *not* a substitute for them. It just adds some distinctly psychological topics.

Apply "The Law of Subjective Rationality"

The evening news gives examples of this law all the time. We hear about someone's shooting several strangers, and wonder why he would do such a thing. Objectively, of course, he is crazy, but his actions are *subjectively* rational: They make sense to *him.* He believed the CIA or the Martians or the Mafia was going to kill him, so he shot first. I am *very* serious.

What does this have to do with poker? Everything. If you can get into the other player's head, understand why he plays poker, what he wants to do, and how he sees the situation, you can understand actions that are now utterly inexplicable.

They may seem ridiculous to you, but they almost always make sense to the person taking them. For example, one wealthy farmer would raise and reraise, sometimes without looking at his cards, because "Looking at your cards just slows the game down."

He played like a maniac, but he was not one bit crazy; he knew exactly what he was doing and what it would cost him.

He always played in low limit games because he could play wildly without losing enough money to bother him. He was playing to relax, blowing money he could afford to lose, and getting something he wanted. His poker playing was no crazier than buying a Rolls-Royce, a Rolex watch, or a race horse, and it was much saner than getting drunk or using cocaine.

That kind of "irrationality" can be seen all the time. A pessimist folds a positive expectation draw because "I never make a flush." A calling station calls a raise from a rock to draw dead because "maybe he's bluffing." A few hold 'em players will raise with weaker hands, but not with pocket aces because "people always draw out on me when I raise with them."

If you agree with the myth that "winning is the only motive," you can't make sense of these plays, but you have certainly seen them. To read people's cards you must set aside your ideas about what people *should* do, get into *their* heads, learn how *they* think, and what *they* are trying to do.

Are they out to win the most money? Or to have a wild time? Or to pass the night cheaply? Do they think a flush draw is worth a raise head to head? Are they superstitious about lucky cards such as a pair of tens?

Beware of "The Egoistic Fallacy"

Everybody — you, me, Doyle Brunson, Sigmund Freud — falls victim to it from time to time. We try to "put ourselves in the other's shoes," but see his situation with our own eyes, not his.

This fallacy can really hurt your card reading. For example, when trying to put a raiser on a hand, you might think of what kind of hand you need to make that raise, then assume that he thinks the same way you do. Since you would not raise without a certain hand, you may misread his hand.

I've made that mistake many times. In fact, I folded a winner a few hours ago because I assumed another player would not have bet unless he could beat my marginal hand. He wasn't bluffing; he thought he had a good hand (and he had a winner after I foolishly folded).

The subjective rationality and egoistic fallacy principles are closely linked, and they cause people to make all kinds of objectively foolish decisions: Check or fold winners, raise with losers, play in games they can't beat, and so on. To read cards accurately, you must understand *this player's* motives and beliefs.

Avoid the "We're Different Fallacy"

You may object that people in other games make these and other mistakes, but the people in your game are tighter, looser, more sensible, better card readers, more deceptive, whatever. Don't believe it; it's the "we're different fallacy."

Everyone wants to believe that *we* are different, that people might do this or that in small games, or in another casino, or in Las Vegas, "but in our game we ..." However, we are all subject to the same motives, fears, and foolishness. In your game these weaknesses may be less obvious, or they may be expressed in different ways, but none of us can help being human, with all the weaknesses it includes.

If you doubt it, just think of the rich, brilliant people who have taken extremely stupid actions. If Bill Clinton could risk his presidency for a little sex, or Mike Milken could destroy himself by stealing when he was a billionaire, you, and I, and everyone else can make foolish mistakes.

Restrain Your Own Impulses

Three thirsty people look at a glass of expensive wine.
The pessimist whines: "It's half empty."
The optimist rejoices: "It's half full."
The poker winner unemotionally says: "Measure it. I want to know *exactly* how much wine is in the glass."

That's what you have to do to read cards well. Set aside your natural impulses and look objectively at the facts. Tight-passive players are too pessimistic; they are so afraid of losing that they look for excuses to be cautious. None of the signals suggest it, but maybe, just maybe, the other guy has a big full house; so they just call with a small full house, losing a profit.

Loose-aggressive players are too optimistic; they look for excuses to gamble. The tightest rock in town has just raised, but maybe, just maybe, he has set aside the habits of a lifetime and decided to make a wild raise; so they reraise, get capped, and lose to a lock.

Control your impulses — your fears and your hopes — and ask: "What do the *facts* say he has?"

Develop This Skill When You are Not Playing

When your money is at stake and you have to make an immediate decision, you cannot read cards as well as you do when you are just observing. You should therefore work on this skill when you are out of the hand and/or out of the game. This time should also be used to develop another simple, but essential skill, counting the pot. All good players do it automatically, but it is hard to develop the right habits while playing. So practice while you are not playing.

During the game you have a great deal of "dead time." You have folded, or the hand is over, and the cards are being shuffled. Most people waste that time, but winners keep working. They watch the action, trying to understand how people play. Between hands they review the action and make mental notes. "Tom will not raise unless he ... Charlie is a little on tilt. Sue calls with ...."

Don't think of it as work or try to do it every hand. Regard it partly as a way to relieve your boredom. You can get so tired of folding that you play weak hands or chase with marginal ones. Working on your card reading after folding will relieve the boredom, make the game more interesting, and, of course, improve your skills.

It will also help you to see things you never even considered before. Nearly all of us resemble spectators at a football game: They just watch the ball and miss lots of important things, such as the quarterback's being intercepted because he did not see an open receiver and threw to a closely guarded one. On TV the instant replays show us these things, but we miss them at the stadium.

There are no instant replays in poker, but, if you work at it, you will see lots of things that you miss while playing. Then you are too intent on your own cards and the betting to see that Bill holds his cards one way when he is going to fold, another way when he is going to bet. Suzy looks intently at the bettor when she has a weak hand, but away from the action when she has a powerhouse. Tom fakes disappointment when great cards hit and looks elated when he misses. These things are happening right in front of you, but you will miss many of them while playing.

The best way to improve your card reading is to focus completely on it. Take a golf analogy. If your chip shots are weak, don't play eighteen holes; instead, hit fifty chip shots and discuss them with a coach.

Watch a game from the rail, or sit behind a friend and try to read everybody's cards. Make notes. When you get a chance, quietly discuss selected hands. You will both benefit from it. Even if he reads better than you, your observer role will let you see and understand things that he misses or misinterprets.

If you do it for a few minutes a week, you will develop more card reading skill than you can develop in many hours of play. If you doubt it, just look at your current skill level. You would not be reading this book if you were satisfied with it, but you have played thousands of hours. Since more of the same probably won't help much, try something new.

Verbalize Your Analysis

This form of visible thinking was mentioned earlier, but it is particularly helpful for card reading. Explicitly put people on specific hands and state your reasoning, including each player's style. If you make a mistake, decide where you went wrong, then adjust your reasoning the next time. Let's take a few examples.

Example No. 1: When the third heart comes on fourth street in hold 'em.

A. The button is very loose-aggressive. You were the big blind and bet your queen high flush draw on the flop. There were two callers before him, and he did not raise. The third heart makes your flush; you bet and one player calls before he raises. What do you do?

Reraise! Your verbalization should go something like this: "Because he is a very loose-aggressive player, he would have raised with an ace or king high flush draw or other draws on the flop. Since he doesn't have that high a flush, I've got the best hand now."

B. The button is very tight-passive. There were three callers, and you just called in the big blind with two black jacks. The flop is

You bet; nobody calls, and the button raises. You call, but do not reraise because a very tight-passive player is unlikely to

raise with anything you can beat except AT or KT.[7] The turn is the

making you top set, but making a flush possible. What do you do?

Bet. Your verbalization should go something like this: "Because he is a tight-passive player, he would not raise on the come, especially heads-up. He therefore can't have a flush. Because he is so tight-passive, I cannot check for a raise; he will probably just check behind me."

Note that both of these plays require considering the player's style. You can be confident that the loose-aggressive player does not have a big flush because he would have raised on the come, and equally confident that the tight-passive player does not have a flush because he would not raise on the come (except for maybe a hand like 8♥7♥).

Can you be certain? Of course not. People do act out of character, or you may have misunderstood a player's style. But, to develop yourself you have to have enough confidence in your judgment to back it up with money.

Example No. 2: "Go for a check-raise?" Two players limped in, then the button, a loose-passive player, raised before the flop. You called in the big blind with

---

[7] Still a reraise may be right. However for the sake of this example we will assume you just called.

The flop is

rainbow (three suits) giving you top two pair. What do you do?.

Check-raise. Your verbalization should go something like this. “He can’t have a set because a loose-passive player would not raise with a pair of anything on the board. He probably has a big pair or two big cards such as AK. If we all check to him, he will probably bet. If I bet, he will not raise. Either of the callers could have a gut-shot draw, and the pot and implied odds justify their calling for one bet. If he bets and I raise, they will either fold a gut-shot draw, or be making a mistake by calling with it.”

Example No. 3: Calling the probable straight. In seven-card stud a loose-passive player raised when she caught a queen on fifth street, giving her

She cannot have three queens because two queens are out. You started with

and bet on fifth street when you caught the third ten. There are nine big bets in the pot and no other callers. What do you do?

> Flat call. Your verbalization would be something like this: "That queen made her a straight because a loose-passive player would not raise with queens up, and she can't have trip queens. If I make a full house it is a certain winner. The pot odds justify my calling now and on sixth street in the hopes of filling up. If I fill up, she will certainly pay me off. If I don't fill up, and she bets (which she might not do) I will fold."

There is nothing new about this method of thinking; you do it semi-consciously all the time. Just make it more visible to yourself by verbalizing it as you play. Then, if you are surprised by a later bet or the cards you see at the showdown, you can review your analysis, decide where you went wrong, and become more accurate in the future.

Please note that you cannot wait until it is your turn to act to start this process. Each time a player acts, you must make a mental note of who he is and what he did. "Joe would not raise in that position without ..."

You must also automatically count the pot, and, of course, you have to know how many outs you have. If you wait until decision time to consider what players did earlier, and to start counting the pot and your outs, you will not have enough time to make an intelligent decision.

Listen to the Bets

This technique is just another way to verbalize your analysis. Try to think of what the bet is "saying" to you. Sometimes bets make a statement, and you can "tune in" if you listen carefully.

Let's take a stud example. You have

The player on your left has

The king and queen of hearts are dead, meaning your AQ flush would beat his flush. The tight-passive player to your right has

The ace of diamonds has not been exposed.

On sixth street the pair of fives and you both check; the four hearts bet, saying, "I have the flush or a draw to it." You put him on the flush, and the pot odds justify your call.

You both call, saying: "We can't beat the flush, but we are drawing to hands that can beat it." (There is a slim possibility that the pair of fives is also saying: "I don't believe you have the flush.")

You catch a small club, making you an AQ flush. The fives check, and you check, planning to raise because you can beat his flush.

The four hearts bet, reinforcing the previous message: "I have an AJ flush."

The pair of fives raises, saying: "I can beat your flush."

What do you do?

There is only one thing to do, fold! It hurts to fold an AQ flush, but the bets have said it's a loser. Remember, the raiser is a tight-passive player. He would not raise with any hand that can't beat an AJ flush, and you can barely beat it. He's got you beat.

The *best way to hear a bet's message is to say it to yourself.* Don't just sit there passively. Ask yourself: "What is that bet saying?" Then answer your question and listen to the answer. Does it sound right? If not, ask why you don't believe the message. Perhaps you are letting your own hopes or fears affect your thinking.

Discuss Poker Seriously When You are Not Playing

We all have to wait for a seat, but we don't use that time to develop our skills. If we talk about specific hands, the usual topic is bad beats. I have never learned anything from a bad beat story except how to beat the person telling it.

But you will enjoy the game more and play better if you discuss it seriously once in a while. If you look, you can certainly find a few people to discuss specific hands and strategies with while you are waiting for a game or eating lunch. Pick people who play well, and start the conversation in a way that captures their attention. For example, you might say, "I had a hand recently, and I'm not sure I played it properly...". Or, "I saw the way you played that flush draw, and I wondered why you ..."

Lots of people love to criticize, lecture and give advice, and you might start a valuable conversation. The next time you wait for a game or see a good player in the coffee shop, try to discuss a recent hand or two. You might be pleasantly surprised.

There are discussion groups on the internet. I particularly recommend the Two Plus Two Forum (www.twoplustwo.com) because Sklansky, Malmuth, and Zee often contribute; the emphasis is upon strategy; and the site is well organized.

You can also try rec.gambling.poker, www.pokercentral.com, and www.universe.digex.net. They are wider ranging, but disorganized. These discussion groups can give you lots of new ideas plus reactions to your own thoughts and plays. Try them at least once.

Understanding Tells

Some great players have an uncanny ability to read tells. Since you and I don't have that gift, we need a system, which is exactly what Mike Caro provides in *The Body Language of Poker*. Instead of telling war stories, he explains how various tells signal a player's motives and thoughts. Buy and study it. It will pay for itself in no time.

He identifies the actions that *suggest* that someone is bluffing, has a big hand, etc. However, some tells "are simply powerful cues you should use along with other factors to make your decision." You must go beyond generalities and treat players as individuals. What does it mean when *this player* bets forcefully or looks you right in the eye?

This point is particularly true for people who have read Caro's book, which includes most highly skilled players. Because they know what you are looking for, they may deliberately send you false signals.

Study his book, but go beyond his general principles and record every *specific* tell you see because *they* are nearly 100 percent reliable. For example, some players *always* bluff by throwing their chips forcefully, while others *always* bluff by betting neatly and gently. If you spot a specific tell and do not record it, you may forget it or fail to look for it. So make a note.

Seeing Telegraphs

Poker authors rarely discuss this subject, probably because the people in their games don't often telegraph their intentions, but it happens frequently in middle and lower limit games (and occasionally in big games). (I even saw a former WSOP Champion telegraph his intentions on five consecutive hands because he was on tilt.) A *telegraph* is any signal of what people are *going to do.* Some telegraphs are subtle, just a tension or relaxation that you may miss without concentrating, but some are extremely obvious, literally unmistakable.

For example, many people hold their cards or put them on the table in a way that indicates they will fold if you bet or raise. These telegraphs are particularly common and noticeable before the flop and on third street in stud because people don't care about the hand. They indirectly invite you to bluff or steal their blinds or antes, and it would be rude to reject such a generous offer.

Telegraphs can also improve your "effective position." You may have three people behind you, but see that two of them are going to fold. Your "effective position" is now further along, allowing you to bet with a hand you had intended to check, to raise when you had intended to call.

Other people show tension, touch or even pick up their chips if they are going to bet, and a few dummies actually take the exact number needed to raise. Since many people bet with their right hand, you can't see the chips, but you can see the movement to pick them up. If you see such a clear, reliable signal, you can confidently slow play a big hand or fold a marginal one.

Some people obviously "threaten" to bet by picking up their chips when they are going to call. Others do exactly the same thing when they intend to fold, because they hope to keep you from betting. *You have to know exactly what each signal means for* this *specific player, and you can't do it without close attention.*

Hesitate and Look Left

Those four words may do more to improve your game than any others you will ever read. If you just hesitate to think for a moment, you will definitely improve your decisions. This quick pause will give you a chance to ask yourself: Why have they checked or bet or whatever? What should I do now? If you doubt the value of hesitating, just remember all the times you acted quickly, then wondered: Why did I do that?

If you develop the habit of looking left before acting, you will often see telegraphs. Better players are less obvious, but even they sometimes telegraph their intentions. Their signals are usually subtle, but, if you look for them in almost any game, you'll be amazed at both how often they occur and the number of people who miss them.

However, be careful not to pause too long. A quick glance should pick up 90 percent of the information that you could get from a longer look. Taking too much time in hope of causing people to act out of turn slows down the game, irritates many people, can make the game seem too serious (which can turn off the mood to gamble), and can be seen — correctly — as "angle-shooting." Get the information you need, but keep the game moving.

Consider Many Possibilities

A common weakness is jumping to conclusions, then ignoring any contrary evidence. Virtually everyone does it, not just when playing cards, but all the time. It's just a natural human weakness. For example, researchers have found that psychiatrists very quickly assign patients to a diagnostic category such as manic-depressive, then ignore any evidence that contradicts their diagnosis.

If psychiatrists, who should certainly know better, can make this mistake, just about anyone can. I have done it countless times.

I put someone on a high pair or a flush draw, then discount or even ignore other possibilities. This sort of thinking has cost me lots of money.

> This tendency is particularly important when reading hands: "Do not put undue emphasis on your opinion of your opponent's hand. I know many players who put someone on a certain hand and play the rest of the hand assuming he has that hand. This is taking the method of reading hands too far... Instead you must put a player on a few different possible hands with varying degrees of probability for each of these hands." (*Hold 'em Poker,* p. 49, Sklansky.)

The specific techniques for making these judgments are covered in the suggested reading. Now I am just trying to make you aware of how natural it is to fall into this trap. It is not natural to think of many possibilities. It is much more natural to put someone on a hand, then "have the courage of your convictions." But, if you want to read cards accurately, you must continuously fight this human, but destructive way of thinking.

Choosing the Right Games

Where you play is almost as important as *how well* you play. Some mediocre players win consistently by playing with weaker players, while many excellent players are often broke because they challenge even better players or play in the wrong kinds of games.

As Mason Malmuth put it in *Poker Essays*:

> "Once you reach a certain level of competence at poker, your most important decision by far is game selection." (p. 122)

Virtually all winners, but hardly any losers, understand and apply this principle. Winners make carefully reasoned choices, while losers just yield to their impulses. A few general principles can improve your choices.

Set Very Clear Objectives

First, decide what you are trying to do. When written, that principle seems obvious, but most people ignore it. It is derived from the earlier one about understanding why you really play poker.

The game that satisfies one motive will often frustrate others. For example, if you want to make the most possible money, you should pick a different game from the one that gives you the most competitive challenge, or is most relaxing, or has the most pleasant companions.

Poker writers usually ignore this issue because they assume your only motive is to make the most money. Since you have other motives, make sure you consider them when choosing a game.

Consider a Wide Variety of Factors

Although they ignore or minimize all motives except making money, Malmuth's *Poker Essays* and Sklansky's and Malmuth's *Hold 'em Poker for Advanced Players: 21st Century Edition* provide excellent advice on choosing a game, and they describe the way you must adjust to all these factors.

- The type of game: Stud, hold 'em, Omaha, or others
- The stakes and their relationship to your bankroll
- The relationship between antes/blinds and the betting limits
- The types of players: Loose, tight, passive, and aggressive
- The number of players: Short-handed versus full games
- The skill of the other players

However, because they overemphasize profits and minimize other motives, they have generally ignored a subject that should be near the top of the list, your "comfort zone." If enjoyment is important to you, make sure you understand and adapt to your own comfort zone, the stakes, type of game, and players that make you feel comfortable, and the limits beyond which you get uncomfortable.

If you ignore these factors, you will neither enjoy playing nor have good results. For example, if the stakes are too high, you may "play scared," and the other players will run over you. If the stakes are too low, you will probably get bored and make careless mistakes. In fact, when they join a little game some high stakes players become so careless that they lose to greatly inferior players!

Conversely, if you overemphasize your comfort, you may enjoy yourself, but lose lots of money. The game you enjoy most may be one you can't beat. For example, many people yield to their need for action or competitive challenges by playing for stakes they really can't afford, or against players who are too tough for them.

In poker, as in almost everything else, you need balance, and you can't get it without thinking objectively about who you are and what you can do.

Experts consider all of the factors listed earlier — plus their comfort zone — when they choose a game. Most people never even think about them. They just do what feels good, and it often costs them dearly.

Don't Try to Prove Anything

The most costly mistake is trying to prove something by selecting a game that is too tough for you, and it happens all the time. Lots of people regard poker as a macho contest, like the battle between Edward G. Robinson and Steve McQueen in *The Cincinnati Kid*. It was the crude equivalent of a Hollywood gun fight. Two tough guys challenge each other.

"This town isn't big enough for both of us."

"Get out, then."

"No, we'll have a fair fight to see who's the better man.

They stand dramatically facing each other, wait with their hands away from their guns to show they are fighting fairly, draw, and fire. One of them dies.

It is fun to watch such gunfights or their equivalents in poker movies, but they never happened, at least not between professional killers. The gunfighters who survived to a ripe old age had the same approach as winning poker players. They would not even think of trying to outdraw another professional in a fair fight; in fact, they would not fight unless they had an edge, even if they had to fight only amateurs or shoot somebody in the back.

When poker winners recognize each other, they do not have a macho contest. If there are enough weak players in the game, they divide their money while avoiding each other. Of course, if they happen to have good hands at the same time, they compete, but they generally avoid confrontations with the other winners. It is not "professional courtesy." They just value money more than macho.

If there are too many good players, some of them "say" without uttering a word, "This game isn't big enough for all of us, so I'm leaving." It is not heroic, but winners don't care about being heroic; they care mostly about winning.

Top players do compete with each other in tournaments, but they are just dividing the "dead money," the thousands or millions of dollars paid by weaker players who are quickly eliminated. Without that dead money, they would not enter tournaments because it is not profitable to play against each other.

As Othmer put it:

> "Our strategy should be not to play against advanced players.... We don't want to prove we are the best player in town, we just want all the money." (p. 173)

All winners know and apply two old poker maxims:

1. "It is no good to be the tenth best player in the world if the top nine are in your game."
2. "If you look around the table and don't see a live one, you're it."

Be Honest About Your Limitations

This point is clearly related to the previous one. If you overestimate your abilities — and many people do — you will often find yourself in games you can't beat.

As we saw earlier, even highly skilled players can make that mistake. Nick "The Greek" blew his bankroll trying to beat Johnny Moss, and hundreds of home town champions saved for years to challenge Las Vegas, but went home busted.

Conversely, if you are honest about your abilities and carefully select your games, you can be a consistent winner — even with moderate skills. For example, some barely competent players win regularly by playing only in soft games. They are called "walkers" because they walk around, looking for the right game. If they do not find it, they keep walking.

Some of them play only when the games are weakest such as weekends, holidays, and vacation seasons, particularly late at night. Tourists and weekend players are generally softer than regulars, and the softest games occur early Saturday and Sunday morning. There are lots of tourists, and the worst players stick around long after most people have gone to bed. They may be losing heavily and trying desperately to get even, which makes them even softer than usual.

They are also tired, and many of them have had too much to drink. Even average players can easily beat these games, and a few "scavengers" play only then. They sleep until midnight, then play when they are rested and their opponents are tired, drunk, and desperate.

I vividly recall one Labor Day weekend game. My friend and I were the only competent players, and we were doing wonderfully. After profiting from some particularly stupid mistakes, my friend whispered: "We should have this game freeze-dried so that we could thaw it out whenever we need money." It was not at all macho to beat up a bunch of weak players, but we loved it.

Learn Which Games Favor You

In addition to looking for generally soft games, winners know which kinds of games favor them. The game that is best for you may not be so good for me, and vice versa. Winners keep records which teach them that, for example, they do better in short-handed rather than full games, or that they have poor results when a maniac is playing.

Many players love to play with maniacs because they lose so much money and make the game exciting, but some winners avoid them because they care more about low volatility results than excitement.

Most players do not know what kinds of games favor them, and they would not even consider keeping detailed records. They just sit down wherever they can find an open seat.

There are so many variables that nobody can tell you exactly which game to select. You have to consider all the factors mentioned earlier, plus the styles of the players and some other variables.

The chapters on styles will provide general guidelines for each kind of player, but only accurate records can provide the specific information you need to make the best decisions. After each session describe the game as completely as possible, record your winnings or losses, plus any other relevant information such as how well you enjoyed the game, aspects you liked and disliked, and which adjustments are needed. If you do it regularly, you will slowly learn which kinds of games are best for *you.*

Don't Play Without an Edge

Then you must use that information to make intelligent choices. If you can't find the right game, don't yield to your impulses and sit down in the wrong one. Prove that you have that essential self-control by waiting for the right opportunity.

Unless winning and losing are much less important to you than other motives such as testing yourself against tough players, you should never play without an edge. That edge can come from any of the factors we have already discussed, but no winner plays without it. If you don't have an edge — because the players are too tough, or it's the wrong kind of game, or any other reason — *don't play.*[8]

---

[8] There is an important exception. You may sometimes be willing to sit down in a game that is a little too tough because you expect it to get better. This frequently occurs when a game is first starting. By sitting down you assume that the game survives and will be available for the expected "live ones."

Part Three
Styles and Ratings

Styles and Ratings

Introduction

Part Three lays the foundation for the remainder of the book, which analyzes players' styles. You obviously should know what the ratings mean and how to make them before considering how to adjust to other players' styles or improve your own.

"The styles grid" explains why you need a grid to help you identify and remember the styles of all players you encounter. It also discusses the limitations of the grid or any other rating system. It then describes the grid and provides an overview of the major types of players.

"Rating players" describes both a simple and a complicated method to rate players, then tells you how to "fine-tune" those ratings, rate yourself, and get more information about other players.

The Styles Grid

Many experts have written about the importance of adjusting to different kinds of players, but there are no common definitions. Various champions use the same term with conflicting definitions, and different terms for the same kind of people.

To reduce that confusion we will use a simple Styles Grid to put people into clearly defined categories. Later chapters will tell you how to adjust your strategy for each type.

Why Use a Grid?

Blake and Mouton's Managerial Grid and similar systems have been used to rate tens of thousands of managers, salespeople, doctors, accountants, and many other "occupations." They make it easier to rate people quickly, compare them to each other, adjust your strategy, and, perhaps most important for poker players, remember how you rated them.

If you always play with the same small group of people, you may not need a grid system. You can slowly learn how everyone plays. But most of us often play against new players. By the time we learn how they play, they have cashed in, and we have to study somebody else.

A grid system is particularly valuable if you play at lower limits. You may not be that skilled at reading players, and you have far more players to read. In many low limit games, people tend to play briefly; the pool of players is huge; and in just a few sessions you may play with dozens of people.

The next time you see a player, you may have forgotten most of your previous thoughts and have to start all over again. It is immeasurably simpler to make and remember a mental note, "Sam is 8,2 (very loose-passive), or Christine is 3,7 (tight-aggressive)." Once you remember that simple number, you know how they play and how to adjust to them.

The grid may seem too simple and general. You naturally want to know how somebody would play a specific hand, and the grid score just describes his general style. Alas, to be really specific, you need the masters' intuition, concentration, and experience, and we don't have them.

All a simplifying system can do is provide general guidance about how to play against various types of players. To adjust to *this particular player and this specific hand*, you must add your own judgment and consider other factors.

David Sklansky used the same logic with his rating system for the first two cards in hold 'em. He divided the hundreds of possibilities into several groups and stated the general rules for playing each group. However, he never encouraged readers to apply his rules mechanically, nor does he play that way himself. A later book stated the underlying logic.

> "In fact, the starting hands actually move up and down the hand rankings depending on the circumstance. Because of that it can be a mistake to rigidly adhere to the hand rankings." (*Hold 'em Poker For Advanced Players: 21st Century Edition*, p. 14)

We will do the same thing: Rate players and fit them into a grid. Expect them to play about the same as other people with similar ratings, but look for and adjust to other information.

In other words, you should use the grid cautiously, and accept that there is no substitute for knowing how this particular player is feeling and acting *now*. Maybe Christine was winning last time and playing her "A" Game, but tonight she's had some bad beats, is on tilt, and is raising on hands she would usually fold. You must obviously adjust your strategy.

The grid can help you to get a quick and basic picture of each player, but don't think that assigning a two digit rating to a player means that you can stop studying him. Later chapters will tell you how to build on the grid's foundation, but for the moment, let's create that foundation.

The Grid

Looseness and aggression are the most important stylistic dimensions, and they are independent of each other. A player can be high, average, or low on both, high on one, but low on the other, and several other possibilities.

Lots of writers have made this point, but nobody has dealt with it systematically. The styles grid will help you to adjust quickly by portraying each player and game as a two digit number. The *first digit* is the *tight/loose* score, and the *second* digit is the *passive/aggressive* score.

Players are rated on each dimension from 1 to 9. "1" (for the first digit) means extremely tight or (for the second digit) extremely passive, while "9" means extremely loose or extremely aggressive.

By using numbers rather than words, we can consider different degrees of looseness or aggression. Since an 8,2 player is looser and more passive than a 7,3 player, you should treat them somewhat differently.

Figure II: The Styles Grid

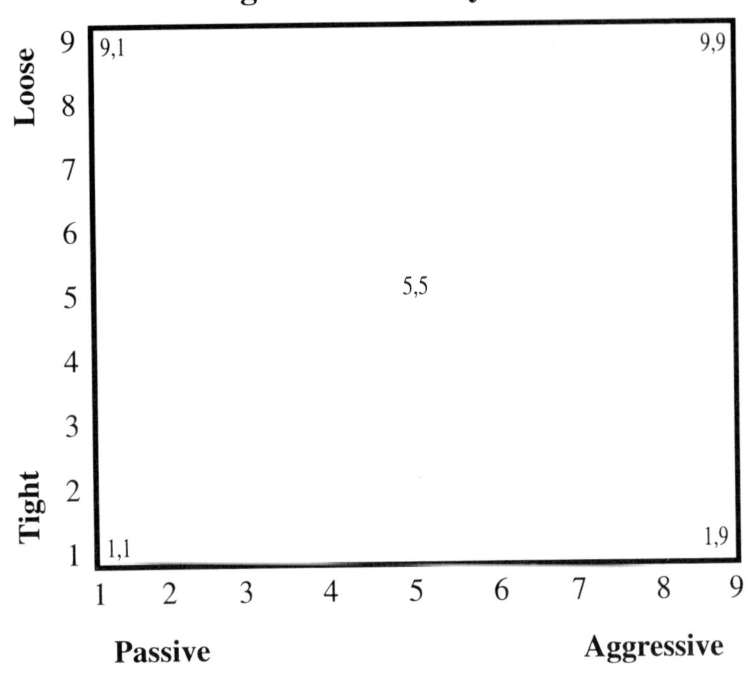

Since the system's purpose is to help you to adjust to different styles, it generally ignores the average players, the ones in the middle of the grid. It focuses on the corners, the players and games with high or low scores on *both* dimensions because you must adjust to them.

To help you to see the overall picture we will name and describe the most extreme players, the ones at the corners. They are caricatures, but it is easier to see the pattern with them. Besides, there are a few extreme players such as rocks (1,1) and maniacs (9,9).

Learning how to spot and deal with them will help you to deal with similar, but less extreme players. For example, you just soften the rules for dealing with a calling station (9,1) to deal with less extreme loose-passive players.

There are very close links between people's styles and their motives, fears, and other drives. In fact, these drives usually *cause* the style. The way people play depends upon the kind of people they are.

This principle is particularly true for people with extreme styles (except tight-aggressive). The closer someone is to any other corner of the grid, the more his style is caused by his fears and desires, and the more rigidly and ineffectively he will play. We will just touch upon these drives here, then discuss them more thoroughly in later chapters.

The grid and the entire book are organized by two digit scores, but we will use other numbers later to "fine-tune" the ratings. Let's ignore these distinctions now to clarify the big picture.

Figure III: The Extreme Players

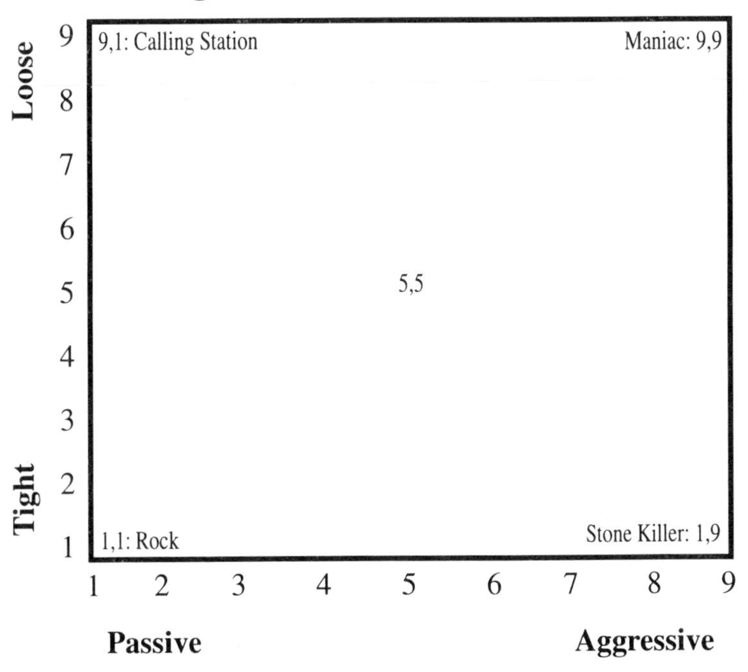

Extreme Style 1,1: The Rock (extremely tight-passive). We have all played with rocks, and it is usually neither pleasurable, nor profitable. They sit there, waiting for great cards, folding hand after hand.

All tight-passive players prefer to win small amounts most days rather than have large swings between winning and losing sessions. Instead of looking for action and competitive challenges, they wait until they have a big edge. The complete rocks are dominated by their own fear of taking risks. They don't just want the edge; they want a lock (unbeatable hand).

Some rocks also want to pass the time. The most common rocks are retired people with limited incomes and nothing else to do. Playing an extremely tight-passive style allows them to play a long time on a limited bankroll, and they may even grind out a small profit.

They can be so quiet and passive that they "blend in with the wallpaper." Some players hardly notice them and make the mistake of gambling with them. Perceptive players learn to avoid them, which reduces the rock's profits. They wait for good cards, but cannot take advantage of them; they don't get action because they don't give action. Good players run over them by bluffing and stealing their blinds and antes, but also recognize that, when the rock bets and raises, they are against a strong hand and run away.

They do best in low limit games because so many players are loose, and lots of them are oblivious. They do not quickly recognize the rock, and they may not adjust even when they do so. When a rock finally plays a hand, he has a head start in a short race. The other players are chasing him, and they often can't catch up.

Extreme Style 9,1: The Calling Station (extremely loose-passive). The calling station is everyone's favorite, except their spouse's. They almost always lose because they stay in nearly every pot, calling bet after bet, but they rarely bet or raise, and they almost never bluff. People soon learn how they play, which creates the worst possible combination: They give action, but do not get it. When they finally get a winner and raise, good players run for the hills.

Many calling stations lack card reading skill, confidence in their judgment, or both. They may not even try to read other people's cards, and they can't read them well, nor do they have the confidence to act on their judgment. Some of them are so afraid of being bluffed or feeling foolish for folding a winner that they just call and call and call. We have all heard them say, "I know you've got me beat, but I'll call."

Calling stations do not play to win. They want to pass time and socialize. The cardroom acts as a club, a place to meet people, talk, and let the hours roll by. Many of them are dominated by their fear of conflict and competition. They want to "be nice," and it isn't nice to raise or bluff. Some of them don't even bet locks when they are heads up because they don't want to "take advantage" of people.

Extreme Style 9,9: The Maniac (extremely loose-aggressive). Maniacs raise, reraise, and even cap (make the last raise allowed) with hands you should throw away. They lose more money and lose it faster than virtually anyone else, but they can easily destroy your bankroll and occasionally will leave the table a huge winner.

Their wildness distorts the game's entire logic: Hands that make sense in a normal game become uneconomic because they cost so much to play. Reading hands becomes nearly impossible because they treat garbage like gold. Other players either tighten up or go on tilt, and some of them move back and forth from one to the other. One minute they are folding the winner; the next they are raising on little more than their anger.

Maniacs are literally addicted to action. They need it the way a junkie needs a fix, and it costs them dearly. They get great action on their winners, but they give too much action on their losers. The inevitable result is huge losses.

Extreme Style 1,9: The Stone Killer (extremely tight-aggressive). They are the people you can't beat. They don't play anything but profitable hands, and they play them in the most profitable way. Nearly all of the very best professionals are "Stone Killers" or close to it.

They don't come to play. *They come to win.* Poker is not a game for relaxation; it is their livelihood or their "second job" or a personal testing ground. They enjoy it, but they are there for the money and the challenge, not for casual fun. They do not care about socializing or passing the time, and they are neither afraid of, nor addicted to taking risks. Risks are just a part of the game that should be calculated and controlled.

When they don't have the edge, they fold. When they get the edge, they attack mercilessly (if appropriate).[9]

Extreme Style 5,5: The Average Player. Average players are not really an extreme style, but we still need to mention them. In fact, they are just what you would expect: Average or close to it on both dimensions. Some of them score 3 or 7 on one dimension, but their scores are usually from 4 to 6.

They have neither extreme needs, nor extreme fears. Their motives are mixed, even confused: They hope to win, are afraid to lose, and want to relax, pass time, socialize, get a little excitement, and challenge the competition. They play about as many hands as other people, raise about as often, reraise once in a while, rarely cap.

The average player varies from game to game, and the definition of the more extreme types should be adjusted accordingly. For example, if about half of the players in a game call on third street (in stud) or before the flop (in hold 'em or Omaha), then the average player (on looseness) is someone who calls about half the time. If more or less players call, then the

---

[9] Actually the best players are more like 2,8 or 3,7 since there are few games where the best strategy is extreme tightness and extreme aggression.

average and all other ratings must be adjusted upward or downward.

The same principle applies to most human qualities. For example, among the general population a six foot three inch man would be called "tall," but professional basketball players might call him "Shorty."

Figure IV: The Five Groups

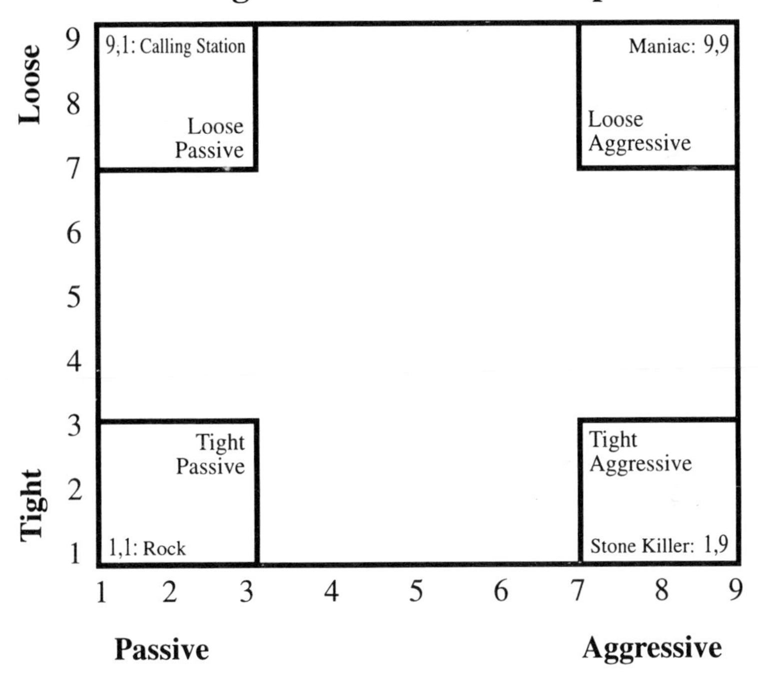

Look at Figure IV. It is almost identical to Figure III except for highlighting the four corners. The players at the corners are separated from those with one or more scores in the middle. For example, someone with a 7 or higher on looseness, *and* a 3 or less on aggression is "loose-passive."

A score between 4 and 6 is in the average range for that dimension. Players with scores in the average range are not discussed further because you do not have to make large adjustments to them.

We will focus only on the players near the grid's corners because you must adjust to them. The more extreme a player's scores are, the more closely he resembles the rock, calling station, maniac, or stone killer, and the larger the adjustments you must make.[10]

Later chapters are organized by the four corners. There are two chapters on "tight-passive," "loose-aggressive" and so on. The first chapter covers that type of opponent, and the second one is titled "If You Are a Loose-Passive (or whatever) Player."

The first chapter of each pair starts with a description of that style, then discusses five topics:

1. Quick recognition signals
2. Strengths
3. Weaknesses
4. Playing against that type of player
5. Playing in that type of game

The second chapter of each pair also covers five topics:

1. Accepting the consequences
2. Understanding your motives
3. Improving your play
4. Choosing the right game
5. Getting your act together

This consistent structure enables you to make quick comparisons and adjustments. You can easily compare two different styles on several specific dimensions and see exactly what you must do to adjust to a tight-passive rather than a loose-aggressive opponent. Before considering those comparisons and adjustments, let's describe the ways to rate players.

---

[10] You would also need to adjust to players with ratings like 4,9; 1,5; etc. But these are very rare "birds." See page 91, "Dealing with 'Mixed Styles' "

Rating Players

Rating players is not easy at first, but it is worth the time and frustration. Just doing it will automatically improve your game by "forcing" you to think about how other people play, comparing them to each other, and deciding how you should adjust to each one.

Most people don't think about these subjects, which is one of the reasons they don't do as well as they could. By taking the time to think about how people play and planning ways to adjust to them, you are becoming *pro*-active, while most people are *re*-active. You are getting ready in advance, while they just wait for things to happen to them, then react without any clear plans.

Most significant winners are pro-active, which is a major reason they win. So take the time to rate players, especially the ones you encounter frequently. The more accurately you rate players, the better you will play. This chapter will describe how to rate players, discuss ways to fine-tune these ratings, and suggest ways to get more information.

There are two methods, a simpler and a more complicated one.

1. (Simpler) You just assign numbers that fit the descriptions.
2. (More complicated) You establish benchmarks (standards of comparison) for each rating, then compare other people to these benchmarks.

The second method takes time to learn, but is more accurate and easier to apply to strangers. If you want to save time, just use the simpler method. You might also start with the simpler system to get an immediate payoff, then shift to the complicated one to improve your accuracy and ability to rate strangers quickly. Or you could use the more complicated method only for the people you encounter frequently or have trouble beating.

The Simpler Method

Just use the numbers as "shorthand" to describe people that fit the descriptions. For example, "1" means "extremely tight" or "extremely passive." "8" means "very loose" or "very aggressive."

Work with only one dimension at a time to minimize confusing looseness and aggression. The next section explains the reasons for doing so.

Compare people to your usual game, not to some idea of how they "should" play. If, for example, about half of the players see the flop in your hold 'em game, someone who sees about half the flops would be rated "5" on the loose/tight dimension. You might think that only three people should see the flop, but you have to adjust to the players in your own game, not in some ideal one.

Apply the "bell curve" principle. The more extreme a rating is, the fewer people it describes. You can see the "bell curve" everywhere. Let's say we rated height on our 9 point scale:

- #7, tall 6' to 6'6"
- #8, very tall 6'7" to 7'
- #9, extremely tall over 7'

We would have lots more #7's than #8's, and lots more #8's than #9's.

Assign a #8 rating about half as often as a #7, and a #9 about half as often as a #8. Having fewer extreme ratings matches reality; it also helps you to concentrate on the players who require the largest adjustments. You must make the largest adjustments to the people with the most extreme styles, and you want to make large adjustments to only a few people.

Before rating anyone, read the next section and apply its general principles. For example, rate each dimension separately and work from the extreme people toward the average ones.

The More Complicated Method

Benchmarks convert abstract numbers into real people, and it is much easier to compare strangers to benchmarks than to try to remember the exact meaning of, say, a #8 rating on looseness. With this method #8 is assigned to anybody as loose as Tom (the benchmark for #8 or "Mr. 8"), looser than Charley ("Mr. 7"), and tighter than Charlotte ("Ms. 9").

The hard part is establishing benchmarks. After that you just compare other players to the benchmarks and assign the rating of the benchmark they most resemble. To use this method, take the following steps.

General Principles

1. *Use players you know well as the benchmarks.* The better you know them, the more accurately you can rate them, and the easier it is to compare them to strangers.
2. *Select your benchmarks when you are NOT playing.* You are not used to rating people, and trying to do it while playing will confuse you, mess up the ratings, and disturb your play.
3. *Work with one dimension at a time.* Trying to rate both dimensions simultaneously will partially defeat the purpose of having a two digit rating. You may confuse looseness with aggression.
4. *Start with the tight-loose dimension.* Otherwise, you may confuse looseness and aggression. For example, if you rated aggressiveness only on the total number of raises, you might rate a tight-aggressive player as only average on aggression because he raises about as often as the average player. You must remember that he usually folds. *Aggression should be measured, not by the total number of raises, but by the ratios of raises to calls and bets to checks.*
5. *Start with the extremes and work toward the middle.* The extremes are the easiest to see. You can easily identify the

tightest, loosest, and most aggressive or passive players, but it gets harder to make distinctions as you approach the average.

6. *Consider only their normal game.* Most people's style varies because of their mood, the other players, whether they are winning or losing, the size of their stack, and so on. For both benchmarks, and other players, ignore these variations and consider only the way they usually play.
7. *You should be the benchmark for your specific rating.* It is certainly easier to compare a stranger to yourself than to anyone else.
8. *Don't waste your time setting benchmarks for nearly average ratings (4-6).* You don't have to adjust too much to them. Focus on the more extreme players. However, you should make notes about the issues we discuss later such as over-protecting blinds or attitudes toward bluffing.
9. *Use pencil.* You may want to change some benchmarks or ratings of other players.

Establishing Tight/Loose Benchmarks

Start with the loose end of the dimension (#9) because it is much easier to see who plays the worst garbage than to distinguish between degrees of tightness.

Table III: Tight/Loose Ratings

Rating	Benchmark	Explanation
#9, Extremely loose	________	Pick someone who is *typical* of the loosest few players in your game. If one player is much looser than everyone else, do *not* make him Mr. 9 because he is not typical.
#8 ,Very loose	________	Pick someone who is noticeably tighter than Mr. 9.
#7, Loose	________	Pick someone who is noticeably tighter than Mr. 8.
#6, Slightly loose	________	Don't bother to make a benchmark.

Stop! Instead of continuing to move down from the loose end of the dimension, jump down to #1, the tightest players (#1), and move up from there.

Table III: Tight/Loose Ratings (Con't)

Rating	Benchmark	Explanation
#5, Average	________	Don't bother to make a benchmark.
#4 ,Slightly loose	________	Don't bother to make a benchmark.
#3, Tight	________	Pick someone who is noticeably looser than Mr. 2.
#2, Very tight	________	Pick someone who is noticeably looser than Mr. 1.
#1, Extremely tight	________	Pick someone who is *typical* of the tightest few players in your game. If one player is much tighter than everyone else, do *not* make him Mr. 1 because he is not typical.

Stop! Review all the benchmarks.

- Is each benchmark noticeably tighter than the one immediately above him?
- Do the numerical ratings and descriptions seem appropriate? For example, would you describe "Mr. 8" as "very loose?" If the description does not fit any benchmark, select someone who does fit.

- Can you easily compare the other players to your benchmarks? Do you have a clear enough picture of how each benchmark plays to say "The new player is about as loose as Mr. 8, looser than Ms. 7, but not as loose as Mr. 9?" If not, either select new benchmarks or study the benchmarks until you can make those comparisons.

Rating Other Players on Tightness/Looseness

To rate everyone else, just compare them to your benchmarks. Remember to rate only this dimension to avoid confusing looseness and aggression.

Because of the bell curve, fewer people should receive a certain rating as you move away from #5, average.

Establishing Passive/Aggressive Benchmarks

Start with the aggressive end of the dimension because it is much easier to distinguish between degrees of aggression than between degrees of passivity.

Table IV: Passive/Aggressive Ratings

Rating	Bench-mark	Explanation
#9, Extremely aggressive	______	Pick someone who is *typical* of the most aggressive players in your game. If one player is much more aggressive than everyone else, do *not* make him Mr. 9 because he is not typical.
#8 ,Very aggressive	______	Pick someone who is noticeably less aggressive than Mr. 9.
#7, Aggressive	______	Pick someone who is noticeably less aggressive than Mr. 8.
#6, Slightly aggressive	______	Don't bother to make a benchmark.

Stop! Instead of continuing to move down from the aggressive end of the dimension, jump down to #1, most passive player, and move up from there.

Table IV: Passive/Aggressive Ratings (Con't)

Rating	Bench-mark	Explanation
#5, Average	________	Don't bother to make a bench-mark.
#4 ,Slightly passive	________	Don't bother to make a bench-mark.
#3, Passive	________	Pick someone who is noticeably less passive than Mr. 2.
#2, Very passive	________	Pick someone who is noticeably less passive than Mr. 1.
#1, Extremely passive	________	Pick someone who is *typical* of the most passive few players in your game. If one player is much more passive than everyone else, do *not* make him Mr. 1 because he is not typical.

Stop! Review all the benchmarks.

- Is each benchmark noticeably more aggressive than the one immediately below him?
- Do the numerical ratings and descriptions seem appropriate? For example, would you describe "Mr. 8" as "very aggressive? If the description does not fit any benchmark, select someone who does fit.
- Can you easily compare the other players to your benchmarks? Do you have a clear enough picture of how each benchmark plays to say "The new player is about as passive as Mr. 2, less passive than Mr. 1, but more passive than Ms. 3?" If not, either select new benchmarks or study the benchmarks until you can make those comparisons.

Rating Other Players on Passivity/Aggression

To rate everyone else, just compare them to your benchmarks. Remember to rate only this dimension to avoid confusing looseness and aggression.

Because of the bell curve, fewer people should receive a certain rating as you move away from #5, average.

After Rating Players on Both Dimensions

After rating players on both dimensions you need to do the following:

1. Place them into the grid and expect them to play about the same as the others in that part of the grid.
2. Make mental or even written notes about everything else you know about each player, especially the ones you encounter frequently and/or have trouble beating.
3. Decide how to play against each individual player.
4. Watch for changes that occur repeatedly. For example, many people play differently when they are ahead or behind, have

drunk too much, are tired, etc. The question is always: How is he playing *now?* If necessary, adjust your strategy.

5. Watch for signs that your rating is incorrect. Perhaps you misread him, or he has changed his style. If necessary, change your rating.

Dealing with "Mixed Styles"

The next group of chapters focuses on each of the grid's corners, such as loose-aggressive players. People who are average on both dimensions are not discussed because there is no need to adjust to them. However, if someone is extreme on one dimension, but near average (4-6) on the other, some adjustments are necessary. For example, you usually don't want an aggressive player to your immediate left regardless of how loose or tight he is.

People who have one extreme (1-3 or 7-9) rating and one near average (4-6) rating are called "mixed." To deal with them, focus on the extreme rating and apply a mixture of the recommendations for the two styles which share that extreme rating. For example, someone who is 5,8 (average on loose/tight, but very aggressive) requires a combination of the adjustments for loose- and tight-aggressive players.

Fine-Tuning the Ratings

Fine-tuning applies a principle called "exception reporting." Well-managed companies do not waste people's time with unnecessary reports, but they do want to know about anything that breaks the pattern. For example, if sales or customer complaints increase, they want it reported.

The two digit rating gives you a quick idea of a player's style, but a few refinements will make it more useful. For example, many players' styles change when they are drinking, losing, or winning heavily. A few people play differently on early and late streets. Others bet aggressively, but raise conservatively.[11] Some tight-passive players bluff frequently.

Although these refinements will help you to adjust your strategy, they make the system more complicated and harder to use. Use them only if the exceptions are large or frequent enough to require adjustments. You might also ignore them until after you have mastered the basic system.

Temporary Changes in Style

Many players' styles change when they are winning or losing, drunk or sober, tired or awake, short of money, and so on. If these changes are predictable, make a note. For example, you probably know players who fit these descriptions.

- Sober 7,7 (loose-aggressive); drunk 9,9 (Maniac).
- Usually 3,3 (tight-passive), but 7,3 (loose-passive) if losing heavily.
- Usually, 7,3 (loose-passive), but 3,3 (tight-passive) if short money.
- Usually 5,5 (average) but 7,7 (loose-aggressive) right after a bad beat (e.g., makes "steam raises").

Distinctions Between Early and Late Streets

A few players are looser on early streets than they are on later streets. They will call with weak hands on the first or second round of betting, but will not chase if they do not catch something soon (especially in flop games because luck is so important between the first and second rounds). Even fewer players have the opposite pattern: They are slightly tight early, but will keep chasing with weak hands. (This pattern is more prevalent among

---

[11] A fairly common trait that is important to notice.

stud players since the pot gets larger while the amount of luck increases with each round due to the increasing number of combinations that each card brings.)

Some players play more or less aggressively in early than in later rounds. For example, they will not raise without strong cards before the flop, but will raise with fairly weak hands on the flop or turn. Others have exactly the opposite pattern.

Use hyphenated numbers to describe this distinction. The number before the hyphen refers to the early round(s), and the one after the hyphen refers to later rounds. For example, someone who will see the flop with garbage, but will fold unless he gets a good piece of the flop could be rated 8-4 on the loose/tight dimension. Someone who rarely raised before the flop, but was slightly aggressive after it might be rated 3-6 on the passive/aggressive dimension.

Note that the previous examples used a 4 and a 6 rating, even though the system usually ignores near average ratings. They were used to distinguish the player's pre- and post-flop play.

Over-Protecting Blinds

Most people's attitude toward protecting their blinds is consistent with their style rating. Loose players protect them, while tight ones don't. However, a few tight players over-protect their blinds, especially the big one. When making this evaluation, take account of the raiser's position. Good players will more readily call a raise from someone in late position — who might be stealing — than from a player in early position (whose raise is probably legitimate). Just note "OPB (over-protects blinds)," then adjust your play.

Distinguishing Between Betting and Raising

Most people are consistently passive or aggressive, but a few of them bet much more aggressively than they raise. They will bet weak or marginal hands, but they will not raise without a very strong one.

To describe this pattern make separate ratings for betting (B) and raising (R). Let's say a hold 'em player is loose-passive before the flop, bets weak hands aggressively after the flop, but does not raise then without a strong hand. He could be rated 7,3-7(B)-3(R).

Remember, the comma comes between the loose/tight and passive/aggressive ratings, while the hyphens divide the early (pre-flop) and later rounds. That small group of numbers immediately tells you all the information in the sentence just before it. It is obviously much easier to record and remember than all those words.

Betting on Weakness and Position

Some players — even somewhat passive ones — will bet almost anything if everyone checks to them on the flop in hold 'em or Omaha. Whenever this sort of player is last, you should consider checking anything. If you have a good hand, you can confidently check for a raise. Because this pattern is so important, make a note of it.

Check-Raising

If someone check-raises about as often as most people with similar ratings, no change is needed. For example, aggressive players check-raise much more often than passive ones, and loose-aggressive players do it most frequently. Make a note of any exceptions to that pattern such as passive players who check-raise frequently or aggressive players who rarely do it.

Betting or Raising on the Come

This issue is extremely important. If you know that someone routinely bets or raises with draws, you should usually consider raising or reraising with your marginal hands, especially if you can knock out other players. However, if no one else is in, you may want to switch to a more passive strategy to encourage them to bluff. Conversely, if someone never bets or raises on the come, you should fold some hands that you might normally call with (unless the pot is very large).

Most aggressive players, especially loose-aggressive ones, bet or raise on the come, often foolishly. For example, they may reraise heads up with a poor draw because, "If it hits, I want to win a good pot." If this player's attitude toward acting on the come are different from people with similar ratings, make a note of it, then use that information against him.

Bluffing

Make a note only if a player does it more or less often than similarly rated players. Note also *when* he bluffs. Some players will almost automatically bluff in certain situations, such as after everyone has checked on this street or the previous one.

This information is the purest gold. You can invite him to bluff when you have the right kind of hand. Conversely, if you know he never bluffs, or will not bluff in a certain situation, you can fold when he bets. Since this information is so valuable, make sure you make a note of it.

Superstitions

Many players have superstitions, even if they don't call them that. For example, they may have a favorite hand such as a pair of deuces or jack-ten suited that they overplay. Others may underplay certain hands for superstitious reasons. For example, they may raise with a pair of jacks, queens, or kings, but not with aces because they foolishly believe that raising causes them to lose.

Sometimes they will directly tell you their superstitions. For example, one player said he plays "five-seven" in hold 'em because he was born in 1957. With other people you have to ask questions such as: "Why did you play that hand?" or "Why didn't you raise?" Get in the habit of asking questions; you will be amazed at how much you learn.

Taking Notes

Most people are reluctant to write notes, but you simply cannot remember everything. A few minutes spent on notes after a hand or a session can put lots of money in your pocket. An excellent investment is a small dictating-machine; as you drive home, you can easily dictate your observations about players, your own play, ways to improve, etc.

However, you must be very discreet when taking notes. Away from the table is always best. Many people play mainly for recreation, and you don't want to let them know that:

1. There is much more to the game than they think there is, and
2. You take the game that seriously. You could start converting them from an easy to a tough opponent. See *Hold 'em Poker for Advanced Players: 21st Century Edition*, pages 153-156 for an extended discussion of this issue.

Rating Yourself

Rate yourself, then insert your scores below. Remember to put your loose/tight score first, your passive/aggressive score second.

My styles grid score is ___ , ____

Remember that number. It is the book's most important piece of information. It affects everything you do and how other people see and play against you.

Ask a few friends who know how you play to tell you how they rate your style. Insert their ratings here in pencil.

Name	*Rating*
______________	______,______
______________	______,______
______________	______,______

If their ratings are different from your own, ask them to explain their ratings. Learning how they rate you will help you in two ways. First, it may make your self-ratings more accurate. Perhaps they see things you overlooked or even denied.

Second, it will clarify how other players perceive you. Most other players adjust to their perceptions, not your real style. We will see later that your image and style should usually *not* be the same. If they are, you are too predictable. If a different image would improve your results, plan ways to project a better image. The chapters titled "If you are a loose-passive (or other style)," will contain many specific recommendations.

As you get more information from your friends or other sources, you may revise your self-rating or, hopefully, change your style to a more effective one, but that rating is how you see yourself now.

Look at Figure V which has been copied from the last chapter.

Figure V: The Five Groups

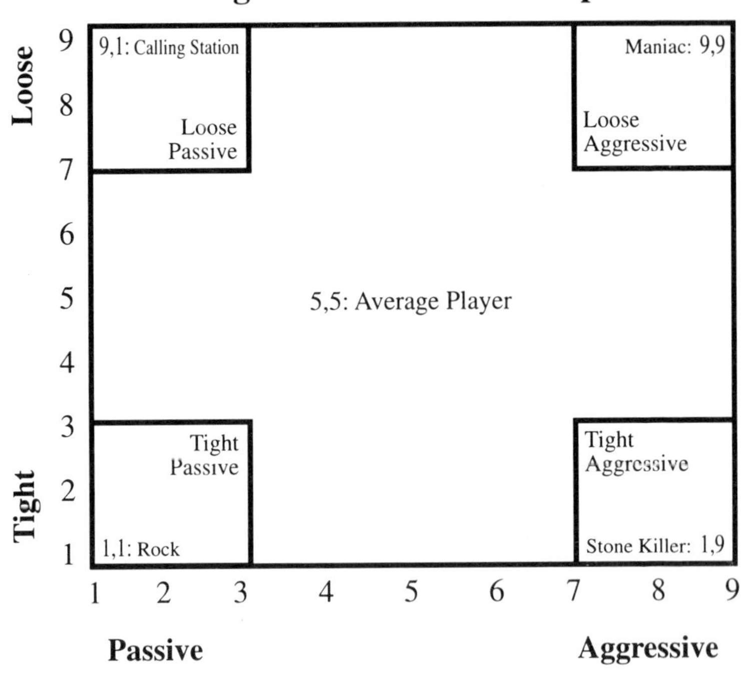

Put a large X at the point on the grid that fits your rating. Do you fit into or come close to one of the corners? If so, you probably play and get the same sorts of reactions as the other people in that corner.

Parts Four through Seven focus on the four corners of the grid (tight-passive, etc.). You might find it useful to go directly to the two chapters on the style closest to you. For example, if you are loose-passive, read Part Five now. It will tell you why you play the way you do, the strengths and weakness of your style, how the good players adjust to you, what results to expect, how to change your style, and which games to choose. You may be very surprised.

But don't forget to come back here. We have lots more subjects to discuss.

Getting Information

Every poker expert would agree that information is power, but they have not written much about how to get it. Here we will discuss a few ways to determine players' styles and idiosyncracies.

If you usually play with the same few people, you can slowly learn how they play. However, because the players constantly change in some games, *you have to read people quickly and remember what you have learned.* The chapters on each style will describe its "Quick Recognition Signals." Now we will cover the three basic techniques: Observing, listening, and asking questions. Then we will discuss a more unusual topic, "listening with the third ear."

Observing

Good players are usually observant, and the best players really work at it. After folding, most of us "tune out." We daydream, look at television, decide what to eat, and so on. Winners stay focused on the game, learning how people play. In fact, they can often learn more after folding than while they are playing. They can think of styles and other long term issues instead of focusing on how to play this hand. That pattern gives us *Rule One for getting information: Watch the action whether you are in or out of the pot.*

Don't try to do too much. If you try to follow the action, count the pot, put people on hands, and learn how several people play, everything can become a blur. Simplify your task by applying *Rule Two: Focus on one or two players at a time.*

Obviously, you should focus on the players who have the biggest impact on you and the game, such as the regulars you can't read or beat. If you ignore everything else and concentrate on just one or two of them, you may be pleasantly surprised at how easy it is to read and beat them. You will probably see habits and weaknesses you never saw before.

You will learn more by applying *Rule Three: Make predictions and verbalize your reasoning.* We discussed this principle in the introduction and the chapter on reading hands. It is such a powerful tool, that virtually all scientists use it. They explicitly say, "If my theory is correct, this will happen because of A and B and C." If their prediction is incorrect, they can quickly determine what they did wrong and revise their theory.

We don't have much theory in poker, but we do try to put people on hands. We might predict that Joe will bet on the next round because we put him on a full house. If he checks and shows down a weaker hand, we realize we made a mistake, and can learn where we went wrong. If we don't make predictions, we might never recognize or correct our mistakes.

Listening

We will learn the most from observing because the most important actions are bets. However, we should also listen because people say lots of things — both at the table and when they are just sitting around — that give them away.

Cardrooms should have a sign with a "Miranda Warning: Everything you say can be used against you." Most people do not realize how much information they give away by talking carelessly. For example, whenever they tell a bad beat story, they let people know how they think and play, and good players will use that information to beat them.

They also give themselves away whenever they discuss other people's hands. Lots of people love to show how "smart" they are by commenting on other players. "He shouldn't have raised because ..." "I would have put him on a flush because ...." "I would never play a hand like that." If you just listen, you will be amazed at how much "free information" is floating around.

Sometimes people will tell you exactly how to beat them, essentially giving you a knife to slit their throats. Later observations confirmed that people were not lying when they made the following statements. The comments after "Thanks" say how you could use that information against them.

- "I'm not aggressive. I won't raise unless I'm almost certain I've got the winner."

  Thanks. The next time you raise, I'm outta here.
- "I'll always bet on the flop, if I'm last and nobody has bet."

  Thanks. The next time I've got a good hand and you're last, I will go for a check-raise.
- "If a pot is big enough, I'll call all the way with anything, but I'm not willing to make loose calls for small pots."

  Thanks. Now I know when to bluff you.
- "I never check-raise because I believe in betting my own hands."

  Thanks. The next time you check, I'll *know* you have a weak hand. I can bluff with garbage or bet a marginal hand without fear of a raise.

You may be thinking, "Nobody in my game would make such stupid remarks," but even major tournament players do it. For example, one player's foolish remark helped Matt Lessinger win the Carnivale of Poker Pot Limit Championship (with a prize pool of over $150,000). Matt emailed me that he had raised with QQ and had been reraised.

> "Initially I put him on a better hand than mine, but after he makes the raise, he turns to me, smiles, and says, 'I just wanted to make sure it was only the two of us.' Now I am sure I have the best hand. It comes to me, and I re-raise $500. He calls. On the flop I put him all in. He calls, shows a pair of tens, and is out of the tournament."

Probing

Observing and listening are relatively passive, while probing is much more active. Questions or other types of probes are attempts to get people to provide information they would not normally offer. Hardly anyone probes enough; we passively wait to be given information, but we will learn much more by using *Rule Four: Ask questions and probe in other ways for reactions.*

If you are too obvious, most people will resist or resent your probes. For example, most people are turned off by questions such as: "What did you have last hand?" They will respond more positively to questions about how they played cards they have already shown.

Many people have a strong desire to be understood; they *want* to tell you how they think and play. For example, after seeing their cards, you might probe by saying:

- "I wonder why you didn't check-raise."
- "I'm surprised that you called with that hand."
- "Why would you try to bluff such a loose player?"
- "That was a strange raise."
- "I never thought you had anything like that. I thought you had ..."

You can often get important information by criticizing people, but do it gently. For example, lots of people defend calling or raising with bad cards by explaining their reasons.

- "I always protect my big blind for one raise."
- "I'll see the next card if I've got three cards to any straight."
- "I raised because they are my lucky cards."

These statements provide you with valuable information you could not get any other way, and that knowledge helps you to understand and beat them.

An indirect criticism could tell you when someone caught a card. "You were lucky to catch that ace on the river." He might defend his play by saying, "I did not. I had it all the way."

Occasionally, someone will object to your probing. So what? Getting information is like panning for gold; it takes a lot of work to get a little bit of it. But it's worth the effort. However, if they seem genuinely irriated it is often best to back off since this might affect the mood of the game and perhaps even drive a weak player from the table.

Listening With the "Third Ear"

You will get insights you could not obtain any other way by employing *Rule Five: Listen with the third ear.* An eminent psychoanalyst coined that term. He said we have two ears to listen to facts, and a third, mental, ear to listen to the underlying meanings, such as people's feelings, hopes and fears. It's like "reading between the lines." That third ear can teach us surprising things, *if we use it.*

You may not use your third ear because you share the common belief that poker is only about money, but we have already shown that nearly all players have many other motives. To understand and adjust to players we have to listen with the third ear and constantly think of all kinds of motives, fears, and thoughts that have rarely been considered by poker authors.

The remaining chapters will discuss some of these "irrational" (i.e., unrelated to winning) motives and fears. We will use the third ear to go beneath the surface, analyze these other motives, and relate them to your own and other players' styles. You will see that people with different styles play for different reasons, see the game differently, and require different counter-strategies.

Part Four

The Loose-Aggressive Player

The Loose-Aggressive Player

Introduction

We will begin our discussion of types of players with loose-aggressive players (LAPs) because they are — by a huge margin — the most visible type. You may not quickly identify the other types, but you can't miss them. They are in almost every pot, jacking it up, making the game, and often making lots of noise as well.

The other players may even have nicknames for them, such as "Mr. Raise," "King Kong," and, of course, "The Maniac." Some people love to play with them because they make the game so exciting and lose so much money. Others can't stand them because their raises and reraises make the game too tense and/or volatile. In addition, many of them make irritating remarks, urging people to gamble and criticizing the "wimps" and "rocks."

The only sure thing is that nobody can ignore them. You may love or hate playing with them, but you always know they are there.

When they have good cards, they win lots of money, more than any other type. When they have average or worse cards, they take huge losses. A few extraordinarily gifted LAPs (who don't play extremely loose, e.g., Stu Unger) have become immortals, but most LAPs are big losers.

Loose-Aggressive Opponents

"Loose-aggressive players" (LAPs) include anyone with scores of 7-9 on both dimensions. Many of these principles and examples refer primarily to maniacs (9,9). The higher a player's scores, the more likely he is to act, think, and feel like a maniac.

Maniacs are so dominated by their addiction to action that their thoughts and actions are rigid and — in a rather bizarre way — predictable. You know they are going to raise and reraise with anything, and you must make huge adjustments in your strategy.

Less extreme LAPs have more self-control and flexibility. When dealing with a 7,7, you must be more cautious in applying these principles. You still have to make the same sorts of adjustments, but you must use more judgement and expect a more effective and unpredictable opponent. You must constantly look for variations in his style and adjust to how he is playing *now.*

All maniacs are heavy losers, but some 7,7 players are overall winners, especially if they pick the right games and read cards well.

If either score is 6 or less, a player is outside of the corner labeled "loose-aggressive," and some of these principles may not apply to him.

Since every one of the four styles we will discuss shares a quality with two of the other styles, there will always be overlaps. For example, LAPs share looseness with loose-passive players, and aggression with tight-aggressive players. They will naturally have some of the same habits, motives, and feelings as these others.

Please remember that psychology is a very inexact science. Regard everything you read here as general principles which may not fully apply to any individual. Start with these general principles, but make sure you carefully observe *this* opponent.

This chapter is the longest one for several reasons. LAPs are the most attractive, exciting, frustrating, and frightening opponents. They create more opportunities and more problems than anyone else. They appeal to our greed and desire to gamble, but they scare and irritate many players with their wild action and attacking words and manner.

Many players are attracted, frightened, and confused. They don't know whether to jump in and gamble with them, hunker down and become a rock, or just go away. In fact, many opponents get so confused that they shift rapidly from one extreme to another; one minute they are gambling wildly; the next they are timid and hesitant, and they finally run away.

Figure VI: Loose-Aggressive Players

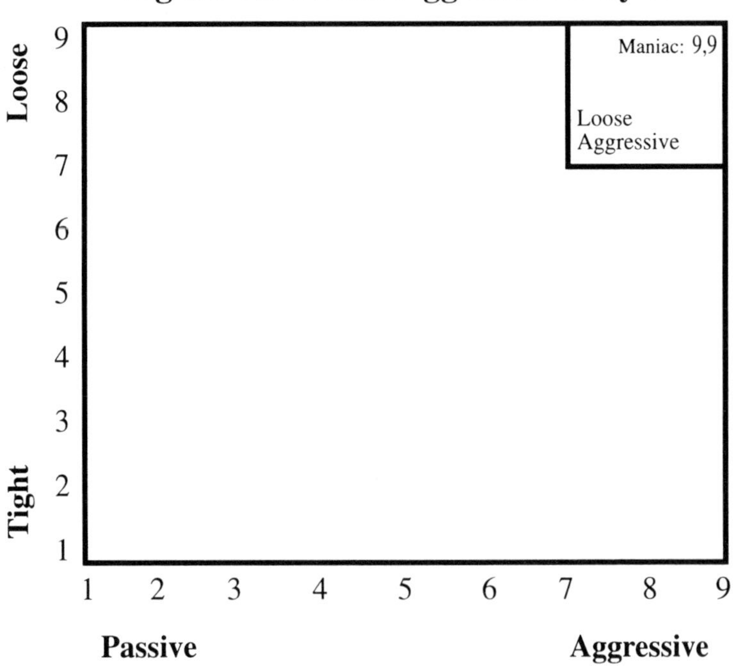

Quick Recognition Signals

This section is based on the common sense idea that people play poker the way they do other things. Their playing style, clothes, voice, gestures, and vocabulary all reveal and express their underlying personality.

However, you must be cautious. These signals are only moderately reliable, and the more sophisticated the player, the less reliable they become. Sophisticated players can easily reverse these signals, especially if they have read this book.

The underlying cause for the loose-aggressive style is a lack of control, and you can see it as soon as they start playing. They are usually the center of attention, involved in most pots, raising and reraising. Many of them are also loud or even obnoxious, showing off their machismo, urging others to gamble, criticizing the "rocks" and "wimps."

However, by the time you see those raises and hear those remarks you may have already made some expensive mistakes. The faster you can identify a player, the sooner and better you can adjust. Speed is especially important for LAPs because they can hurt you so quickly and so badly.

This section will describe and explain signals that quickly identify LAPs, perhaps even before they play a single hand. However, individual signals are *not* reliable for three reasons:

1. Psychology is not an exact science.
2. LAPs naturally have a lot in common with *loose*-passive and tight-*aggressive* players.
3. Poker is based on deception. Skilled players may deliberately create a false image, *especially if they believe you have read this book.*

You should regard these signals as just hints or cues. If a stranger's clothes, voice, words, and gestures suggest aggression, impatience, and lack of control, they are probably loose-aggressive. The more signals you see, the more confidence you can have, and the more extreme the stranger is likely to be.

However, you can't be sure until you observe how he actually plays because his play is the *only* reliable cue to a player's style. If he looks, talks, or otherwise appears to be loose-aggressive (or any other style), but plays differently, adjust to the reality, not the image. Here are some specific signals which frequently identify a loose-aggressive player.

Signal No. 1: Loud voice, aggressive words, forceful gestures, and an angry face. Any signs of aggression, anger, and lack of control hint that someone is loose-aggressive. For example, if someone pushes ahead of other people, is abrupt and demanding with waitresses, or loudly critical of other players or the dealer, he is probably loose-aggressive. Why only *loose*-aggressive? Because *tight*-aggressive players are much more controlled.

Signal No. 2: Flamboyant clothes, jewelry, words, and mannerisms. If a man dresses or acts like a teenager trying to impress girls, he is probably an LAP who will show off his machismo by taking foolish chances. If his shirt has two or three buttons open to show his gold chains and hairy chest, make a note. If he also shows off his bankroll, flashes his Rolex, and mentions his Cadillac, the odds get much better.

With women, flamboyancy is expressed a little differently, and it is a less reliable cue. However, you should still take note of bright colors, huge earrings, rings, or other jewelry, huge glasses (especially tinted ones), and hair dyed an aggressive color such as bright red.

Signal No. 3: Men are much more likely to be loose-aggressive than women. It is not politically correct to say it, but men are usually more aggressive and less controlled than women. Perhaps the most obvious example of testosterone's effects is the man who shows off for his girlfriend or the other women in the game.

Signal No. 4: Excessively large buy-in. If someone buys many more chips than necessary, he is either loose-aggressive or trying to intimidate. He will probably play aggressively, but you cannot be sure of whether he is loose or tight.

Flamboyant clothes, large buy-ins, etc. say, "Look at me!" and these people love being the center of attention. They want people to notice them and care about making a macho impression.

Younger people tend to be loose, but they may be either passive or aggressive. People get more conservative as they age, while young people have much less control of their emotions. They are much more likely to yield to their desire for action and need to impress people.

Signal No. 5: Sloppy chips or forceful bets. Always look at a player's stack and the way he makes his bets. A sloppy stack or forceful bets suggests a loose-aggressive style. In fact, some LAPs bet so forcefully that their chips get mixed in with other players' bets. The more forceful the bets and the sloppier the stack, the more confidence you can have that a player is loose-aggressive. However, many new players are sloppy with chips, which lowers this signal's reliability.

Signal No. 6: Posting unnecessarily. In hold 'em and Omaha most new players either wait for the blind to get to them or post in a late position. Posting in a middle or early position clearly signals impatience and perhaps a desire to show off machismo, especially if he says something like: "I didn't come to wait" or "Let's gamble!" Obviously, the less time he is willing to wait, the stronger the signal is. Refusing to wait just one or two hands is a strong signal of impatience and poor control (or simple stupidity).

Signal No. 7: Nervous tension. Aggressive players tend to be much more tense than passive ones. Their desire to attack makes the adrenalin flow, and it affects their entire body. LAPs express that tension in uncontrolled ways such as jiggling their legs, blinking frequently, nervous gestures, and talking too much, while tight-aggressive ones are more focused and controlled.

Don't just look at the player; watch how others react to him. They may already know him. Here are three recognition signals that often give away a loose-aggressive player.

Recognition Signal No. 1: Eager welcomes. If several players seem delighted to see a stranger, and they make a point of encouraging him to sit down, he is probably loose-aggressive or, at least very loose. If their eyes light up with greed and excitement, you can be more confident.

Recognition Signal No. 2: Signs of fear, requests to change seats, or an exodus from the table. Although lots of players welcome LAPs, some people — especially tight and/or passive players — detest and fear them. The combination of eagerness and fear is especially revealing. If the more aggressive and stronger players are glad to see somebody, and the quieter, tighter, and more passive players seem frightened, change seats, leave, or just grumble, the stranger is probably loose and aggressive. However, if the better players leave, you may be looking at a tough opponent.

Recognition Signal No. 3: Very direct remarks. People often comment on new players, especially LAPs. For example, in one $10-20 game, when the "Resident Maniac" sat down, somebody often said, "Now we're playing $20-$40." Others say things such as "He'll liven up the game." These remarks are obvious when you see them written down, but — if you don't listen — they will go right over your head.

Strengths

Nobody can win as much money as quickly as an LAP. He gets action because he overplays many hands. With good cards, he can win lots of money.

Weaknesses

Nobody wins or loses money as quickly as an LAP, but nearly all of them lose in the long run. In fact, *every* very loose-aggressive player (8,8 or higher) is a big loser, but some of them lie about it. Poker rewards patience, discipline, and *selective* aggression, while LAPs are impatient, undisciplined, and *promiscuously* aggressive.

Any extreme style is rigid and predictable (except, perhaps, tight-aggressive), and the combination of looseness, aggression, and predictability can be deadly. They make him the target. People know much more about them than vice versa, and they can easily develop strategies to exploit their weaknesses.

The most obvious are check-raising, slow-playing, inviting them to bluff, and isolating them with hands that normally would be correct to fold (e.g., three betting with

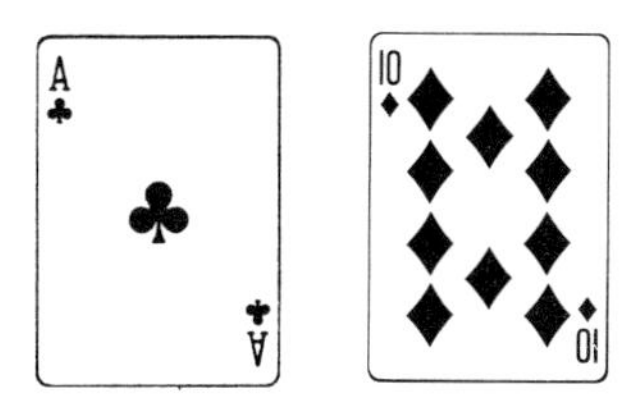

in hold 'em). Even fairly weak players soon learn to let the LAPs build the pots, and the better ones deliberately invite them to bluff. Because LAPs have poor self-control, they fall into the same traps again and again.

Because they are the center of attention, everyone focuses on them, and they give away lots of information with their hyperactive words and gestures. Their opponents — especially the better ones — may learn he is bluffing when he forcefully throws in his chips, is weak when he says "check" loudly or stares at his cards, and is ready to raise when he sits erect. Of course, you must always watch out for *smart* LAPs who will send false signals.

Reading Their Cards

Unless they send out tells and telegraphs, LAPs are among the hardest players to read, and maniacs can be almost completely unreadable. How can you put them on hands when they will raise with garbage?

The complete maniac is often unreadable, but hardly anyone is that extreme. Reading the 7,7 or 8,8 player can be difficult, but it is certainly not impossible. The key is to *remember when he does* not *raise.*

Since he will raise with weak cards, not raising in earlier rounds lets you exclude certain possibilities. For example, if a hold 'em flop has two hearts, and he just called behind two players, he probably does not have a flush draw. Otherwise, he would have raised. If another heart hits, don't be too afraid of a flush.

Or take a hold 'em flop of

If he did not raise before the flop and bets now, he may have a pair of aces or jacks and nines, but he probably does not have any set or aces up because he would have raised with AA, JJ, AJ, or A9.

Playing Against Them

They make the game more exciting, but riskier and more demanding. Because the pots are bigger and the action is wilder, your decisions are more stressful. Whether you like it or not, they will force you to gamble.

You have to make three key decisions. Should you play with them? Where should you sit? How should you adjust your strategy?

Should You Play With Them?

It depends upon who you are. If you like action and play reasonably well, of course, you should play with them. You can have more fun and make more money than in any other game.

If you are a cautious, conservative player, who dislikes risks, wild action, and ambiguity, you should avoid them. You won't like the game, and you may take a serious loss because the LAP may run over you, and the action can distort your judgment. If a maniac sits down, consider getting up.

If you are short of money you should probably avoid them. Your swings will be too large, and you may be so timid that the LAP runs over you. This recommendation becomes stronger if the game is short-handed, especially if there are blinds or substantial antes. Unless you understand short-handed play, you won't like the game or have much chance to beat it.

Everything changes as the number of players gets smaller. Much weaker hands win most pots; fewer pots go all the way to a showdown; bluffing and stealing blinds and antes become essential. If you wait for a good hand, the blinds or antes will destroy you. These characteristics of a short-handed game convert an LAP's style into an asset in games with blinds.

- "To be successful at short-handed hold 'em [or Omaha] you must realize that if you are not careful an individual could have the best of it simply by always betting." (*Hold 'em Poker for Advanced Players: 21st Century Edition*, p. 185)

- Always betting will not work in stud because the ratio of antes to blinds is smaller, but:
  "Short-handed poker can be difficult for people ... who are used to full games [because] many ring game players never learn how to play poor to mediocre hands well...
- "In ring games you can almost always make the assumption that your opponents have, on average, rather good hands. This means you can avoid the lower end of the mediocre hands. But in a short-handed game where other players are playing quite a few more pots you will frequently encounter situations where your hand, as bad as it is, is wrong to fold....
- "Against loose, aggressive players you must not just meekly call with your poor hands. You must occasionally splash around, raising with hands that seem like they are barely worth calling, in order to prevent your opponents from having a big edge from their semi-bluffs....
- "If you find yourself against players who are ... loose and aggressive, you've got to throw in raises with hands that are ... in some case below those you would normally even call with." (*Seven-Card Stud for Advanced Players: 21st Century Edition,* pp. 170-72)

You may find it difficult or impossible to make such large changes in your strategy. If you can't make them, don't play in short-handed games against LAPs.

Where Should You Sit?

That's easy: *To his immediate left so he acts before you do.* Generally, you want to be to the left of loose and/or aggressive players. You can raise loose players to knock out the players behind you, which lets you isolate and take the maximum advantage of their tendency to play weak hands.

If you are to the left of aggressive players, they raise before you act. If your hand is strong, you can reraise. If your hand is weak, you can fold. If you had to act first, you might put in one bet, then another with a hand that you would not play if you had known the pot would be raised.

Since these people are *both* loose and aggressive, being on their left helps you regardless of your hand. There are, of course, exceptions. See *Hold 'em Poker for Advanced Players: 21st Century Edition,* page 131, and the discussion below on telegraphs.

If you have just a fair hand, and he raises, you can quietly fold. If you were to his right and had already put in one bet, you would probably put in another one. If he just calls, you can play your fair hand. However, if a player behind you raised and the LAP now reraised, you will frequently have to fold.

When you have the right type of good hand, you can raise or reraise to go one on one with him. Very few people will call for three bets — and risk being caught in a raising war — even if their hands are a little better than your minimum reraising hand. Since you probably have a better hand than he does, you want to be heads up.

However, note that you need the right *type* of good hand. You want a hand that can win in a showdown without improving. Thus, in hold 'em

(a group six hand) is better than

(a group three hand). In stud a middle pair is much better than most drawing hands.

When you have a great hand, and he raises, you should usually reraise to shut out other players and start a raising war. If it is a *really* great hand (such as rolled up queens in stud) you can just call and get lots of action because many people don't take his raises seriously, and they may hardly notice that you cold-called behind him. They would fold if you reraised, but will call with weak hands and they may even reraise with good ones. Then you can put in another raise or continue to follow a trapping strategy.

However, *if you have a reliable telegraph on him, sit to his* right. Because LAPs lack patience and control, you can see what some of them are going to do. In fact, once in a while they will bet or raise out of turn. Even if they do not telegraph their bets, you can often see that they dislike their hand and will fold.

If you know what the LAP is going to do, being on his right is wonderful. You can fold marginal hands, slow play your great ones, and bluff at exactly the right time. If there are one or two players between you, you can make a squeeze play on them. If, for example, you see that he is going to fold, you can bluff, and the people between you may fold for fear of being overcalled.

Conversely, if you have a great hand, and see he is going to bet, you can squeeze the people behind him. You can check, knowing he will bet, and others will call with weak hands. Then you can raise, and he may even reraise. You may trap them for two, three, or even more bets.

How should You Adjust Your Play?

Although LAPs lose lots of money, they are risky opponents. They increase the size of your swings by essentially raising the stakes. When you are lucky, you will win more. When the cards go against you, you can lose a lot of money very quickly. However, if your raises and reraises can get you heads-up with the maniac, you can sometimes have the lovely combination of increasing your win rate *and* reducing your swings at the same time.

Even though you have varied motives, every recommendation here is concerned *only* with increasing your profits. The next chapter will consider your other motives.

One of these motives, your desire for action, can be your worst enemy. You may want to gamble with them, especially if they publicly criticize you for being too tight or even call you "a wimp." Lots of normally sensible players have gone broke trying to prove their machismo to wild players.

To get the best results, you must restrain your urge to gamble and make the opposite adjustment: *Call less often on the first round and become more selectively aggressive at all times.*

Your objective should be to reduce your losses on your weak and marginal hands, but to isolate the LAP when possible with your better (but maybe not best) hands. Your net will improve for two reasons. First, you won't get trapped with your marginal hands for extra bets. Second, if you raise, you will get less action from people other than an LAP.

People pay much more attention to raisers than to callers. He will get more action on his raises than you would, and they may hardly notice your call. You can win very large pots by quietly calling with especially good or even unbeatable hands when the LAP is jacking it up, and someone else may be reraising. Of course, at the very end, you can raise, but by then the pot may be so large that some people will make "crying calls."

This strategy may not appeal to you. You may get caught up in the gambling mood and become looser and more aggressive, but doing so can be extremely expensive. The bottom line is that you will play less hands which is just not as much fun, even though it improves your long term expectation.

Let's get more specific. Here are some concepts to help you against LAPs.

Concept No. 1: Don't try to bluff them. The temptation to bluff can be almost overwhelming, especially if you have invested a lot of money on a busted drawing hand. But it is usually a waste of money because they call with almost anything. But what about advertising? Forget it. You don't need to advertise to loosen them up. (The one exception occurs on the last round when you have a busted hand with no hope of winning a showdown. Since the LAP may also have very little, a bluff might be in order.)

Concept No. 2: Be less inclined to steal their blinds or bring-ins. These attempts are even sillier since you can gain so little, but lose so much. LAPs will call with almost anything on early streets, and they will often reraise. One failure to steal their blinds can cost you several times your potential profit, especially if you compound this mistake on the later streets.

Concept No. 3: Don't bet positional hands for value. A "positional hand" is a weak hand that seems stronger because everybody has checked to you. Betting these hands is often risky, but it is even riskier now because so many people won't bet okay or even good hands because they fear a raise from the LAP, or they are trying to check-raise.

Let's say you were playing stud, there are three players in the pot (you, a maniac, and an average player), and you are drawing to an ace high flush. You catch a second ace on the river; nobody has a pair showing; and everybody checks to you. If you bet your aces, and it is the best hand, nobody may call. If you bet and get called, it is probably beaten. And what if you get raised? You may call to avoid being bluffed, then feel like a fool for losing two unnecessary bets.

Concept No. 4: Raise or reraise to isolate them. Occasionally, you should become more aggressive. Some hands play better with a small field such as high cards or high pairs before the flop in hold 'em or middle or high pairs on third street in stud. Protect those hands by raising or reraising the LAP.

Let's say you are playing hold 'em in middle position with

and an LAP raises in front of you. Reraise in an effort to get heads up. Do the same thing with a pair of sevens in stud if the LAP raises with a jack showing. (Unless there are several bigger cards behind you. Now it is usually best to fold unless your hand is live and you have a large overcard kicker.)

You can also check-raise if you are first to act, the LAP is to your right. Lots of players — including ones who have you beaten — will fold rather than put in two bets and face the danger of having to put in two more if the LAP and you both reraise. For example, in hold 'em you have

in the big blind; the LAP is the button; there are four players besides you; and nobody raised before the flop. The flop is

You check because you don't like your kicker, want to see what the other players will do, and the LAP will almost certainly bet if it is checked to him. They check; he bets; the small blind folds, and you raise.

You can be fairly confident you have him beat because he would bet anything in that position. Of course, he might have you beaten, but you probably have the best hand, and you want to go one on one. Your raise can scare and confuse the other players, especially if they view you as a tight player. They probably will not put you on Q♦3♣ because they would not check-raise with it.

If you knock out someone with a hand that would have won, you may gain in two ways. You win a pot that he would have won, and he gives you more action in the future. He may remember that you raised him out of "his" pot and go after you the next time (when you might just show him a lock).

Concept No. 5: Bet into, raise, or check-raise them for value on the later streets. If you think that you have the best hand, overplay it. Of course, you will be wrong sometimes, but your gains will greatly exceed your losses. If you would check and call with a normal player, check-raise or bet and be prepared to call a raise. If you have a solid call, put in a raise. Your aggression will yield four benefits.

1. It will increase your profits on your winning hands.
2. It will occasionally knock out a better hand. For example, if you aggressively bet sevens up in stud, you may get a call or raise from the LAP with just aces, and a timid player may

fold a better two pair or a hand that would become best. If you knock out the winner just once in a while, it will more than compensate you for the bets you lose here and there.

3. It may "turn on" the LAP. They get a bigger kick out of playing against somebody who "gambles" with them than with the more conservative players. If you give them action when they perceive your hand as just being OK, they will give you more action when you've got a big hand.
4. It will do wonders for your image. You will look like a much looser "gambler" than you really are. Many players will not realize that you are not really gambling; you are just exploiting the LAP's weakness. (However, a few of your opponents will realize that you are making sophisticated plays and tighten up against you.)

You may be a little confused by an apparent contradiction. Didn't you read just a minute ago that you should tighten up? Yes, but that recommendation was for your *starting* hands. If you make a mistake with them, it can cost you lots of bets. Now you have lots more information and think you have the best hand. You will probably increase your expectation, but at worst you are just costing yourself a theoretical fraction of a bet.

Concept No. 6: Invite them to bluff. They love to bluff. In fact, many of them get a much bigger kick from bluffing than from winning with the best hand. If you suspect they are weak and might not call your bet on the end, don't bet into them. Just check and call if they bet.

Concept No. 7: Call or even raise them with marginal hands on the later streets, especially the river. You have to call or even raise for four reasons.

1. The pot has gotten so big that losing one or two bets is much less important than losing the whole pot.
2. They will bet much weaker hands than anyone else.

3. They like to bluff. The few bets you lose here and there will be much less than the huge pot you will occasionally win.
4. You cannot afford to be seen as a "folder." Many of them are quite perceptive about timidity, and appearing timid will just encourage them (plus any good player) to take a shot at you.

Sometimes you even have to raise on a marginal hand to prevent an overcall. For example, in a hold 'em game the LAP has bet or raised on every round, making a total pot of 17 big bets. All you have is top pair with a poor kicker, and there is no danger of a straight or flush. If the LAP bets, you should call or even raise to prevent an overcall. You would hate to beat the LAP, but still lose to two small pair or top pair and a better kicker.

If the LAP is Behind You

The following concepts apply whenever the LAP will act after you.

Concept No. 1: Look for telegraphs every *time.* So many LAPs telegraph their intentions that you must *always* look left before acting. They are particularly likely to telegraph folding. If you see a telegraph, take advantage of it. If they are going to fold, play your hand normally except consider your position to be one player later at the table; if they are going to raise or call, adjust your strategy.

Note: The following points are based on the assumption that you have not seen a telegraph.

Concept No. 2: Get much tighter on early streets. Since the chances of a raise are much higher, don't call unless you can stand a raise.

Concept No. 3: Don't try to steal their blinds. They overprotect their blinds, and may even reraise you with weak hands.

Concept No. 4: Check-raise frequently. A check-raise is much less risky and more profitable than with any other player. Since they bet hands that others would check, the danger that everyone will check behind you is obviously reduced, and the profits are greater because many people would fold if you bet, but call if he bets.

Concept No. 5: Use them to knock other players out. If the LAP is on your immediate left, be willing to bet many hands into them so that their likely raise will eliminate any players behind them.

Concept No. 6: Slow play big hands. They will get much more action than you will, so let them make the pot. On the river you can call or raise, depending upon the circumstances.

Playing in a Loose-Aggressive Game

A loose-aggressive game (LAG) has two or more LAPs raising each other or a maniac raising or reraising nearly every pot. Bluffing is common, but often futile because most hands end in a showdown. Huge pots are sometimes won by common hands, but so many players may stay to the river that many pots are won by back door flushes, gut shot straights, and other "miracle cards." The game is wildly exciting, but extremely dangerous.

These recommendations are derived from the ones for playing against an individual LAP, but adjustments are even more important. Poor adjustments to an individual LAP will cost you some money, but not adjusting well to an LAG can wipe out your bankroll.

In an LAG the stakes have essentially been raised, but the antes and blinds remain the same. You can therefore afford to be *much* tighter. Remember that point every time you get tired of folding.

Accept that the Rules are Different

The action is so different from most games that you must change your assumptions and strategy. We will make the same point in later chapters because you should constantly ask: How is this game different? How should I adjust to it? Since LAGs are so different and so risky, thinking and playing the way you normally do can ruin you. The following changes often occur.

Change No. 1: Most players' games have changed. An LAG affects nearly everybody. The action is so fast and the pots are so big that many people go on tilt. Although the term "tilt" is usually reserved for loose, careless play, I'll use it for any emotional foolishness.

The player who disgustedly folds an OK draw because he's angry about paying too much for previously missed draws is as much on tilt as someone who makes a "steam raise" with garbage because someone just drew out on him. They are both acting emotionally, not rationally.

Even people who are not on tilt are affected by the tension. They may become so excited that they think less before acting, and they do not think as well. Instead of coolly thinking of how much this next bet may cost after it gets raised and reraised, or hesitating to analyze why somebody made a bet, they may be thinking about a bad beat or wishing they hadn't folded an earlier hand. They may even act without thinking because the gambling fever has grabbed them.

Since so many people are emotional, the usual rules for reading their cards and playing your own have to be revised drastically. Surprisingly, two completely opposite reactions can occur. Many people "play scared," folding hands they should play. Others become too loose and aggressive. The urge to gamble wipes out their natural conservatism.

We have all been baffled by irrational raises from normally sensible players. For example, one man I know is usually a 4,4 (slightly tight-passive). In a wild hold 'em game he was the small blind with

unsuited. Normally, he would play it, perhaps even call a raise, but he would not even think about raising. After it was raised and reraised, he capped it. When asked why, he shrugged and smiled because he didn't know. The gambling fever or the frustration of being raised out of many hands may have taken over.

A few people even bounce back and forth from one extreme to the other. One minute they are mixing it up with gusto; the next they are checking or even folding winners.

Change No. 2: You and your game have probably changed. You are not immune to emotional reactions. You can easily go on tilt without realizing it. Tilt is always dangerous, but it is particularly dangerous here. The pots are bigger; the risks are greater; and many people are off balance, making you put in more bets every time you play. If you lose control, you can take a real bath.

Change No. 3: The pot odds and implied odds have changed drastically. Many pots become so big that the odds justify chasing with very low probability hands.

Change No. 4: Somebody will draw out on you *much* more frequently. This point is a direct result of the preceding one. So many people will stay with low probability hands that lots more of those hands will be made. Again and again you will lose huge pots to "miracle cards."

Change No. 5: The relationship between the size of the pot and the strength of the hands becomes wildly unpredictable. In most games huge pots often mean that great hands have clashed, but in these games weaker hands will win monster pots. The pot odds and gambling fever will make people pay huge amounts to catch miracle cards; when they all miss, a weaker hand than expected may be the winner.

Change No. 6: Luck becomes *much* more important than usual. Since the game is so wild and unpredictable, and so many hands are won on the river, and huge pots are won with small hands, these games often become "crap shoots." If you get the right hand at the right time, you win big. If not, you lose big. However, if you play these games correctly, your long run expectation is still higher since those good hands do eventually come home.

Concept No. 7: The tension is much greater. All of these factors make the game more exciting and more stressful, which brings us back to the ways everybody changes.

Adjust Your Strategy to Fit These Rules

Since the rules are different, your strategy must be different. In fact, an LAG is so different from the games discussed in most books that their recommendations may be almost irrelevant. The best specific advice is in *Hold 'em Poker for Advanced Players: 21st Century Edition,* pages 213-215 and *Getting the Best of It,* pages 83-86. Here are some adjustments you may need to make.

Adjustment No. 1: Monitor yourself. Your first and most important task is to look at yourself. Are you playing coolly and well or reacting to your own emotions? If ever there is a time to take a walk, it is now. The more you want to do something, the greater the risk that it is a mistake. The last thing you want to do is take a walk and miss the excitement, which is exactly why you need to get off your butt. If you feel your heart pumping and hate the thought of even a brief walk, *beware* because your emotions have taken over.

Every few hours or whenever you make a bad play, get a bad beat, or just feel off balance, take a few minutes to walk around, review your own play, analyze the way the game is going, and decide what to do. If you are playing badly or feel unsure of what to do, *quit!*

It is hard to walk away from a "great game," but, if you are off-balance, you are probably going to lose, and you may lose much more than you can afford, perhaps so much that you become desperate and blow your bankroll, trying to get even.

Adjustment No. 2: Analyze the way other players have changed. If you decide to stay, review the game and the key players' action. How is the game and their play different from usual? Be as specific as possible. Barbara has gotten much more aggressive. Joe is playing scared. Bill is bluffing more often.

Adjustment No. 3: Revise your game plan. Then ask yourself: Exactly how should I change my game plan? Adjust both your overall strategy and the way you will play against the key people. You might, for example, decide to get much tighter, but simultaneously reraise more in the early rounds, and be more aggressive in the later ones. You might want to bluff Joe more frequently and check solid hands to invite Bill to bluff.

Adjustment No. 4: If necessary, change your seat. Your seat is always important, but these games make it particularly important. The best seat is usually behind the aggressors; the worst is right between them. If, for example, a maniac is in seat three, and a 7,7 is in seat one, the best seat is number four, and the worst is number two. In seat four most of the action occurs before you, while in seat two you can get hit from both sides. You may also want to sit as far as possible away from a player who troubles you. Study the action and seating arrangements, then if necessary, change seats. The important point is to make a rational decision, not to take any old seat or to change seats to "change your luck."

Adjustment No. 5: Tighten up on the early streets. Play fewer hands and avoid weak draws. For example, 8,7 suited is a Group Five hand in the Sklansky system, and they say that "from a middle position ... in an unraised pot, you can play all hands in Groups 1-5 when the game is typical or tough."

Note the words "unraised pot." Even if the pot has not been raised *yet*, it is likely to be raised and perhaps reraised. Those raises change things in that most hands that require high implied odds become unprofitable. Let's say you call because the pot is unraised. The LAP raises, and the maniac reraises. Do you put in two more bets? Or throw away your hand? And, if you put in two more bets, you might have to put in another one or two. Then if the flop doesn't help (and most flops don't help), you have to surrender much more money than you wanted to invest. The net result is that your implied odds — total eventual win compared to present investment — have deteriorated dramatically.

The only way to avoid this sort of foolishness is to avoid weak draws (and don't worry about the rare times that they would have won a huge pot). Hunker down and wait for premium cards. Keep in mind that in an LAG small and medium suited connectors go down in value because if you flop a draw you may be charged a lot to make it. Compare this to a small pair where now you want to be "charged" when you flop a set.

Adjustment No. 6: Slow play more often. An LAG is the ideal place for slow playing because so many pots are raised, and the LAP will get much more action than you will. If you get a great hand, say a big full house, on fifth street (in stud) or the flop (in hold 'em), don't raise until sixth street or the river. Let the LAP do the raising because they get more action than you will. Besides, you *want* people to make their straights, flushes, and small full houses. You might end up in a raising war with an excellent, but second best hand.

Adjustment No. 7: Check-raise more often. The same principle applies to check-raising in later rounds. The danger that everyone will check is greatly reduced, which makes check-raising less risky and more profitable. Check-raising is particularly valuable in these games because the pots get so big, and your main objective should be to win them since you only rarely have the nuts. A check-raise is much more likely to knock out players than a single bet.

Adjustment No. 8: Don't focus too much on the LAP or maniac. It is natural to focus on them because they are making the game, but some other players may have made huge changes in their game, tightening up, going on tilt, playing scared, whatever. If you focus only on the wild players, the others can quietly take your money. You must also be aware of the size of the pot and the general type of adjustments needed.

Constantly shift your focus back and forth from the raisers to the others, especially the naturally tight players, and the ones who seem to be playing scared. They are in the pot for a reason. Why are they there? That question is particularly important if they acted before the LAP. If they did, expect them to have better hands because they risked being raised.

Adjustment No. 9: Bet or raise good draws with pot odds. Because the pots grow so quickly, the pot odds often justify aggressive betting. If you would certainly call a bet or a raise, it is often better to bet or raise yourself, unless you intend to check-raise.

For example, if on fourth street in seven-card stud you have

you have over a 45 percent chance to make a flush (on average), and it will usually win. You might also catch other cards which give you the winner. If there is a bet go ahead and raise. (Your raise may also knock out a player who would beat you if you just make a pair or two pair.)

You will probably get two or three callers, giving you wonderful odds on your raise. You may also get a free card on fifth street, when the bets double, because so many players almost automatically "check to the raiser."

Adjustment No. 10: Minimize bluffing. Because the pots get so big, somebody will usually call you, and you certainly don't need to advertise to get action.

Adjustment No. 11: Minimize deception and "fancy" plays. In this sort of game subtleties, deception, and "fancy" moves are just a waste of money, time, and energy. Most fancy moves will go right over everyone's head because they are too busy slugging it out. In fact, if you try to make moves, you can easily get distracted and waste your money. Keep your strategy simple, and emphasize the basics..

Adjustment No. 12: Bet for value more often than usual on the river. There is so much money in the pot that you may be eager to show down your hand to find out whether you have won. But the size of the pot virtually guarantees your bet will be called, and most people are unlikely to check-raise. You can bet just OK hands for value, especially if everyone has checked in front of you. Of course, since there are so many players, a good hand could be out there (and afraid to bet), causing you to occasionally throw away an unnecessary bet or two, but selective betting for value will pay off over time.

Adjustment No. 13: Call on the river unless you are *sure* you are beaten. The pots are so big that you are getting overwhelming odds. One correct call will more than cover the cost of several bad ones. Losing a bet is annoying, but losing a pot by folding a winner is a financial and emotional catastrophe. "Crying calls" in big pots have also been called "peace of mind calls." If you fold a winner, you could become so upset that you lose more money by replaying the hand in your head: "How could I have been so stupid. I knew ..." While replaying it, you may make other, even worse mistakes.

Adjustment No. 14: Hesitate and look left much more often than usual. Because the action is so exciting, many people play faster, and you can easily get caught up in the "Let's gamble" mood and act impulsively. Let's discuss why you should slow down.

1. Your decisions have more impact. Raises and reraises are so common that your first bet often commits you to risk much more than you had originally intended. The stakes have been raised, and you need to consider whether you want to take the additional risk *before* getting involved.
2. Your decisions are more difficult because the fast action changes the odds and the way people play. You have to consider factors you usually minimize such as the effects of future raises on the odds and the way some players' styles have changed. Since your decisions are more difficult, you need more time to make them.
3. Your own thinking may be affected. Unless you are extremely disciplined, the fast and furious action is going to disturb and distort your thinking. You can't think as clearly and coolly as usual when your heart is racing. You might also be thinking about previous hands ("If I had just called when ... .") For all these reasons, slow down. A moment or two can make all the difference between a good move and a stupid blunder.
4. People will telegraph more, but you might be less observant. Because people are excited, more of them will telegraph their intentions. Players who normally don't telegraph at all will have their chips in their hands or be ready to throw away

> their cards. Or they will be staring disgustedly at their cards, showing they missed a draw. Or they will be visibly tense, just waiting for a chance to play. In fact, if you hesitate briefly, some of them will bet or fold out of turn!

Winning is easy when you know their intentions, but your own excitement may make you miss obvious signals. So briefly pause and look left.

If You Are a Loose-Aggressive Player

You are a loose-aggressive player (LAP) if *both* of your scores are seven or higher. In that case this chapter focuses directly on you. Before reading any further, write your styles grid scores from page 96 of "Part Three: Styles and Ratings."

My styles grid scores are: ____,____

Figure VII: Loose-Aggressive Players

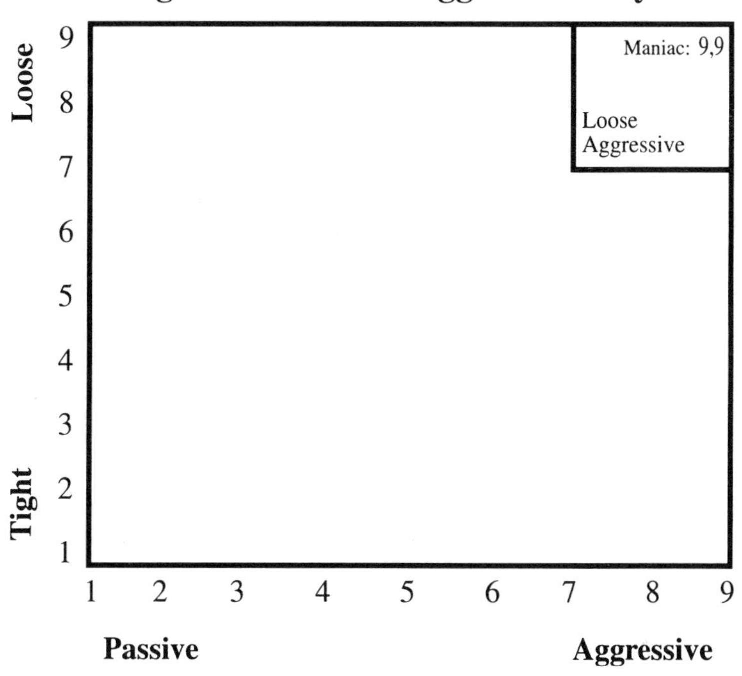

Place an X on Figure VII at the point that matches your grid scores. The closer that X is to the top-right corner of the grid, the more loose-aggressive you are, and the more relevant this chapter is to you.

Although anyone with two scores higher than seven is an LAP, most of the examples and principles refer primarily to the *extremely* loose-aggressive player, the "Maniac," 9,9. If either of your scores is less than 9, everything here is off, maybe a little, maybe a lot.

If either of your scores is less than 7, you are not an LAP, and much of this chapter does not directly relate to you. For example, if you are a 7,6, you are loose and slightly aggressive. Some of this chapter will fit you, while other parts may be quite inaccurate.

This chapter is divided into five sections.

1. Accepting the Consequences
2. Understanding Your Motives
3. Improving Your Play
4. Selecting the Right Game
5. Getting Your Act Together

We begin by discussing the general consequences because virtually all loose-aggressive players get the same overall results. The next four sections will help you to understand why *you* play that way and what you should do about it. Most comments will be addressed to "you" rather than "him" or "they" because I'm writing directly to you.

Accepting the Consequences

If you are an LAP, particularly an 8,8 or higher, you may not like the next few lines, but you should take them seriously. The consequences of your style are fairly obvious.

- You will lose lots of money.
- You will be welcome in almost any poker game.
- Many players will be secretly contemptuous, and a few players will be openly hostile.

Losing Lots of Money

You will lose because poker rewards patience, discipline, and *selective* aggression, while you are impatient, undisciplined, and *promiscuously* aggressive. You will have a few great nights, but many terrible ones. Unless you play for tiny stakes, the long term total losses can be substantial. Here are your major strengths.

1. When the cards are right, nobody can win as much as you can because you will get great action from them. People give you action because you overplay so many hands.
2. You may also take control or even "own" the table, which can create an edge in some situations, but cause problems in others. The other players may "hold their breath," waiting to see what you will do. If you raise, they may jump in and gamble with you, or run away because they are afraid of you.

   However, owning the table has negative effects. When the pot is large, you often want others betting so that you can raise to knock out players. Owning the table also makes you the target, a subject we will discuss in a moment. Being the center of attention sounds like fun, but it often has a "boomerang effect." It comes back and hits you in the head.

Here are your major weaknesses.

1. Despite your strengths, you need great cards to have a winning night. If your cards are just average — as they usually are — you will lose. Over the long term, you will certainly lose unless you play in exactly the right games.
2. Those losses can be painfully large because your style is so risky. You play too many hands, and you play them too aggressively. Nobody loses so much money as quickly as an LAP, and nearly all lose heavily, but lots of them deny it. They remember the good nights, and forget or minimize the bad ones.
3. Any extreme style is rigid and predictable, and the combination of looseness, aggression, and predictability is deadly. Even owning the table has a down side. It makes you

the target. People study you more than other players, and they often develop counter-strategies to minimize your strengths and exploit your weaknesses.

The most obvious are check-raising, slow-playing, and inviting you to bluff. Even fairly weak players soon learn to let you build their pots, and the better players will also check betting hands to invite you to bluff. Since you crave action, you may fall into their traps again and again.

4. Good players will focus on you and trap you with their better hands. They will spend much more time studying you than other players because you make the game. If, like many other LAPs, you get "hyper," with lots of hand movements, gestures, and nervous conversation, you may tip off your intentions. Other people may give off equally obvious signals, but most players miss them because they don't study those players. They study you because you are in the pot so often, betting and raising, dominating the action.
5. The better players will also get position on you. Weak players don't know how important position is, or they just don't care about it. They just sit anywhere or choose their "lucky seat." The good players know how important position is, and they will use it against you. You will often end up in the worst seat: The weaker players will be to your right, and the stronger ones to your left.

Any one of these factors would make it hard for a very loose-aggressive player (8,8 or higher) to win; the combination of all of them virtually guarantees that he (you?) will lose very heavily in the long run.

Being Welcome

Loose-aggressive players are welcomed almost everywhere, and maniacs are especially welcome. Many players welcome them because they make the game exciting and lose lots of money. The house appreciates them because they make bigger pots, increasing the rake and prolonging the game; people who planned to leave stick around when a maniac is playing. The dealers love them because they usually tip well, and the other players tip better because the pots are bigger.

You can often recognize a maniac before he plays a single hand. If lots of people welcome somebody, or they nudge each other and point him out, he's probably a maniac. Do you remember that wealthy farmer who raised blind because "looking at your cards just slows the game down?"

He played in a small California town with only one lowball table at $1-$5. If the game was full, he would offer $25 or so to buy a seat, and the other players would chip in about $5 each. A player could sell his seat for over $50, and most players would not take the money and leave. That's how welcome he was.

He knew he would lose about $500, but so what? He said our "little game" was the only place he could relax, and he didn't care about the "few bucks" he lost. If you feel that way, and you can afford to lose a "few bucks," you can have the same wild time and warm welcome.

Warren Buffet, America's greatest investor, rephrased the classic proverb: "A fool and his money are soon parted." He was talking about foolish investors, but his words also fit wild gamblers: "A fool and his money are welcome everywhere."

Hostility and Contempt

Not everyone welcomes wild players. In fact, when one of them sits down, some conservative players will grumble, and a few of them will leave the table. They like a quiet, peaceful game without too much risk and excitement. They also resent the fact that some LAPs make nasty remarks about "Rocks" and "Wimps."

Even the people who seem so glad to see you may be secretly contemptuous. They welcome your money, not you. They may smile and shake your hand, but they are trying to put their hand into your pocket.

They may also have the contempt of predators for their prey. No matter what they say to your face, behind your back they call you a "Maniac," "Wild Man," or "Total Live One."

Understanding Your Motives

The first question is: *Why do you play poker?* And the next one is: *Why have you chosen such a self-destructive style?* You certainly are not playing primarily to win money because you are a loser. Come on, stop kidding yourself. You know you have lost your share.

Let's find out why you *really* play. Go to the: "Why Do You Play Poker?" chapter in "Part One: The Right Stuff." Quickly review it, then copy your answers from page 35 into the "Self-ratings" table below.

The next few paragraphs may change the way you see your motives.

Table V: My Motives for Playing

Make money	______%
Socialize, meet people	______%
Relax	______%
Get excitement of risk	______%
Test self against competitive challenges	______%
Sense of accomplishment from winning	______%
Pass time	______%
Other (specify)	
______________	______%
______________	______%
______________	______%
Total (must be 100%)	______%

Every player should know why he has chosen his style, but this self-knowledge is especially important to you because your style is so risky. *If you do not understand why you are an LAP, you can easily lose much more money than you can afford.*

LAPs just love action, and some of them are literally addicted to it. The term "addiction" means an uncontrollable, destructive craving, and that is exactly what they have. The thrill of gambling often outweighs everything else: Judgment, strategic concepts, awareness that a game is too tough, even their major responsibilities.

You can see this pathological pattern in many casinos late at night. Small children are sleeping on the floor because their parents are gambling. People are desperately trying to borrow money from their friends, relatives, or even strangers to get back in action. Or look at main street in any gambling town; there is one pawn shop after another. People will pawn almost anything — even their wedding rings — to get back in the game.

Some very loose-aggressive players (8,8 or higher) are pathological gamblers; they cannot control their addiction to action, and they keep playing foolishly until they lose everything. Like all addicts they make excuses and deny reality. "I'm sorry, honey, but it was such a good game that I couldn't leave." "I know I can beat that game, but I was just so unlucky." "I'm sorry I blew the down payment for the house, but I'll never do it again." Of course, they do it again, and again, and again because they can't control their addiction.

Less extreme LAPs (say 7,7) may be somewhat successful at the poker table, especially if they select their games carefully and develop good hand reading skills, but many of them blow their winnings — and the rest of their bankroll — playing craps, sports, or the horses. They know they can't beat those games, but their need for action makes them act foolishly.

Another motive for choosing the loose-aggressive style is the desire to meet competitive challenges. LAPs — and lots of other people — like to test themselves, to see how good they are. We already discussed Nick "The Greek's" testing himself against Johnny Moss.

If you are loose-aggressive, you may take foolish risks just to challenge yourself. For example, you may play in games that are too big or too tough for you; you *know* you are battling uphill, but you can't resist the challenge.

You may play long shot hands partly because it is more of a challenge to win with them. You probably bluff frequently because stealing a pot is a much bigger kick than winning it with the best cards. And bluffing a good player is an even bigger kick.

This hunger for risks and challenges can be extremely destructive. You may look at your hand, realize that the odds are against you, but call or even raise. The thrill of action and the challenge of trying to win with a weak hand outweigh your desire to make money.

You may know the odds and strategy, but deny them. In fact, the entire casino industry is built on this denial. People lose billions every month trying to buck the odds on craps, the horses, whatever. In poker you can make the odds work for you by playing conservatively, but that isn't you. You get your kicks from action, and you are willing, consciously or unconsciously, to pay for them.

One very loose-aggressive player (8,8) even told me: "I have a theory. I believe that flushes occur more often than the books say they should." I wonder if he also believes in the tooth fairy. He is the only person who directly told me his "theory," but lots of people share his fondness and draw to many hands when the pot size does not warrant it. I once asked an LAP (7,7) with my tongue in cheek: "Have you ever met a flush draw you didn't like?" He laughed and said, "No."

Some extreme LAPs enjoy the "status" of being welcomed and the feeling of dominance they get from lots of betting and raising. It gives them the same kick that other people get from being high rollers at the crap tables, owning the fanciest car, or being welcomed by headwaiters at expensive restaurants. They like standing out, being welcomed into the game, being the "main man."

I have deliberately used a teenager's expression because they act like silly adolescents showing off on skateboards. They essentially say, "Look at all the crazy chances I'm taking. Aren't you impressed?" The good players are impressed all right. They quietly say to themselves: "Another live one with a big stack of chips."

All these motives are potentially dangerous. That farmer could afford to lose $500, and he expected to do so. If you can't afford your losses, and you are hooked on making the action, testing yourself by taking risks, and being "welcomed," you may have a serious problem. If you think you might be a pathological gambler, get help by calling 1-800-GAMBLER.

Enough of that heavy stuff. Let me tell you a lovely story about a classy lady. Doreen is an LAP (7,7), but quite sane (beyond the craziness that all of us players share). This story shows the positive side of loving action more than results.

> In a small hold 'em game Billy bet, she raised, and he reraised.
>
> She said, "I'm not going to take advantage of you. I flopped four tens, and I'll just call."
>
> Billy smiled as he turned over his cards. "I wouldn't have minded if you raised because I have a Royal Flush."
>
> She *instantly* applauded and smiled. She did not curse or complain or even hesitate.

She had just had a memorable experience, one she would talk about again and again. That pleasant experience was far more important to her than the money she lost.

Take another look at the ratings of your motives. If you did not put some serious points next to "excitement" and "competitive challenge," and something about "status" or "taking over the game," you are kidding yourself. You are definitely not playing just to make money or whatever you wrote. In the final section, "Getting your act together," you may want to revise your ratings.

Improving Your Play

If you are loose-aggressive, especially an 8,8 or higher, you can't improve your game until you accept the central truth: *If you don't change your style, nothing else really matters.*

You can master the odds, read all the books, become a great card reader, and do whatever else you think will help, but, *if you continue to use a very loose-aggressive style, you will continue to lose heavily.*

I apologize for offending you, but you have known it for years. You may have denied it and wished that there was some way to win and still get the kick of raising and reraising wildly, but you can't do it, and it is time you stopped kidding yourself.

General Stylistic Changes

In terms of the styles grid you should move down from the top right corner toward the bottom right corner, and the further you go, the better. You already have half of a good game: You can act very aggressively. (Though perhaps a bit less aggressively than you are now.) You just have to do it much more selectively.

Figure VIII: Improving the Style of the Loose-Aggressive Player

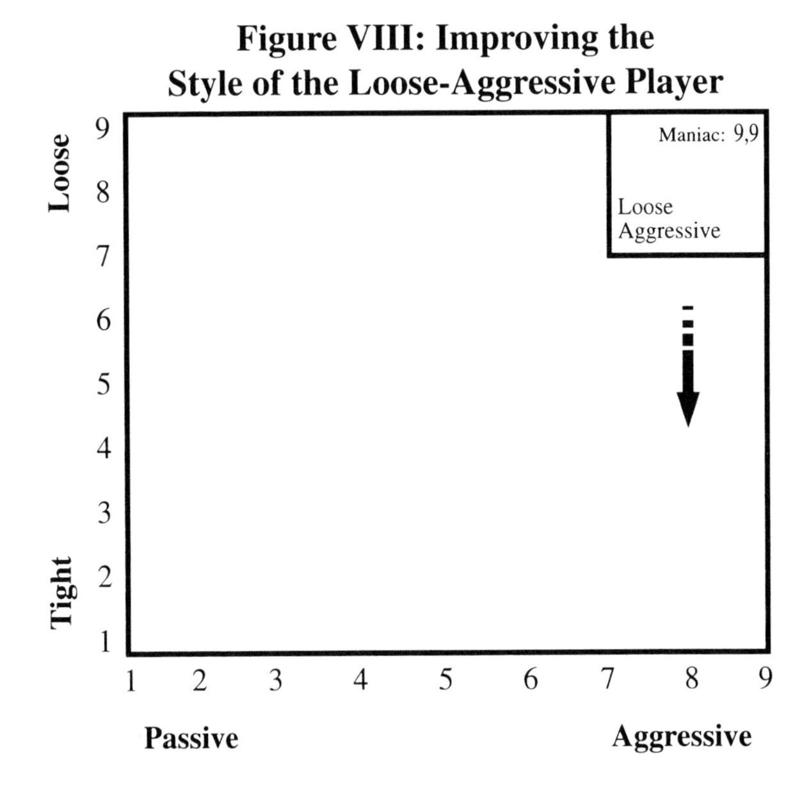

Specific Changes

We will consider only ways to affect your chances of winning because it is impossible to deal with all of your other motives. You should: *Calm down, tighten up, become more selectively aggressive, attack weaker players and avoid stronger ones, develop card reading skill, exploit your image, and select your games carefully.*

Specific Change No. 1: Calm down. Your emotions are your biggest problem. They may make you call or raise when you should fold, join games that are too big or too tough for you, and keep you playing long after you are too tired or distracted to play well.

You know you have done lots of foolish things. Again and again you have asked yourself, "Why did I raise that hand? I knew he had me." "Why did I play with them? I know I can't beat them." "Why did I keep playing when I was so tired I could hardly keep my eyes open?"

Your problem is not knowing; it is doing. You have to get a grip on yourself, take a deep breath *before* you make the mistake, then say to yourself, "No thanks. I'll pass."

Specific Change No. 2: Tighten up. Nothing will improve your game faster than tightening up. *When you have garbage, dump it.* When the action clearly says you are beaten, *get out*. If you are weak and haven't improved, *run* (unless the pot odds justify a call).

Lots of people have told you to avoid foolish gambles, but you have kidded yourself about how much they cost you. You do it because the excitement is more important to you than the money, but you often kid yourself that only bad luck makes you lose. You have to decide whether you want to get honest with yourself and stop losing so much money. To do so you must tighten up.

Specific Change No. 3: Be *selectively* aggressive. It is almost as important as tightening up. Every top player is capable of being very aggressive, but they are selective, while you are promiscuous. You are aggressive all the time, while they pick those spots where they gain by forcing the action.

Just focus your aggression. You do not want to be a passive player, nor should you even try to become one. *Save your aggression for the players that will gamble with you, the hands that deserve it, and the situations that demand it.*

Specific Change No. 4: Attack the weaker players and avoid the stronger ones. This is one form of selective aggression. Over time the strong players are going to beat you because they have more skill, a better style, and position over you. To win you must reduce your loses to the stronger players and increase your gains from the weaker players.

Since the strong players generally have good cards, you must give them more respect. Check your marginal hands, then usually fold if they bet. Given your reputation, they will not bluff often (unless you telegraph your weakness). If you would normally bet or check-raise with a hand, just call with it. If they raise, fold marginal hands. In other words, since they play only good cards, keep away from them when you have weak ones. Save your wild gambling for the weaker players who will gamble with you.

Alas, this strategy directly conflicts with your competitive urges and need for action. It's more fun to gamble with the better players. They present a bigger challenge, and they will raise and reraise right along with you, while most weak players are passive. But you may have overlooked something. *The better players are* all *tight (except for a few exceptional situations); they will give you lots of action* only *when they have the edge.* You must avoid them when possible and act cautiously when you can't avoid them.

Specific Change No. 5: Develop card reading skill. Developing it is more important to you than to any other player because your style is so risky. Without it you can't be *selectively* aggressive. The "Reading Hands" chapter in "Part Two: The Right Skills" discussed ways to develop this skill, but just studying it won't do much for you. Card reading is not like memorizing the odds; it requires judgment and reflection, and you are an extremely active person, not a reflective one. You like mixing it up, not sitting back and analyzing.

You, more than anyone else, should follow the recommendation to sit behind a highly skilled friend and try to read the other players' cards. When you get a chance, quietly discuss selected hands. As a passive observer you will see and understand things that now go right over your head, and those discussions will open your eyes further.

Specific Change No. 6: Exploit your image. Because people know you as an action player, you are going to get great action. If you mix up your game and get a *little* tighter and more selectively aggressive, you will still get lots of action, but you will get it with better hands.

Because you have a high profile, the other players will focus on you, and the very good ones will quickly recognize and adjust to your new style. Fortunately, there are not that many good players, especially if you play at the lower limits, where many players almost ignore how someone else plays.

You can tighten up and still get lots of action for a long time. When they have seen and adjusted to the new strategy, put them off balance by briefly reverting to your old style, then tightening up again. The key point is to avoid being predictable. If you are *always* loose-aggressive, you have to lose. If you are *selectively* loose-aggressive, you can become very tough indeed.

Selecting the Right Game

Choosing the right game is part of selective aggression. Select games that allow you to play the way you enjoy, but improve your chance of winning (or at least reduce your chance of losing). The looser and more aggressive you are, the more important it is to select these kinds of games.

- The lowest limits you can tolerate.
- Lots of other loose players, preferably aggressive ones.
- Short-handed games.

There are two main reasons for picking low limits. First, you will lose less money. Remember that maniacal farmer who was not really crazy? He could have gone to much bigger games in other places, but then he would have had to play more conservatively or lose a lot more money. He chose to play wildly in our little game where he would lose "only" $500, which was chump change to him. If he had gone to Las Vegas, Atlantic City, or some of the large California cardrooms and played $50-$100 or higher, he could not have played wildly without losing serious money.

Second, low limit games are usually looser, and the players are less skilled than in bigger games. You have a much better chance of beating a little game, but will probably lose in bigger ones. You may not like playing in small games, but please remember that you are not playing to make a profit.[12]

You may make that claim, but you would be kidding yourself. You are playing for action, competitive challenge, status, and other primarily psychological satisfactions. The money is just the way of keeping score, and winning a few dollars is much more fun than losing lots of them.

You should not even think of playing in a game without lots of other loose players. Tight players are going to beat and frustrate you. With lots of them in the game you don't have a chance, and you won't have much fun. So play with people who love action almost as much as you do. They will gamble with you and love it, win or lose. You will have more fun and get better results with them than with anyone else.

Short-handed hold 'em games can cause major problems for tight players who won't call enough. If they just sit there, waiting for a hand, you can bet every time and cause them to lose money. (See *Hold'em Poker for Advanced Players: 21st Century Edition* and *Seven-Card Stud for Advanced Players: 21st Century Edition* for more discussion.)

---

[12] This is actually another topic that is worth addressing. Many players who would otherwise be winning poker players insist on staying broke by continuously playing in big games where they are only mediocre players at best.

Getting Your Act Together

If you are a loose-aggressive player, this chapter has told you a lot about yourself and your playing style. Let's relate it to the questions you answered earlier.

Whenever it says to review and copy scores from a previous chapter, you might find it useful to skim that chapter to remind yourself of the content.

This exercise will take some time, and the answers you write today may be revised as you develop yourself. It may be boring or irritating to spend so much time, but it could pay huge dividends.

Your Right Stuff Ratings

Go to "The Right Stuff Questionnaire" on page 294. It should be dog-eared or paper-clipped. The next few lines are identical to that page. Look at the answers you wrote some time ago. Do they still seem correct? If not, revise them and write your answers here.

Which right stuff dimensions are assets, liabilities, or neutral for you?

Assets	*Liabilities*	*Neutral*

How can you take advantage of your assets?

How can you reduce the effects of your weaknesses?

Your Card Reading Grid Scores

Go to page 47. It should be dog-eared or paper-clipped. Answer the following questions.

My score is closest to the corner named _____

I have the following similarities and differences from that sort of player

Similarities:

Differences:

How do these similarities and differences affect your poker playing?

What are you going to do about it?

Your Styles Ratings

Look at the styles rating that you wrote on the first page of this chapter. Write it here.

My styles grid scores are: ____,____

Now that you have read this chapter, does that rating seem accurate? Circle the appropriate answer. Yes No. If you circled "No," write a more appropriate set of scores here ____,____

If you changed either or both scores, briefly state why you did it. The more you write, the more benefit you will get.

Your Motives for Playing

Look at your self-ratings on motives from page 140 of this chapter. Copy them into the "Self-Rating" column of the following table. Use pencil and make sure they add to 100 percent.

Table VI: My Motives for Playing

My Motives	Self-Rating	Revised Rating
Make money	____%	____%
Socialize, meet people	____%	____%
Relax	____%	____%
Get excitement of risk	____%	____%
Test self against competitive challenges	____%	____%
Sense of accomplishment from winning	____%	____%
Pass time	____%	____%
Other (specify)		
____________	____%	____%
____________	____%	____%
____________	____%	____%
Total (must be 100%)	____%	____%

Based on all you have read, do those percentages seem accurate? If not, insert better numbers in the "Revised Rating" column. Use pencil and make sure that they add up to 100 percent.

General Questions

Write the answers to these very general questions:
My current style *satisfies* these motives:

My current style *frustrates* these motives:

I should *change* my general style *from:* __ , __ *to* ____,____ because I want to:

Specific Actions

Review the entire chapter and write down *specific actions* you will take.

I should *play in* the following kinds of *games:* ___________
because they ______________________________

I should *avoid* the following kind of *games:* ________________
because they ______________________________

I should make the following *specific changes in my strategy:*

1.

2.

3.

4.

Dog ear or paperclip these pages. From time to time review your plans, note how well you have implemented them, and, if appropriate, revise them.

Good luck!

Part Five

The Loose-Passive Player

The Loose-Passive Player

Introduction

Loose-passive players (LPPs) are the easiest to beat, and there are lots of them, particularly in the smaller games. They are so dominated by their need to get along with people and their fear of conflict that they never get the message: *Poker rewards patience and aggression.*

Instead of waiting for a good hand, then attacking, they play too many hands, and they play them too passively. They are so uncomfortable with aggression that they let other players control the action. Instead of betting and raising, they just call, call, call. The inevitable result is a long string of substantial losses.

They are not as visible as LAPs because they do not raise either their bets or their voices, but you can quickly spot them. In addition to being in every pot and playing passively, their entire manner is often gentle and passive. They are the sorts of people you would like to have as neighbors or in-laws, but they haven't got a chance to win at poker.

Loose-Passive Opponents

"Loose-passive players" (LPPs) include anyone with scores of 7-9 on the tight/loose dimension, and 1-3 on the passive/aggressive dimension. Many of these principles and examples refer primarily to calling stations (9,1). The closer a player's scores are to that extreme, the more likely he is to act, think, and feel like a calling station.

Calling stations do not play to win. They may say it, but even they know they don't mean it. They are so dominated by their passivity and desire to get along with other people that they take actions they know are foolish.

Less extreme LPPs have more self-control and flexibility. When dealing with a less extreme player such as a 7,3, you must be cautious in applying these principles. You will still have to make the same sorts of adjustments, but you must use more judgment and expect a more effective and unpredictable opponent. You must constantly look for stylistic variations and adjust to how he is playing *now*.

All loose-passive players are heavy losers. They lose more consistently than anyone, even maniacs. Once people have identified an LPP's style, they bet into and raise him with abandon. They know he will call, even when he is clearly beaten. When he finally gets a hand and raises, nobody calls because they know what he has. LPPs have the worst possible combination: They give action, but don't get it, making them the easiest opponent to beat.

If either score is outside of the pattern (below 7 on looseness or above 3 on aggression), a player is outside of the corner labeled "loose-passive," and some of the principles may not apply to him.

Since LPPs share looseness and passivity with the adjacent corners, some parts of this chapter will overlap with the chapters on loose-aggressive and tight-passive players.

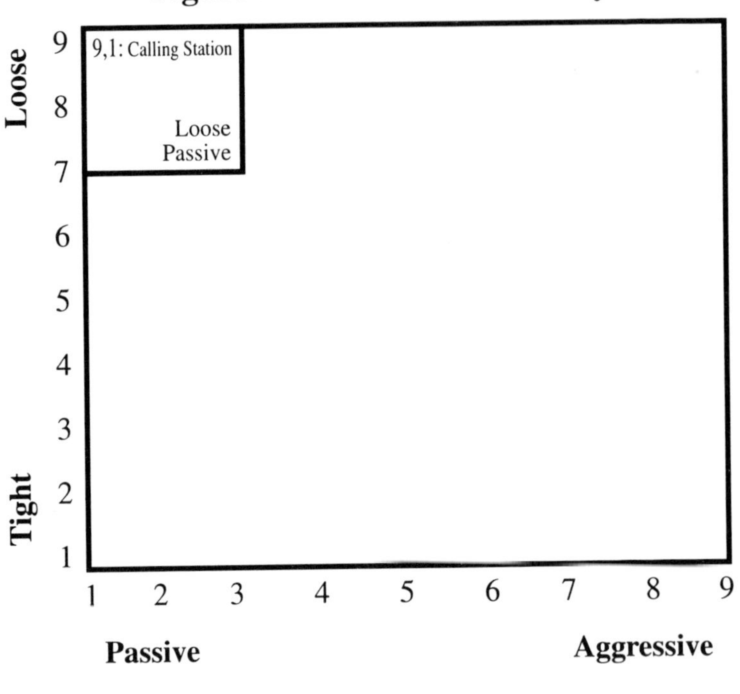

Quick Recognition Signals

This section is based on the principle used in the previous chapter: People play poker the way they do other things. Passive people play passively; careless, impatient people play loosely. If someone's voice, manner, and gestures suggest passivity and a lack of control, he probably plays a loose-passive game. The more signals you see, the more confidence you can have, and the more extreme the player is likely to be.

However, we must repeat an earlier warning: Poker is a game of deception, and some players — especially ones who have read this book — might mimic an LPP to deceive you. Make sure their play correlates with these other signals. If not, ignore these signals and adjust to their play, *and* expect them to be deceptive in other ways.

Loose-passive players are easier to identify than everyone except loose-aggressive ones. You will naturally notice them because they play almost every pot, and they tend to be open and honest: What you see is what you get. A few of them will even tell you how they play.

Besides, it is not that important to identify LPPs quickly. They can't hurt you very much — except by drawing out on you — nor can you have much influence on them. For example, if you try to bluff or run over them, they will do probably what they would do anyway, call your bets.

Below are some characteristics that you can use to identify an LPP.

Characteristic No. 1: Soft voice, passive words and gestures, an accommodating, friendly manner, and a placid face. If someone looks placid and friendly, the odds are he is a passive player, but not necessarily a loose one. If he also seems loose, relaxed, and friendly, expect looseness. Look at how he relates to non-players, such as waitresses, dealers, and spectators. An affable, non-demanding manner toward them suggests that someone is loose-passive.

Characteristic No. 2: More interested in socializing than winning. This pattern is an extremely reliable signal that someone is loose-passive. For example, if he pays little attention to the cards, does not know who raised or what the action is, chatters away as if he was playing party bridge, you can be almost certain he is loose-passive.

Characteristic No. 3: General relaxation. Passive players are more relaxed than aggressive ones, and loose-passive players are the most relaxed of all. Some of them even resemble the cover boy of *Mad Magazine*, Alfred E. Neuman. Their whole manner says, "What, me worry?"

Characteristic No. 4: Nondescript clothes, jewelry, words, and mannerisms. Anyone who "blends in with the wallpaper" is probably passive, but not necessarily loose. Once you recognize passivity, you can assess looseness in other ways.

Characteristic No. 5: A gentle or even timid betting manner clearly suggests passivity. For example, if they gently place their chips so close to them that they seem afraid of intruding or want to pull their bets back, they are probably passive. Again, you have to make a separate estimate of looseness.

Characteristic No. 6: Posting unnecessarily. Anyone who posts in a middle or early position clearly signals looseness. Obviously, the less time he is willing to wait, the stronger the signal is. Refusing to wait just one or two hands is a strong signal of impatience or indifference to economics, which are closely related to looseness. The way he posts can give a hint about aggression. Loose-aggressive players may do it forcefully or say something to express their machismo, but loose-passive ones will just post their blinds quietly, and a few of them will seem apologetic. Their manner almost says, "Sorry to butt in."

As always, *observe how others react to him.* They may already know him.

Here are two recognition signals that often give away a loose-passive player.

Recognition Signal No. 1: Very visible welcomes. If several players seem to welcome him, and they look as if "lunch is served," the new player is obviously a weak player, but what kind of player is he? If he is loose-aggressive, you will often see some fear and grumbling, and a few players may want to leave the game. If someone is obviously welcome, but nobody seems apprehensive, grumbles, or wants to leave the game, the new player is probably loose-passive.

Recognition Signal No. 2: Very direct remarks. People do not say much about an LPP, but someone may occasionally say something like, "Here comes a calling station." or "He never saw a hand he didn't like."

Strengths

From a financial perspective, they have no strengths. They nearly always lose. Once in a while they get lucky and win a few dollars, but they soon give it back.

Socially, they do very well. Everybody but the macho fool who yearns for challenges likes to play with them. They are easy to beat because they give action, but don't get it. They are also so pleasant and undemanding that they never cause trouble.

Cynics may snicker because they think that poker is just about money. They don't understand that people play poker for lots of reasons, and to these people winning is not at all important. Their style clearly indicates that fact. They are not stupid; they *know* they are going to lose because they lose so often. In fact, some of them are quite successful in business or other areas.

But they do not change their style because it satisfies other needs. They call because they want to be involved; we even use the term "family pot" for one involving everyone. They don't raise because they want to "be nice" and to avoid confrontations. Remember the "Law of Subjective Rationality." Their actions make sense to them because they satisfy *their* motives, not the ones you would have in their situation.

For example, in many casinos you will see women playing because they want to do something while their husbands gamble. They may not particularly like poker, but it is better than watching him throw away his money shooting craps, and, as several of them have said, "How much shopping can you do around here?" A few husbands do it, but it is much more common for wives.

Or take some of the older regulars. They have retired, are often widowed or divorced, live far from their children, and don't have another hobby. They can choose between playing poker, watching TV, going to the senior center or library, or sitting in a bar. The poker room offers a place to go, something to do, and people to talk to, and the expense is not that great (if they stick to the small games).

You can see the same pattern in a few stock brokers' "boardrooms." People sit in a spectators' area, watching the "tape." Their conversation resembles what you hear in some poker games. They talk about their lucky and unlucky investments, and they may even tell "bad beat" stories:

> "My son-in-law, 'the genius,' told me this stock couldn't miss, so I bought 200 shares. One week and it's down *six* points! What a jerk. I don't know why my daughter married him."

The commissions they pay and any money they lose are essentially just the "club's dues." The money involved is not always trivial, at either poker or stock brokers' offices. Most amateurs who try to trade stocks lose — even in bull markets — because the commissions have the same impact as the poker room's rake. Brokers would not provide that expensive real estate if it did not generate substantial commissions, and purely social players can be seen in almost any poker game.

Poker is generally cheaper than playing the stock market, slot machines, craps, or blackjack, and it costs much, much less than a yacht or a race horse. Besides, the socializing and conversation are much better than you will find at a slot machine or a crap table.

Regulars can meet each other, and the game provides something to talk about. People rarely review interesting spins of a slot machine; when the wheels stop turning, it is over (except for a brief complaint or exclamation). In fact, many slot players don't talk at all; they seem almost hypnotized by the machines.

The action is too fast to talk much while playing craps, black jack, roulette, etc. If you tried to say more than a few words, you would be treated as a pariah. But in a poker room interesting hands are often discussed, especially by the people who lost them.

Their motives may seem irrational to you, but you will do much better if you understand, accept, and adjust to them.

Weaknesses

The obvious weakness is that it costs a lot of bets to call, call, call, and they do not win much when they make a hand because they do not bet aggressively. When they do bet out, they often do not get called because they are so easy to read. Thus, they nearly always lose, and they lose fairly quickly.

Another result of their constant calling is that many players are secretly (and occasionally openly) contemptuous. You have certainly heard — and you may have even made — nasty remarks when they win by catching miracle cards.

As Rodney Dangerfield would put it, they "Get no respect." Poker is a macho game with a macho culture. It values toughness, control, aggression, and deception, which are about as far from them as you can get.

Reading Their Cards

Reading their cards is almost impossible. Since they will call with almost anything, you can't figure out why they are in the pot.

Reading their bets is fairly easy. They do not bet without solid hands.

Reading their infrequent raises and extremely rare reraises couldn't be easier. If they raise, they have a very good hand. If they reraise, they have a lock or close to it.

What about a bluff? Don't worry about it because they rarely bluff, and, when they do it, they may look embarrassed. If you think an LPP might be bluffing, look for signs of discomfort. If he seems comfortable and confident, bless his honest heart and fold unless you can beat a good hand he would bet.

Playing Against Them

This section considers three decisions:

1. Should you play with them?
2. Where should you sit?
3. How should you adjust your strategy?

Should You Play With Them?

Unless your motives are extremely different from most people's, the answer is: *yes, yes, yes.* They are the easiest people to beat. If you can't beat them, take up solitaire. There are only two reasons to avoid them:

1. They are so easy to beat that it's boring. There is no challenge, and winning may not be satisfying.
2. You will get frustrated when they draw out on you, and they will do it again and again with some *terrible* hands.

Where Should You Sit?

Loose-passive players have one quality you want on your right (looseness), and one you want on your left (passivity). You want passive people on your left because you don't have to fear a raise. If they raise, you can confidently fold everything but a powerhouse. However, having them on your left makes it difficult to steal the blinds/antes, buy the button, etc.

In addition, if a *loose*-passive player is to your right, you can raise them to try to knock out the other players, which lets you take maximum advantage of their tendency to play weak hands. One of the best situations is heads up against a loose-passive player.

Even though they have qualities that you want on both sides of you, the reasons to have them on your right far outweigh the reasons to have them on your left. If you tend to be passive, you should force yourself to play more aggressively when they are on your right.

If you can chose between a tight or loose passive player on your left, choose the tight one. You can steal antes, and his bring-ins or blinds with hardly any risk, but, as already mentioned, you can't steal anything from a loose-passive player. He will almost always call.

How Should You Adjust Your Strategy?

They are the softest opponents, but you must control yourself and relate to them on *their* terms, not yours, to get the best results. Here are some concepts that you can consider. Note that the first principle may be especially hard.

Concept No. 1: Be nice. Don't be greedy and try to get every last bet. You can easily get it, but doing so can make them feel you are "mean" or "ruthless." They may leave the game or tighten up against you.

That advice may go against your competitive instincts and greed, but you will actually make more money by giving them an occasional break. For example, if you are heads up and have a lock, you might show it without betting. Sure, you lose a bet, but so what? Good business people invest money to build good will with their best "customers." (Similarly if you are first to act and think you can get a check raise in, just come out betting instead.)

The second aspect of "being nice" is to make sure that you *never* criticize their play. You may have read it many times, but countless people ignore that advice. They criticize the LPP for not raising, or, more frequently, they express outrage when the LPP gives them a bad beat.

> "How could you make such a stupid call? The odds were 20-to-1 against you. If you keep playing that way, you'll go broke."

Such remarks are always foolish. They may educate the LPP (and any other weak players who overhear them), and they can drive away your best customers. These points are true for everyone, but they are especially true for LPPs.

They are not playing to win; they want to enjoy themselves, to be part of a group, socialize, and pass the time. The personal qualities that make them weak players cause them to be very sensitive to criticism and rejection. Your thoughtless remarks can really hurt them, and they are much more likely to leave than anyone else. They may move — perhaps permanently — to another game or even another casino where people are "nicer."

They may also become much tighter and tougher if they realize that their loose-passive style costs them *both* money and respect. They can probably afford the money, but not the loss of respect.

Concept No. 2: Don't make plays that humiliate them. As already mentioned, resist the temptation to get an extra bet — for example, by check-raising them when you are heads up. (It's OK to check-raise when there are several players.) In addition to offending a good "customer," you run the risk of changing his attitude."He is no longer there to have fun. He is there to beat you." (*Hold 'em Poker for Advanced Players: 21st Century Edition*, pp.155.)

You should also compliment them whenever possible. When they make a hand, smile like you mean it and say, "Nice hand." If they win a good pot by catching a miracle card, compliment them on their courage. "I never would have had the nerve to make that call." Of course, don't be too obvious about it; you could appear patronizing.

These compliments are rewards for doing exactly what you want them to do, keep making those loose calls. People repeat rewarded actions, and compliments are extremely cheap and effective rewards. You may have to grit your teeth when you compliment somebody on having the courage to draw out on you, but it will put lots of money in your pocket.

Concept No. 3: Bet and raise for value with weak or questionable hands. You can bet quite weak hands for value because they will call with even weaker ones. If you check in a two handed pot, they will check behind you. So bet hands you would normally check. If they raise, fold. Of course, sometimes they will just call and beat you, but over the long run you will make lots more by betting than checking.

Betting weak hands for value when there is another player behind the LPP can occasionally have wonderful results. The LPP calls with a weaker hand, and the other player is afraid to overcall with the winner. Let's say, for example, that you are playing stud and hold

and are high on board. You bet your 7's up. The LPP calls you with a pair of tens. The person on your right looks at his higher two pair, sighs, looks again, and folds.

When he sees you win with a weak hand, he may bitterly criticize the LPP for calling, but that is not your problem. He may also remember you as the "guy who bet 7's up" and decide to get you next time. Boy, is he in for a rude shock when he calls you with a weak hand.

Incidentally, LPPs hardly every check-raise. If they have a good hand, they almost always either bet out or check and call. If they check, you can bet without fear of being raised.

We have focused on the river, but the same principles apply throughout the hand. Since they call with junk, you can raise them in the early rounds with questionable raising hands. Let's say you are playing hold 'em. An LPP called under the gun, nobody else called, and you are in the big blind with:

With most players you would have to respect their calling under the gun, but you can raise because he probably ignores position.

If you like the flop, bet, and you will probably get called with a weaker hand. If you don't like the flop, check. The LPP will probably check behind you if he cannot beat your hand (and may check if he can beat your hand). If he bets, fold.

You should bet particularly aggressively when you put an LPP on a straight or flush draw. They will often buck the odds to gut shot straights and back door flushes. If they bet, you can frequently fold because they very rarely bluff.

Concept No. 4: Don't bluff. Bluffing is usually a mistake. First, it will probably fail because an LPP is going to call you with all but the most hopeless hands. Second, a few of them will be a little offended by your trying to steal "their" pot. Since you don't need to advertise with them, don't bother.

Concept No. 5: Don't call with marginal or even okay hands (unless the pot size justifies doing so). Since they do not bet without a good hand and they hardly ever bluff, fold marginal ones automatically, and think carefully before calling with just okay ones. Of course, if the pot odds justify a call, make it, but these odds have to be higher than usual since you can't add in a good chance that your hand will win without improving.

Concept No. 6: If they raise, run. They do not raise without very good cards. If they raise, run, even if you have a good hand. If you do not have enough to reraise an average player, you should probably fold.

Playing in a Loose-Passive Game

A loose-passive game (LPG) is classic "no fold 'em hold 'em" (NFHE) or its equivalent. There are several LPPs, a few average players, and no more than one slightly aggressive player. Many players and a few writers believe that NFHE occurs only in lower limit games, but there are loose-passive games at all levels.

> "It is not uncommon, even at higher limits, to find many players who not only play too many hands, but go too far with them. These games, *usually* at lower limits, are referred to as "no fold 'em hold 'em." (Sklansky and Malmuth *Hold 'em Poker for Advanced Players: 21st Century Edition*, page 152)

Some pots are quite large because so many people stay in, long after they should have folded. However, others are fairly small because many players call on the first round, then everybody checks on later rounds. There are few raises and hardly any reraises. There might never be a capped pot. Nearly all hands end in a showdown, and several people may call the final bet.

Look for these games because they are the easiest to beat. The rules for playing in them are derived from those for playing against an LPP, but there are some significant additions.

Be Nice

The first and most important principle is the one we mentioned before: *Be nice.* Don't try to get every last bet; never, ever criticize; and compliment people for their courage and luck when they win, even if they made a mistake. In addition, never make a play that makes a fool of a person. You may be tempted to get another bet by, for example, check-raising, but "if it is heads up and you are against one of those 'weakies' who is there for the fun of it — perhaps a tourist — don't do it." (Both quotations are from *Hold 'em Poker for Advanced Players: 21st Century Edition,* page 155. Unless otherwise indicated, all the quotations come from pages 151-181 of that book. Its principles apply to all loose-passive games, not just hold 'em. See also the discussion of loose games, pages 131-157 in *Seven-Card Stud for Advanced Players: 21st Century Edition.*)

Accept that the Rules are Different

The principle is the same here as it was for a loose-aggressive game. The action is so different from most games that you must change your assumptions and strategy. If you just think and play the way you normally do, you will probably win, but not as much as you should win, and you will probably become quite frustrated. Sklansky and Malmuth make the same point:

> "Most good players underperform in very good games. They do not adjust enough to optimize the amount of extra profit that can be made when someone [or the entire table] is playing badly." (Page 153)

You can expect the following changes.

Change No. 1: You will lose with many hands that would normally win. That's the bad news. Somebody is going to draw out on you again, and again, and again. Frequently, there is nothing you can do to prevent it. You can raise, check-raise, or make any other moves, and they will often stay in there and catch those miracle cards. You will find it extremely frustrating, but read on.

Change No. 2: The increased size of your winning pots will more than compensate you for your unexpected losses. That's the good news. Sometimes your carefully selected hands will hold up, and you will win so much more than usual that your total profits will be much greater than in a normal game.

Most players either do not know or ignore that fact. I'm sick of hearing people whine: "In that game I can't protect my hand." And countless bad beat stories begin: "I had pocket aces, and this jerk called my raise with garbage." That complaint and the stories are based on frustration, not economics. From a purely economic point of view, *the more people who draw against your great hands, the more money you will make over the long term.*[13]

Take the best hold 'em hand, pocket aces. They will win more than 80 percent of the pots with only two players, but only about 30 percent of the pots with ten players. If nine players call all the way, somebody is going to beat you *most* of the time. The more people against your aces, the more often you will lose.

That's frustrating, but the profits on your infrequent victories will average being more than three times as much as you would win heads up. Let's say you played showdown (there are no additional bets) 100 times for $1 per hand.

With only one opponent the aces would win $80 on the 80 winning hands and lose $20 on the 20 losing hands. The net profit for 100 hands would be $60.

$80	won on 80 winning hands
-20	lost on 20 losing hands
$60	net profit

With nine opponents the aces would win about 30 times for a total of $270 ($9 per hand times 30 hands). They would lose about 70 times for a total of $70 ($1 per hand times 70 hands). The net profit for 100 hands would be $200.

$270	won on 30 winning hands at $9 per hand
-70	lost on 70 losing hands at $1 per hand
$200	net profit

---

[13] There are a few slight exceptions that occur rarely that need not be addressed here.

That $200 is more than *triple* the $60 the aces would win in 100 two-handed pots, and a return of 200 percent on the $100 wagered. It is absolutely impossible to get much more than a 100 percent return on your investment in a heads up pot using this model. The people who complain about loose calls and their inability to protect their hands don't know what they are talking about. They are expressing their frustration about being drawn out on because it hurts *now*, and the long term return on investment is just an abstraction to them.[14]

If you play in an LPG, you just have to accept that *you often can't protect your hand, but you will get paid well for your frustration.* They are going to call you and draw out on you, no matter what you do. If you have aces, the best thing for you would be to get a head-to-head raising war and win a huge pot, but it is not going to happen very often.

Pages 151-181 of *Hold 'em Poker for Advanced Players: 21st Century Edition* describe some plays that will reduce this problem and its frustration, but there is no way to eliminate it. When they draw out on you, smile and congratulate them; they'll give the money back, with fabulous interest.

Change No. 3: Pots quickly become so big that the LPPs mindless calling is almost justified. So many people call that the pot odds often (and the implied odds) justify or nearly justify calling with very weak hands.

Change No. 4: You have to show down the best hand to win. Nearly every hand will go to a showdown; you are not going to bet or bluff them off their hands, no matter how bad they are. However, you should often try to reduce the number of callers to increase your chances to take the pot.

---

[14] Of course the model that I used in the example does not do a good job of representing real poker since play on the later streets is not accounted for. Nevertheless, it does help to make the point.

Change No. 5: You will usually need a better hand to win. It is very simple mathematics; the more hands there are, the better hand you need to win. Because so many people call, lots more straights, flushes, and full houses will be made. You aren't going to win as often with a pair of aces, or aces up. Even a set of aces will occasionally get beaten.

Change No. 6: High cards and unimproved pairs go way down in value, while drawing hands become much more valuable. Drawing hands become much more valuable because the pot odds and implied odds are so favorable. Since nobody raises, it does not cost you much to draw.

Because good hands are made so often, high cards and unimproved pairs (other than aces) lose much of their value. Othmer's computer simulations of stud hands (p. 36 of his book) showed that the profit on AA2 continues to rise as more players call, but the profit on every other pair declines after a point, and that point occurs sooner as the pair gets smaller. For example, KK2 peaks at four opponents, QQ2 or less at about 2 opponents. His simulations do have the problem that the opponents held random cards and automatically go to the river, but in some LPGs a few people seem to play any hand dealt to them.

Because so many people play, big cards and unimproved pairs are going to lose far more hands than in a normal game. The odds still favor them, but not nearly so much as you might like.

Adjust Your Strategy to Fit These Rules

Since the rules are different, your strategy must be different. In fact, an LPG is so different from the games discussed in most books, that their recommendations are not optimal. Most are based on typical higher stakes games, which are usually (but not always) much tighter and more aggressive. The strategies that work there will still win in these games, but they won't win as much as is possible. Instead, you should read Othmer's book and the discussion of "loose games" in *Hold 'em Poker For Advanced*

Players: 21st Century Edition and *Seven Card Stud For Advanced Players: 21st Century Edition.*[15] The following strategic changes are consistent with their recommendations.

Adjustment No. 1: Make winning the pot your first priority. Virtually every action you take in any game requires a trade-off (for example, between increasing the size of the pot and your chances of winning it). In other games you often take actions (e.g., slow-playing good hands) which reduce your chances of winning, but can greatly increase the size of the pot. In loose-passive games the pots quickly become so large that you should often bet, raise, check-raise, or do anything else to reduce the number of players, thereby increasing your chances of taking the pot. "When the pots become very large, the most important aspect to your strategy should be to win them." (p. 180)

Adjustment No. 2: "Play more hands than you would if the players were better." (p. 159) If you are too tight, you will miss lots of opportunities. Since nearly everyone will stay, and raises are rare, you can cheaply see fourth street in stud and the flop in hold 'em. You should play hands you would normally fold because you are getting such great odds. Of course, on the rare occasions that somebody raises, run (unless the odds justify calling).

Since there will usually be lots of calls and few raises, you can play almost as if you were the last to act and several people have called in front of you. It is the same principle of anticipation that we applied to the loose-aggressive game. There we suggested becoming tighter in anticipation of raises, while here we suggest becoming looser in anticipation of many calls and few raises.

In hold 'em use the Sklansky Hand Groups, but play one or (if the game is extremely LP) even two groups looser than they

---

[15] All the following adjustments are from *Hold 'em Poker for Advanced Players: 21st Century Edition* unless otherwise noted.

recommend for a normal or tough game. You can play Group Five hands in early position, Group Six or even Seven in the middle, and Group Seven and even Eight when you are late. Sklansky and Malmuth make exactly that point: In middle position "in a loose, passive game, it is all right to play Group 6 hands... The weaker your opponents are, the more hands you can play." (p. 27) Within each group, be more liberal with the hands that play well in multiway pots, the pairs and suited connectors rather than the unsuited big cards.

Adjustment No. 3: Put greater value on drawing hands. The increased pot odds and implied odds make many drawing hands playable. For example, it will often pay to draw — even on third street in stud — to gut straights or small open-ended straights. In hold 'em you can sometimes justify drawing to gut shot straights, or backdoor flushes. The large number of players create excellent pot odds, and, if you make your hand, you will almost always get paid off, frequently by more than one player.

In hold 'em, place a slightly higher value on the drawing hands than the high cards within each group. "If your hand is suited in these loose games, it is a *giant* advantage.. [for certain kinds of flops] people now play hands that can't beat your hand if you hit it." (p. 173)

Small pairs are also drawing hands, and they become much more valuable in these games because your implied odds are so good. If you make a set, you attack. If you miss, you can fold cheaply. In fact, there is a simple little rule: *No set, no bet.*

Adjustment No. 4: Frequently bet or raise primarily to get more money in the pot. The simple fact is that you often can't protect your hand with a bet. Lots of people will call for even two bets just as quickly as they will call for one. However, since most loose calls have a negative expectation, it pays to bet and raise with most good hands.

Let's return to the pocket aces example. We saw that the aces would earn 200 percent on the amount you bet against nine random hands. The calls in an LPP game are not quite random, but they are often close to it. Some people call with nearly hopeless hands. You would obviously raise with aces, but you should also bet and raise with much weaker hands than normal such as a pair of nines before the flop in hold 'em or four cards to a flush on fourth street in stud. You will lose most of the time, but the increased size of the pots you win will more than cover your losses. In addition, against this type of opponent, your raise is more likely to "buy you" a free card.

Again, it is simple mathematics. If a bet has a positive EV (expected value), the more money you bet and the more often you bet, the more you make. Since you have the edge, it often pays to get as much money into the pot as possible.

For example, on the flop in hold 'em, you can bet or even raise with top pair and a weak kicker or middle pair and an ace kicker. Somebody may have you beaten, but lots of people will call with the middle pair and a smaller kicker, bottom pair, or a gut straight draw. In these games the pot odds will often justify these calls. A few lost souls may even call with less than that. (However, if a raise will knock some players out you may be better off not betting and going for a check-raise, or perhaps trying to raise on a later round where the betting limits double.)

The good draws will call in any game, but you will beat them most of the time. The odds against their making their hands are about 2-to-1. Since the pot odds are much more than that, their call has a positive expectation. But so does your raise. Since the odds against them are 2-to-1, you are getting as much as two-thirds *of the additional money*.

What additional money? There is only one pot and one winner. But the pot consists of two parts, the money that is already in there, and the money that goes in now or later. For example, on the flop in hold 'em the existing pot creates the positive EV for the draw, but two-thirds of the time you are going to win. Over the long term you get 67 cents out of every additional dollar that goes into that pot (in heads-up situations).

There is, however, a down side to raising, especially before the flop. If a raise makes the pot too large, it may convert your opponents' natural tendency to call with weak hands from a mistake to "accidentally correct or close to it... Thus, ... a lot of hands that seem like automatic raises should not be raised because you want your skill to mean more on further rounds." (p. 159) But if they really do play terribly, and come with almost anything, you will be giving up too much by not making the raise.

Betting and raising often involve trade-offs, and the factors affecting these trade-offs are too complicated to discuss here. See the discussion of "Loose Games" in *Hold 'em Poker for Advanced Players: 21st Century Edition* and *Seven-Card Stud for Advanced Players: 21st Century Edition.*

Adjustment No. 5: Raise with strong draws. This recommendation is just a specific application of the two preceding ones. Since lots of people are going to call, and strong draws frequently have an immediate positive expectation on each round of betting. Thus the more money you get into the pot, the more you expect to win in the long run.

For example, before the hold 'em flop, if you are the button, and six players have called, you can raise with

or

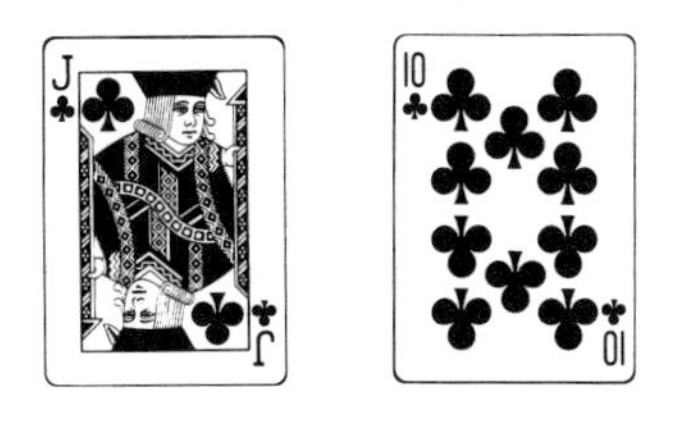

and even

or

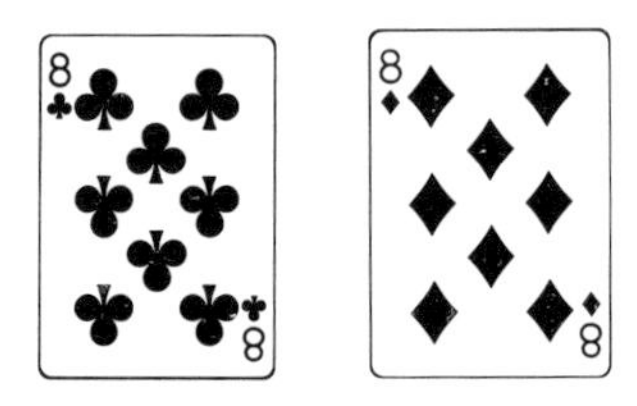

The more callers ahead of you, the weaker hand you need to raise because nearly all of them will call, and one or more of the blinds will probably call, giving you 7 or 8-to-1.

If you get a good piece of the flop, you can bet aggressively. If you get a little piece, you may even see the turn for nothing because LPPs very frequently "check to the raiser." You can also bet in late position to get a free card on the turn because they will probably check again.

If the flop doesn't help you, and somebody bets, you fold, and all you have lost by raising is one small bet. If they check to you, and you bet on the flop, and somebody bets into you on the turn, you can be fairly confident they have you beat (because loose-passive players will usually remember your earlier raise and again "check to the raiser").

In stud you would normally not raise with an open ended straight or a flush draw on fourth or fifth street with several players behind you because it would knock people out, damaging your pot odds and implied odds. You usually want to draw cheaply and have lots of potential callers to pay you off if you make the hand. (However, if your hand has other aspects such as a couple of high cards or a made pair, you may want to make this raise and try to get heads-up or thin the field.)

In an LPG lots of people will call the raise, particularly if they have already called the bet. In effect, they will shrug and say to themselves: "It's only one more bet." If you also have position, you may get a free card on the next round because they will "check to the raiser."

The same logic applies to the flop in hold 'em. If, for example, there has been a bet and four callers ahead of you, and you have a one card draw to a flush, and there is no pair showing, raise. The odds against your making a flush are about 2-to-1, and you are getting 5-to-1 on that raise because all of them will probably call. Your expectation is extremely positive, about a $1.00 profit for every dollar you bet.

You will win about one-third of the time, and lose about two-thirds of the time. Repeat it 100 times with 5 callers, and you will lose $67 on your losing hands, and win $165 on your winning hands producing a profit of $98.

$98 = $165 - $67

In fact, some "no fold 'em hold 'em" games are so loose that you can raise with good draws even if only one or two players have called because lots of people behind you will cold call the raise with garbage.

An additional reason to raise is that it will usually buy you a free card on the turn because of their passivity and tendency to "check to the raiser." This fear can work even if you are in an early position with players behind you. They may be so afraid of a check-raise that you get a free card. If they give you one, your raise has had the best possible effect: It has given you *both* a positive EV on your raise and a lower cost to draw when your first card misses (two small bets on the flop versus one small bet on the flop and one big bet on the turn).

Adjustment No. 6: Bet or raise with weaker hands to increase your chances of winning the pot. Although you have little chance to force everyone out, many pots quickly become so large that you should often bet or raise *even when you think you are beaten.*

> "You do this not just because there is a slight chance that you might win ..., but because betting [or raising] gets out those hands that will cost you the pot a small percentage of the time when your hand improves. Remember, you were going to call anyway." (p. 169)

At times this principle combines with others, such as raising with good draws. Let's say you have

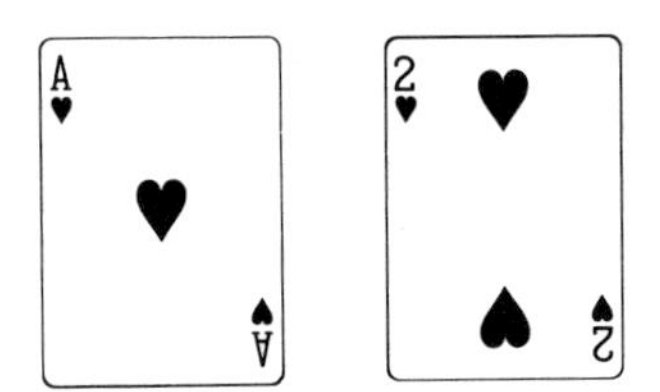

and the flop comes

There was no raise before the flop, and you are second to act with six players behind you. If the first player bets with an apparent pair of kings, raise. You will probably not knock out everyone, but you might knock out people who have A3 to AQ. Then, if you hit an ace, you can win a pot that you would have lost without raising.

I call this process, "buying outs." If someone has an ace and a bigger kicker, your only outs are the nine hearts that make your flush (excluding the very long shot of catching two deuces or an ace and a deuce). If your raise knocks out that player, you have eleven outs, nine hearts and the two remaining aces (unless someone would still beat your pair of aces). Since your priority is to win the pot, a raise that buys outs or increases your chances to win it in other ways is an excellent investment.

Adjustment No. 7: Resist the temptation to make certain raises. Because so many people call, the temptation to raise with some good, but not great, hands can be hard to resist. Let's say you are playing hold 'em on the button with the

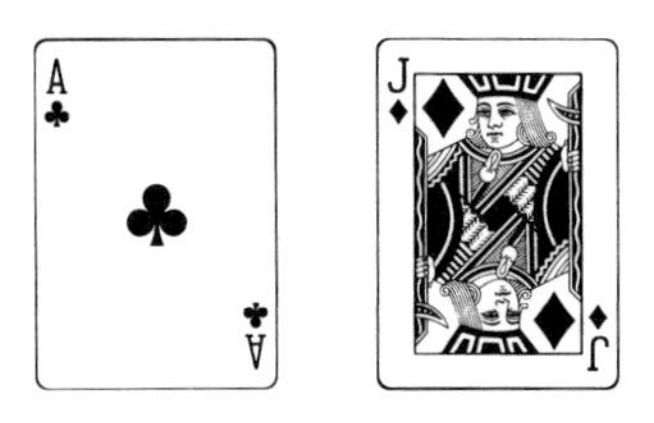

and six people have called. You know lots of them, maybe even all of them have weaker hands, but you should probably resist the temptation to raise.

Everybody will probably call, and your raise makes the pot so large that the pot odds may justify their calling on the flop or even the turn with weak hands, increasing the chances that someone will draw out on you. Calling with a gut shot straight or bottom pair would be a mistake if there are seven or eight bets in the pot, but it is the right play if your raise makes the pot 14-16 bets. Your raise has essentially converted their natural tendency to call on the flop or even the turn from a mistake into a proper play. However, as previously mentioned, if they play really terribly and come with anything, then you are giving up too much by not raising.

The same principle applies in many other situations. If too many people call a bet or a raise in an early round, the pot will often become so large that the LPP's mindless tendency to call with almost anything will often become the right thing to do. This subject is covered more thoroughly in *Hold 'em Poker for Advanced Players: 21st Century Edition* (pages 157-172) and *Seven-Card Stud for Advanced Players: 21st Century Edition* (pp. 141-149).

Adjustment No. 8: Minimize bluffing. Somebody will almost always call you, and there is no need to advertise to get action on later hands.

Adjustment No. 9: Minimize "moves." One of the silliest things to do in an LPG is to try for fancy plays. These people are so oblivious that these plays go right over their heads.

Adjustment No. 10: Minimize check-raises. If you check, everybody else may do the same. You have to bet your own cards because passive people are not going to bet them for you. However, in a few situations you can try to protect very vulnerable hands.

Let's say you have

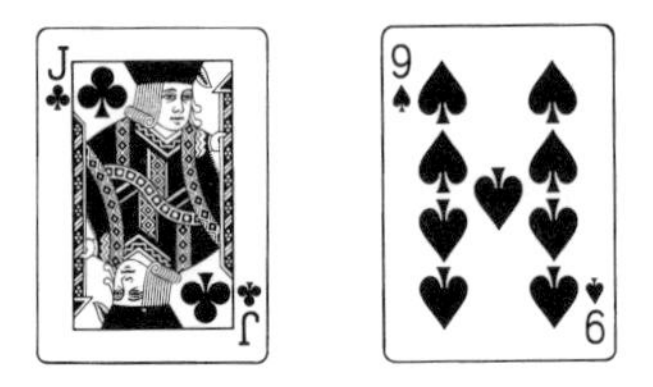

in the big blind in hold 'em; there are seven players behind you; and the flop is

You naturally want to protect your hand, but most or all of them will call if you bet. If you check, a late player may bet, and you can raise. A few of the weaker hands such as QT or 75 may fold, increasing your chances of winning the pot.

Adjustment No. 11: Don't slow-play good hands. Slow-playing runs the same risks as trying to check-raise. People may not bet or raise. If you've got a good hand, bet or raise with it. Otherwise, you will lose money on this round and increase the odds of someone's drawing out on you.

If You Are a Loose-Passive Player

You are a loose-passive player (LPP) if your tight/loose score is seven or higher, and your passive/aggressive score is three or lower. In that case this chapter focuses directly on you. Before reading any further, write your styles grid scores from page 96.

My styles grid scores are: ____,____

Figure X: Loose-Passive Players

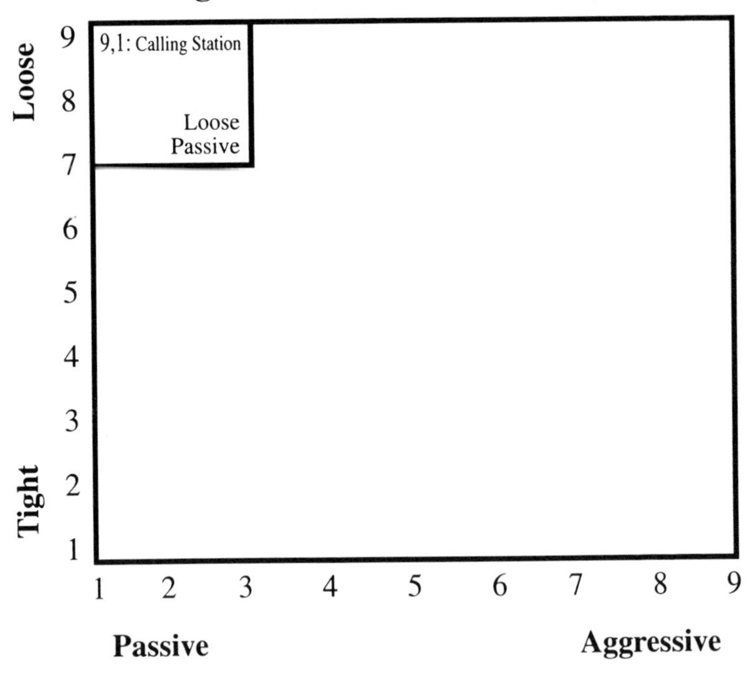

Place an X on Figure X at the point that matches your grid scores. The closer that X is to the top-left corner of the grid, the more loose-passive you are, and the more relevant this chapter is to you.

Although anyone with this pattern of scores is an LPP, most of the examples and principles refer primarily to the *extremely* loose-passive player, the "Calling Station," 9,1. If either of your scores is between two and eight, everything here is off, maybe a little, maybe a lot.

If your tight-loose score is less than 7, or your passive/aggressive score is more than 3, you are not an LPP, and much of this chapter does not directly relate to you. For example, if you are a 7,4, you are loose and slightly passive. Some of this chapter will fit you, while other parts may be quite inaccurate.

This chapter is divided into five sections.

1. Accepting the Consequences
2. Understanding Your Motives
3. Improving Your Play
4. Selecting the Right Game
5. Getting Your Act Together

We begin by discussing the general consequences because virtually all loose-passive players get the same overall results. The next four sections will help you to understand why *you* play that way and what you should do about it. Most comments will be addressed to "you" rather than "him" or "they" because I'm writing directly to you.

Accepting the Consequences

If you are an LPP, particularly an extreme one, you may not like the next few lines, but you should take them seriously. The consequences of your style are fairly obvious.

- You are going to lose money, perhaps a lot of it.
- You will be very welcome in almost any poker game.
- You can relax and socialize at the poker table.
- Many players will be contemptuous.

Losing Money

You *must* lose because you have the worst possible pattern: You give action, but don't get it. You lose too much on your bad hands, and you do not get remotely enough profit from your winners. You also lose many pots by giving free cards that beat you.

In fact, your losses can be much greater than you can afford. It costs a lot to call, call, call, particularly when you do not get much back when you have a winner, and you let people draw out on you for free.

Once in a while you get lucky and win a few dollars, but you soon give it back. Even if you do not care about the money, losing so frequently probably bothers you.

Being Welcome

Socially, you may be quite contented; in fact, that contentment is probably a major reason for playing. You are welcome almost everywhere. *Everybody* except the macho fool who needs to challenge tough players wants you in their game. You are easy to beat and good company.

Relaxing and Socializing

Your style demands very little effort. You don't have to study the players, count the pot, compute the odds, or do any of the tiring things that serious players do. All you need is enough chips to keep calling.

Your style allows you to relax and socialize. Poker is not a particularly social game. In most games you can't chatter away as people do at bridge games or cocktail parties, but poker is immeasurably more social than most casino games. You can meet people, talk between hands, and the game gives you something to talk about.

Contempt

Many players are secretly contemptuous, and a few of them will be openly nasty. As Rodney Dangerfield would put it, you "get no respect." Poker is a macho game with a macho culture. People look up at winners, down at losers. The primary values are toughness, aggression, and deception, which are exactly the opposite of you.

They welcome you because you lose, but lots of them are much more interested in your money than your company. You have certainly seen this contempt, especially when you make a loose call, catch a "miracle card," and give somebody a "bad beat." The smiles suddenly turn to abusive remarks about your play and intelligence.

Understanding Your Motives

The first question is: *Why do you play poker?* And the next one is: *Why have you chosen such a self-destructive style?* You certainly are not playing to win money because you lose so consistently. Come on, don't kid yourself. You know you do.

Let's find out why you *really* play poker. Go to the "Why do you play poker?" chapter in "Part One: The Right Stuff." Quickly reread it, then copy your answers from page 35 into the "Self-ratings" column below.

The next few paragraphs may change the way you see your motives.

Table VII: My Motives for Playing

Make money	______%
Socialize, meet people	______%
Relax	______%
Get excitement of risk	______%
Test self against competitive challenges	______%
Sense of accomplishment from winning	______%
Pass time	______%
Other (specify)	
____________	______%
____________	______%
____________	______%
Total (must be 100%)	______%

Every player should know why he has chosen his style, but this self-knowledge is especially important to you because *your style is hopeless* (from the perspective of winning). *If you do not understand why you play this way, you can easily lose much more money than you can afford.*

Take another look at those self-ratings. If you did not assign at least 75 percent to a combination of socializing, relaxing, passing time, and excitement of risk or similar motives in the "other" category, you are kidding yourself. You are definitely not playing to make money or to meet competitive challenges. In the final section, "Getting Your Act Together," you may want to revise your ratings.

You probably did not consciously choose the loose-passive style; you just acted naturally. I can't imagine anyone's deliberately deciding: "I'm going to pick the worst possible style."

Instead of choosing, you just played the way you do everything else. You are a people person who is friendly and cooperative, and you dislike conflict, competition, and confrontations. You call so frequently because you want to be included in the group, and you rarely raise because you want to be nice and may even fear being rejected for being greedy or pushy.

In my *Negotiate to Win: Gaining the Psychological Edge,* I used the term "dependent" to describe your basic style. A few excerpts seem appropriate.

> "Extremely dependent people crave love, acceptance, understanding, and approval from others. That is, they really are *dependent* upon others' feelings about them.
>
> "They are warm, friendly, and sincerely interested in other people. They ... enjoy most social gatherings. They are gracious and welcoming, with a natural ability to make others feel welcome and comfortable...
>
> "They communicate openly and honestly and expect the same from others. Because they know they can be trusted, they tend to trust other people, even when they should be more cautious and skeptical. (Used car salesmen love this kind of customer.)
>
> "They are cooperative, flexible, and compliant...
>
> "They also tend to be givers. They want to help people...
>
> "some people, especially dominant ones, can easily manipulate and exploit them...
>
> "[They] are afraid... of all forms of conflict (including competition.)" (pp. 186f)

Does that sound like you? If it does, I wonder why you play poker because aggression, competition, and deception are the heart of the game. Damon Runyon once wrote that there really is no such thing as a friendly game of poker because we play poker to take each other's money.

Millions of people play bridge, canasta, pinochle, and dozens of other card games without ever betting a penny, but hardly anyone plays poker without gambling. Unlike most other card games, poker requires betting decisions, not card management. Poker does not involve bidding or deciding how to play your cards; it involves only betting (except in draw poker).

Since betting is the core of the game, and betting well determines your success and the respect you get, you might get a lot more pleasure — and immeasurably better results — if you learned how to bet properly.

Improving Your Play

You can't improve your game until you accept the central truth: *If you don't change your style, nothing else really matters.*

You may have read a few poker books, but you certainly never seriously studied them. If you did, you would not play this way. You can study them now, but it will not make much difference. *If you continue to use a loose-passive style, you have absolutely no chance to win.*

I apologize if I have offended you, but you already knew or at least suspected that fact. Your friends may not have been that blunt, but they have often told you to change your style.

"Why did you play that hand? It was garbage!"

"I don't know why you called his raise. You knew you were beaten."

"Why didn't you raise? I'd kill for a hand like that, and you just called."

You have ignored them, perhaps even been annoyed by their nagging. You may have even denied the reality they tried to communicate because you wish that there was some way to win while playing in your natural style. Alas, you can't do it.

Since winning is not that important to you, let's look at it another way. Many LPPs essentially have a budget for poker. You may not explicitly allocate so many dollars to "poker losses," but you quit after losing a certain amount (if you don't, you really have a problem, and I suggest you get help by calling 1-800-GAMBLER).

If you follow a few suggestions, you will lose less frequently and more slowly. For the same number of dollars you can play more hours. Or, if you play the same number of hours, you will lose a lot less money.

You will also enjoy those hours more. It is more fun to be involved, to do more than call without thinking. I am *not* suggesting that you should take the game as seriously as the books or some of your friends suggest. You should improve your play for the same reason that duffers take golf lessons. Neither of you will ever be champions, but it is more fun to play reasonably well than badly.

You don't have to try to memorize all those odds, and remember all those exposed cards, get bored by folding hand after hand, or get into macho confrontations with aggressive raisers. That's not you, and you wouldn't enjoy it. Just study *one* book, get a *little* more involved, play a *little* tighter, try to figure out a hand *once in a while*, make a raise *every now and then.* If you do it you will not just be more successful, you will have more fun, *and get more respect.*

I guarantee that last point. Virtually all poker players, even those nice folks in your game, respect good players and look down on weak ones. They may enjoy taking your money, but they look down on you and may feel bored or a little deprived because it is so easy to beat you.

General Stylistic Changes

In terms of the styles grid you should move as far as you can toward the center because your style is self-defeating on both dimensions. If you are now a 9,1, try to become a 7,3. If you are less extreme, say, 8,2, try to become a 6,4, or even a 5,5.

Don't set an impossible goal for yourself such as becoming tight-aggressive. You probably can't do it, and you would not enjoy playing if you did it. It is like trying to lose weight; you can lose a few pounds, but trying to lose too much will make you get discouraged and give up. Just try to play a *little* more tightly and aggressively for a while, then a little more later on.

Figure XI: Improving the Style of the Loose-Passive Player

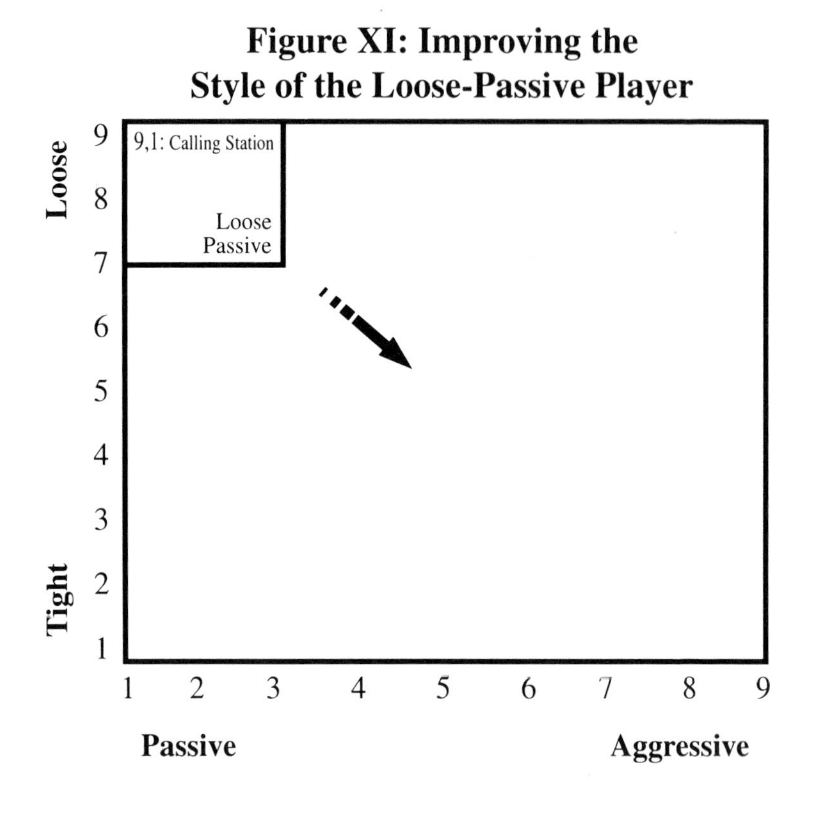

Specific Changes

We will consider only ways to affect your chances of winning because it is impossible to deal with all of your other motives. You should: *Study a little, tighten up, play more aggressively, sit to the left of the aggressive players, develop card reading skill, and exploit your image.*

Specific Change No. 1: Study a little. Note that I said "study," not "read." You may have already read a few books, but you should study one or two books seriously. Read them a couple of times, maybe even make notes and discuss them with somebody.

Compare your play to the book's suggestions. You will certainly see that your game has hardly any resemblance to a winning strategy.

Then, most importantly, apply whatever parts of their strategy you can accept. Don't try to do everything they recommend. The authors want to maximize their own profits, and they assume you feel the same way. Just pick and choose the things you can do and still enjoy yourself.

At the end of the book there is a list of "Suggested Reading." Each book has a few comments. Do not read the books for advanced players. You need to work on the basics. If you play hold 'em, I recommend *Hold 'em Poker* by David Sklansky.

If you play stud, try Oliver's *Low Limit Seven-Card Stud, Casino Strategy* because it is simple and includes practice hands. They give you a chance to test yourself and learn by doing. After reading it, try Percy's *Seven-Card Stud, the Waiting Game.* You need his emphasis upon patience, but you could never play as tightly as he suggests. Read it for the general message, tune out his exhortations to become a rock, and ignore the boring charts. Just take his basic principle to heart and play more of a waiting game.

Specific Change No. 2: Tighten up. Nothing will improve your game faster than tightening up. *When you have garbage, dump it.* When the action clearly indicates that you are beaten, *get out* (unless the pot odds justify calling). If you started with nothing and haven't improved, *run.*

Learn the basic odds and the techniques for computing pot odds; don't try to calculate them exactly, but develop a clear grasp of them. When the odds are too unfavorable, *head south.* I gave exactly the same advice to loose-aggressive players, but it applies even more to you because they get big profits when they hit, while you don't get paid off.

Specific Change No. 3: Play more aggressively. Note I did not say *be* more aggressive. You will not change your personality, nor should you try to do so. It works in most places. But poker is a *game*, and its rules and culture are different from those you encounter elsewhere. Most people accept and adjust to these differences, but you have ignored them.

Poker *requires* aggression, and most *players accept aggression as perfectly legitimate*, just a natural and *enjoyable* part of the game. Poker allows us to express our inherent aggression in relatively harmless ways. You are too timid to bet many hands, but you will call with even weaker ones. That pattern means you give other players value for their hands, but do not get value for your own hands.

The worst effect of your passivity is giving free cards, and you do it all the time. Some of them will beat you, costing you pots you would win if you bet properly. You *must* check less and bet more.

In addition, you rarely raise or bluff, partly because you think — consciously or unconsciously — that people will resent it and like you less. You certainly don't like being raised or bluffed, but most people feel differently. They regard raises and bluffs as just part of the game. The man or woman who would get angry at you for pushing in front of them or — God forbid — stealing their wallet, will not take it personally if you raise them or even steal "their" pot. It is just the way the game is played.

Playing more aggressively will not just improve your financial results. It will actually *cause most other players to like and respect you more.* I guarantee it. A few of them will miss the old you, the doormat they could exploit, but what do you care about them? The worthwhile people will welcome the changes because they like you, and it will be more fun to play with you. It is no challenge to beat you right now.

Specific Change No. 4: Sit to the left of the aggressive players. You want to avoid them, so sit where they have to act before you do. Then, if they raise, and you do not like your hand, you can fold for free. If they are on your left, you may call a bet from somebody in front of you, then feel you have to call their raise. If you had known they were going to raise, you would not have called in the first place (at least I hope you wouldn't).

Specific Change No. 5: Develop card reading skill. It is one of your glaring weaknesses because you have not paid much attention to it; you just called without trying to figure out what other people had. The general principles are discussed in Part Two. Study it carefully, but just studying won't do much good. You have to become more actively analytic. Instead of just sitting there, throwing in your money, try to put people on hands whether you are in or out of the pot.

Just shifting your emphasis from calling to understanding will automatically save you money. You will soon realize that it is much easier to read cards when you are not in the pot. You will pick up more signals and understand them better after you have folded. You may then fold a little more often, which will save you lots of money.

You should also take the role of a passive observer. You play so many pots that you rarely observe. You can learn much more when you are not playing. You call too often partly because it is boring to fold, then have nothing to do.

Trying to figure out people's cards will relieve that boredom. Treat it like watching "Jeopardy." You don't get a prize when you get the right answer, but we all try to do it. If you learn how to read cards better, you will get the fun and a prize.

Specific Change No. 6: Check-raise more often. Many LPPs do not check-raise often enough, and a few don't do it at all. They may dislike taking such an "aggressive" action or even feel that it "isn't nice." But check-raising is not just a legitimate tactic; it is an *essential* one. Your passivity and desire to "be nice" is already crippling you. Don't tie one hand behind your back by refusing to use this essential tactic.

If the other players know that you will not check-raise, every time you check you give away too much information. The other players know they can bet marginal hands or bluff without fear of being raised, and they will do it to squeeze out another bet or, worse yet, to steal your pot. Don't let them get away with it. Once in a while, check-raise.

You will gain in three ways. First, you will get more profit from your winners. Second, you will protect your future hands because people will be much less likely to bet marginal hands or to bluff you. Third, you will get more respect. Poker players respect toughness, and punishing them for trying to run over you will actually increase most players' respect for you.

Specific Change No. 7: Exploit your image. If you remember only one word from this book, let it be this one: *Bluff!*

If you do not make any other changes in your game, except to bluff once in a while, it will make an immense difference in your financial results *and in people's respect for you.*

Select a game with people who look at you and silently say: "Lunch is served." They see you as a pushover. They jump on you when you have weak cards because you will call, but do not give you action when you bet because they know you have a good hand.

Pick your spot well. Wait until you are heads up with a rock or a near rock, a 1,1 or a 2,2, someone who does not check-raise, and folds again and again. Wait until he checks to you. Then bluff, watch him fold, and take the money.

Don't show your hand! You may be so thrilled by your victory that you want to announce it, but your passive image helps you bluff, and you do not want to tarnish it. Besides, it is bad manners to rub it in. Wait for another carefully selected spot, then bluff again. You may get away with it many, many times before you get caught.

Once you get caught, you may be surprised to see new respect in people's eyes. The pushover isn't that easy any more. Then they will start calling you when you have a good hand, increasing your profits on your winners. You will be amazed at the difference it makes.

Selecting the Right Game

Select games that allow you to play the way you enjoy, but give you a chance to win (or at least reduce your losses). The more extreme your style is, the more important it is to select games with:

- The lowest limits you can tolerate.
- Lots of other loose-passive players.
- A friendly, relaxed atmosphere.

There are four reasons to select low limit games. First, you will lose less money. Unless money is completely irrelevant to you, that factor seems worth considering.

Second, low limit games are usually looser and more passive. You will often see "family pots." Everybody calls, and nobody raises.

Third, the players are almost always less skilled than in bigger games. The weaker they are, the better your chances, and the more you can relax.

Fourth, little games are usually friendlier, more sociable, and less cut-throat. Serious players go to big games, and some of them treat poker as their job or second job. The little games are full of people somewhat like you. They are more competitive than you, but they play primarily to relax, socialize, and pass the time.

However, not all little games are that way. Some of them are too intense and aggressive for you. You have to "shop around" to find the right game. Do it; don't stay where you are unless you really like it.

While shopping, consider the ambiance — the mood and conversation and whether people relax or focus on winning — but pay particular attention to how loose and passive the games are. That's where you belong, with people who play like you do. After trying out various games, pick one or a few. You might, for example, play at Casino A during weekday afternoons, but at Casino B nights or weekends. Find games that fit *all* your needs as a player and a person.

Getting Your Act Together

If you are a loose-passive player, this chapter has told you a lot about yourself and your playing style. Let's relate it to the questions you answered earlier.

Whenever it says to review and copy scores from a previous chapter, you might find it useful to skim that chapter to remind yourself of the content.

This exercise will take some time, and the answers you write today may be revised as you develop yourself. It may be boring or irritating to spend so much time, but it could pay huge dividends.

Your Right Stuff Ratings

Go to "The Right Stuff Questionnaire" on page 294. It should be dog-eared or paper-clipped. The next few lines are identical to that page. Look at the answers you wrote some time ago. Do they still seem correct? If not, revise them and write your answers here.

Which right stuff dimensions are assets, liabilities, or neutral for you?

Assets	*Liabilities*	*Neutral*

How can you take advantage of your assets?

How can you reduce the effects of your weaknesses?

Your Card Reading Grid Scores

Go to page 47. It should be dog-eared or paper-clipped. Answer the following questions.

My score is closest to the corner named _____

I have the following similarities and differences from that sort of player

Similarities:

Differences:

How do these similarities and differences affect your poker playing?

What are you going to do about it?

Your Styles Ratings

Look at the styles rating that you wrote on the first page of this chapter. Write it here.

My styles grid scores are: _____,_____

Now that you have read this chapter, does that rating seem accurate? Circle the appropriate answer. Yes No. If you circled "No," write a more appropriate set of scores here ____,____

If you changed either or both scores, briefly state why you did it. The more you write, the more benefit you will get.

Your Motives for Playing

Look at your self-ratings on motives from page 188 of this chapter. Copy them into the "Self-Rating" column of the table below. Use pencil and make sure they add to 100 percent.

Table VIII: My Motives for Playing

My Motives	Self-Rating	Revised Rating
Make money	____%	____%
Socialize, meet people	____%	____%
Relax	____%	____%
Get excitement of risk	____%	____%
Test self against competitive challenges	____%	____%
Sense of accomplishment from winning	____%	____%
Pass time	____%	____%
Other (specify)		
____________	____%	____%
____________	____%	____%
____________	____%	____%
Total (must be 100%)	____%	____%

Based on all you have read, do those percentages seem accurate? If not, insert better numbers in the "Revised Rating" column. Use pencil and make sure that they add up to 100 percent.

General Questions

Write the answers to these very general questions:
My current style *satisfies* these motives:

My current style *frustrates* these motives:

I should *change my* general style *from:* __ , __ *to* ___,___
because I want to:

Specific Actions

Review the entire chapter and write down *specific actions* you will take.

I should *play in* the following kinds of *games:*_________
because they___________________________

I should *avoid* the following kind of *games:*___________
because they___________________________

I should make the following *specific changes in my strategy:*

1.

2.

3.

4.

Dog ear or paperclip these pages. From time to time review your plans, note how well you have implemented them, and, if appropriate, revise them.

Good luck!

Part Six

The Tight-Passive Player

The Tight-Passive Player

Introduction

Tight-passive players (TPPs) are fairly hard to identify quickly, and — unless you adjust to their style — it is even harder to beat them. They are called "Rocks" because that is the way they play: They just sit there and fold hand after hand, waiting for premium cards. When they get them, they play them very conservatively, even timidly.

They are hard to spot because you naturally pay attention to the people who are in the pot, not to the ones who have folded. Most of them also have a low personal profile. They may say little, and a few of them say almost nothing at all. They also tend to make their bets in a cautious, controlled way. They don't throw chips into the pot and loudly say, "I raise." They just carefully place their bet in front of them, usually without a word.

They have the more important half of the proper style (tight-aggressive), and it lets them win consistently if they play in the right games. They do not win much, but they do not expect much. They are content with a steady stream of small wins and infrequent, small losses.

Tight-Passive Opponents

"Tight-passive players" (TPPs) include anyone with scores of 1-3 on both dimensions. Many of these principles and examples refer primarily to rocks (1,1). The lower a player's scores, the more likely he is to act, think, and feel like a rock.

Most rocks are heavily influenced by their inherent conservatism, but they are not as dominated by their emotions as maniacs and calling stations. Those loose players' emotions make them choose a self-defeating style, while the tight-passive style can often lead to success, especially in smaller limit games which have many weak players.

However, like the maniacs and calling stations, rocks are rigid and predictable. You know that they are going to fold hand after hand, call with only premium cards, and raise only with excellent ones.

Less extreme TPPs have more self-control and flexibility. When dealing with a 3,3, you must be more cautious in applying these principles. You still have to make the same sorts of adjustments, but you must use more judgment and expect a more effective and unpredictable opponent. You must constantly look for variations in his style and adjust to how he is playing *now*.

Rocks have half of a winning style, and, if they choose their games carefully, it is enough to win a little. If they do not choose well, they will lose, but they may not not lose much. Less extreme tight-passive players will win more, and they can beat more games.

If either score is 4 or more, a player is outside of the corner labeled "tight-passive," and some of these principles may not apply to him.

Since TPPs share passivity and tightness with the adjacent "corners," some parts of this chapter will overlap with the chapters on loose-passive and tight-aggressive players.

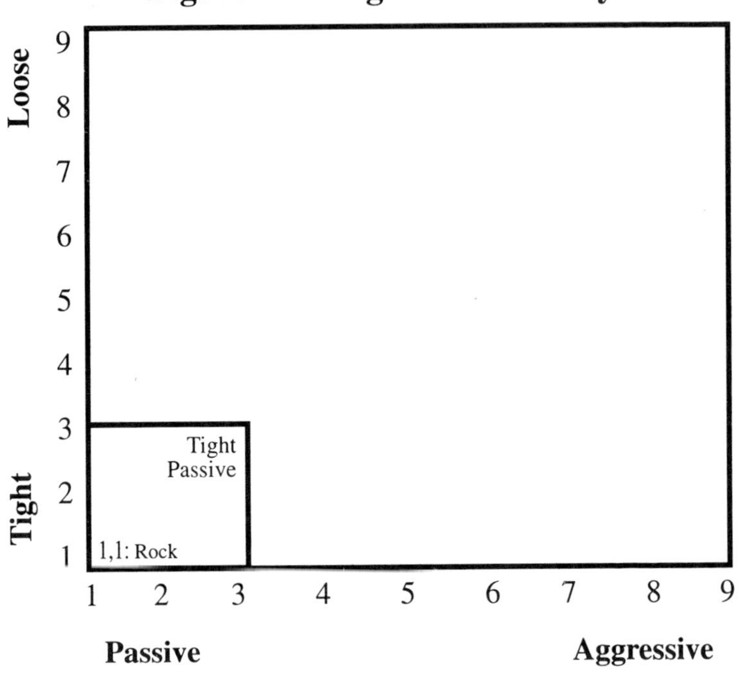

Quick Recognition Signals

This section is based on the same principle as previous chapters: People play poker the way they do other things. Passive people play passively; controlled people play tightly. If someone's voice, manner, and gestures suggest passivity and control, he probably plays a tight-passive game. The more signals you see, the more confidence you can have, and the more extreme the player is likely to be.

You have to work hard to identify TPPs because they have such a low profile. They play very few hands, hardly ever raise, and are usually very quiet. They earned the title "Rocks" by acting like them. You can play with one for hours and not even remember what he looks like, much less how he plays.

However, it is less important to identify them as quickly as aggressive players. They can't hurt you that badly since they rarely play and hardly ever raise. Look for the following signals.

Signal No. 1: All signs of tight emotional control such as neat clothing, little or no jewelry, passive or timid words and gestures (or even their complete absence), an apparent desire to avoid attention, and hardly any facial expressions. TPPs are what Freud called "anal personalities." His theory was that toilet training problems make certain people want to restrain and control *everything* — money, words, affection, whatever.

In modern slang, they are "uptight" or "control freaks." Their primary objective is to avoid risks, and that extreme conservatism affects almost everything they do.

Some signals say more about young people than old ones. For example, wearing a coat and an unloosened tie says a lot about a young man, but much less about an older one. The older man may just be acting habitually, while the young one probably made a deliberate decision.

Pay particular attention to that unloosened tie. The clothing could mean that he just came from work, but the way he wears it says something about his personality. When they play poker, most people take off or at least loosen their ties.

Signal No. 2: Organized chips. Carefully organized chips — such as very neat stacks with the colored bits lined up — show that a player values neatness and control, and tight-passive players have the time to waste arranging chips.

Signal No. 3: Indifference to other people. Showing indifference or not greeting other players, waiters, and dealers suggest a tight-passive style. Miserly tipping supports that inference.

Signal No. 4: Indifference to the action. If someone seems uninterested in the game, he is probably tight-passive, at least for the moment. This indifference can signal a player's general style or just his current state of mind.

People who are distracted by horse races or football games are a special and unpredictable case, particularly if they are betting on them. Some of them will play a tight-passive game while they are trying to pick a winner or see how their bets do; they glance at their cards and fold all but the best hands. Others may play carelessly because they are more interested in the race or game.

A few players watch TV or read. They are usually tight-passive, and they are almost certainly passive. Aggressive players care too much about the action to ignore it.

You can usually read distracted people by the way they act after calling the first bet. If they shift their attention to the game, they probably have a good hand (regardless of their style). If they stay focused on the TV, they are probably loose-passive and/or have weak cards. In either case, you have little reason to fear a raise.

Signal No. 5: A gentle or even timid betting manner clearly suggests passivity. For example, if they gently place their chips so close to them that they seem afraid of intruding or want to pull their bets back, they are probably passive. As I noted in the last chapter, you have to make a separate estimate of looseness.

Signal No. 6: Minimum buy-in. People who make one will usually play like rocks, at least as long as they are short of money. They may have only enough for one buy-in and hope to grind out a few dollars. However, sometimes short money LAPs buy the minimum to "take a shot." Since the styles are so different, other cues will soon help you to distinguish them.

Signal No. 7: Older people obviously tend to be tight-passive. People get more conservative as they age, and many rocks are retired people, trying to fill up their empty hours and make a few dollars.

As always, *observe how others react to him.*

Signal No. 8: Indifference to his arrival. If nobody seems to notice him, he is either a stranger or tight-passive. They tend to be "invisible."

Signal No. 9: Grumbling or rude remarks, especially by loose-aggressive players. Hardly anyone wants to play with them because you can't have much fun or win much money. Listen for comments such as, "This isn't the game for you; we're gambling." If they are *not* made as jokes, the newcomer is almost certainly tight and probably passive.

Strengths

All but the most extreme rocks will win in most games. Poker rewards patience, and they have lots of it. They can sit there all day, throwing away their cards. They are especially successful in the small stud games (such as $1-$5) because the ante is small or zero, and the bring-in is trivial.

Many of them play primarily to pass the time and to supplement pensions or other small, fixed incomes. They satisfy both needs very well. A tight-passive style produces a steady stream of small wins and very few significant losses. It's not exciting to play that way, but it sure beats flipping hamburgers at McDonald's or playing checkers at the senior center.

Their style would bore most people, and it may bore them, but the boredom is not that great. Remember, they are not hoping to win a lot, nor do they crave action. They have lots of time, and they *like* a slow pace, steady wins, and infrequent, small losses.

Weaknesses

A complete rock is going to lose against fairly skilled players, but he probably will not lose very much. He does not get enough value from his winners, is very vulnerable to bluffs, gives too many free cards, and does not steal enough (or perhaps any) pots.

In other words, those who play like rocks should lose against skilled players who play aggressively, but are selective about their hands. The rocks won't win enough on their good hands and they will hardly ever steal a pot; they therefore will not compensate for the money they lose with poor hands or when they are bluffed. Most TPPs are easy to bluff, which good players quickly recognize and exploit.

TPPs are not welcomed by anyone except old friends. They don't give or get much action, and it's boring and frustrating to play with them. There is not much chance to win serious money or have much fun.[16] Even if they play lots of hours, the house and dealers may not value their business because the pots are small, causing tiny rakes and tokes.

The purely social side is mixed. A few of them are "nebbishes," a Yiddish term for "people who are so nothing that, when they leave a room, it's like somebody came in." However, many of them do get some quiet social satisfaction from playing in a way that is not stressful or confrontational.

Reading Their Cards

Reading their cards is very easy because they would not call without a good hand, raise without an excellent one, and reraise without a lock or close to it. As for bluffs, steals, and check-raises, they rarely happen. What you see is what you get.

---

[16] There is an exception. It is in high limit stud games where the ante is relatively large compared to the bet. In this structure tight play is severely penalized.

Playing Against Them

It is boring, but they are fairly beatable. Of course, you usually will not win much, but every little bit helps.

Should You Play with Them?

If there are only a few TPPs in the game and the rest of the table is fairly easy, the answer is usually "yes." Otherwise, it is probably "no."

It is not much fun to play with them, and you can't win much money (except in short-handed games or ones with large antes). They are almost an empty seat, but one which slightly increases the "house cut." They don't give any action, and they take out a little money, so why bother? This subject is discussed in "Playing in a Tight-Passive Game."

Where Should You Sit?

You almost always want passive people — regardless of how loose or tight they are — on your left. Then you don't have to worry as much about a raise behind you. If they raise ahead of you, you can confidently fold everything but a powerhouse. If you have already limped in before the flop or on third street in stud, you can call their bet if the pot odds justify it.

If you can choose between a tight or loose passive player on your left, choose the tight one. You can steal antes and his bring-ins or blinds with hardly any risk, but you can't steal anything from a loose-passive player. He will frequently call.

How Should You Adjust Your Strategy?

Your major problem is to control your own boredom and desire for action. You may be so frustrated by their style that you give them much more action than they deserve (which is exactly what they want). You *must* control yourself.

The central principle is *don't give them any more action than they give you.* Since they don't gamble with you, don't gamble with them. If you gamble, and they don't, they are going to beat you; it's as simple as that. Let's get specific. Here are some concepts to help you against a TPP.

Concept No. 1: Don't call without a good hand. They rarely bluff, nor do they bet marginal hands. If they bet, you need a good hand to call. A good rule of the thumb is: Don't call them without a hand that is good enough to have bet yourself. That rule is particularly important before you get to the river. They might bluff then, but they rarely bluff before then (unless they see great weakness or have a powerful looking board in stud).[17]

Concept No. 2: Don't bet marginal or even okay hands for value, not even after they check. You have little upside, but lots of downside. If they can't beat you, they probably won't call. If they do call, they will probably beat you. Don't assume that checking means they have little or nothing. They will check with hands that other people would bet or even raise.

Concept No. 3: Don't raise without a great hand. Raising them with just a normal raising hand is very foolish. They would not bet without a strong hand, and they will not call a raise without a very good one. If you have the better hand, they will probably fold. If they call, they will probably beat you. If — God forbid — they reraise, fold anything below a near lock (and it probably isn't

---

[17] There is one important exception, especially in the bigger games. There are some rocks who bet few marginal hands for value on the last card, but will bluff with hopeless hands. When *they* bet on the end the chance they are bluffing is now high enough to justify a call with even a mediocre hand.

good enough). For example, if you raise in hold 'em with a king high flush, and a rock reraises, you're almost certainly dead.

Concept No. 4: Don't check-raise. If you do, they will probably check behind you unless they have you beat. If they do bet, you may not want to raise or even call.

Concept No. 5: Don't slow play big hands. The reasons are the same as those for avoiding a check-raise.

Concept No. 6: Bluff and semi-bluff frequently, but selectively. They are the easiest people to bluff because they will fold quite good hands. However, if you bluff carelessly, you can get hurt.

When considering a bluff, remember that they would not be in the pot if they did not have at least a playable hand, and they probably have more than that. They tend to avoid drawing hands. Two, they will check hands that most people bet. If you bluff because they checked, you may be shocked to see a good hand.

Concept No. 7: Steal their blinds or antes. Raise more often than usual to steal the blinds and antes. A TPP will hardly ever call. If he does call, he is unlikely to bet on the flop or fourth street because he is afraid of your raise, and you will get two chances to draw out and win legitimately.

Playing in a Tight-Passive Game

A tight-passive game (TPG) has several tight-passive players, no more than two loose players, and no aggressive players. Lots of hands are not played at all, or there are only two or three players after the flop or on fourth street. Raises are rare, and reraises hardly ever occur. Most pots are trivial, hardly worth winning. Only a few hands go to a showdown, and there is usually only one caller then.

If the game is tight-passive, ask yourself a question: *Why bother to play?* You can't win much; you can easily lose; and it's going to be boring. It's probably better to read the papers, take a walk, or change games.

But let's say it's raining and you've already read the papers. If you really want to play, and it's the only game around (or you're in a tournament and don't have any choice), *prepare for a long siege.* Be prepared to wait and wait and wait.

Don't Expect Much

If you want lots of action, or hope to win a lot of money, forget it. It's not going to happen. In fact, don't be surprised if you lose, and you might lose much more than you expect. This sort of game has little upside and lots of downside. You can't win much, but you can lose quite a bit.

Control Yourself

Self-control is always important, but it is particularly important in a TPG because it is so hard to beat and so frustrating. Your natural desire for action can cause you to play too many hands, and to play them too aggressively.

It happens all the time. The average player, a 5,5, sits down and plays his normal game. He does not lose a lot of money on any single pot; he just slowly bleeds to death. He loses one buy-in, then another one, then a third. He bets aggressively on aces up, but gets beat by rolled up eights. He makes a straight on the river, bets out, and loses to a flush that was made on fifth street. He wins a few pots, but does not win much on them, while losing again and again.

He slowly goes on tilt. At first, he just gets a little looser, calling with marginal hands, raising a little too aggressively. Then he gets mad at the "Damned Rocks" and at himself for playing in "this lousy game." When that happens, he may be on his way to big trouble.

Which brings us back to our first question: Why bother? If you think that you can't make the changes in your style that this game requires, don't sit down. If you cannot control yourself and play *much* more conservatively, don't play at all. If you find that you started conservatively, but are loosening up, *get out.*

If you decide to play, a few principles will help. After realizing what you have to do to win a little in a TPG, you may want to reconsider your decision to play.

Accept that the Rules are Different

The action is so different from normal games that you must revise your assumptions and strategy. Otherwise, you will probably lose, and you will almost certainly be frustrated. Here are a few of the most important changes.

Change No. 1: Fewer people will be in every pot. This obvious point has many consequences.

Change No. 2: Many hands will end before the showdown. You will start with fewer players, and they will usually fold more quickly. The average hand will end about fifth street or the flop.

Change No. 3: The pots will be much smaller than usual. This point is an inevitable result of the two preceding ones.

Change No. 4: Weaker hands than normal will win most pots. Because so few people will contest each pot, there will not be remotely as many straights, flushes, or full houses.

Change No. 5: Pairs and high cards will go up in value, while drawing hands will go way down. An ace, king, or one pair will win many pots. Two pair is a relatively strong hand. You will rarely see straights or flushes because rocks don't play most drawing hands, and the action does not justify other people's playing them. Note: In hold 'em *small* pairs — which are really drawing hands — go down in value because there are not enough callers to create pot odds for the few sets you will flop.

Adjust Your Strategy to Fit Those Differences

Since the rules are different, you must adjust your strategy. Unless you do so, you don't have a chance. Here are some adjustments you should make.

Adjustment No. 1: Become much tighter. If you do not get tighter on every street, you're dead. You must be particularly tight on third street or before the flop. Everybody else is waiting for premium cards, and you must do the same.

You can be a little more liberal in stud than in flop games because you can often play for the bring-in since so few hands are raised.

> "If ... is only the bring-in, and it is unlikely you will be raised, ... many good players probably play too tight in this spot. There are a lot of hands you can play if it's cheap, if your hand is live, and it has the potential to make something big." *(Seven-Card Stud for Advanced Players: 21st Century Edition,* p. 66)

In hold 'em play at least one group higher than Sklansky and Malmuth suggest; for example, if it would be OK to play a Group 6 hand in this position, play only a Group 5 or better, and favor the high cards in that group, not the suited connectors.

On subsequent streets the same principle applies. If somebody bets, he probably has good cards. If a hand would be a marginal call in a normal game, consider folding.

Adjustment No. 2: Become much less aggressive (except for bluffs and semi-bluffs). The same basic logic applies to aggression: If you would not normally consider raising with a hand, don't bet. Unless you would normally consider reraising with a hand, you probably should not raise. However, a raise on the last cheap street will often buy you a free card on the next one.

Adjustment No. 3: Bluff, semi-bluff, and steal the blinds and antes more often. You must do so to make any money in this kind of game, but do it carefully. Follow the rules for bluffing TPPs. Early bluffs are especially profitable. For example, if a hold 'em flop is all small cards, especially with a tiny pair, you can be confident that nobody got a piece of it because they don't play small cards.

Unless someone has a high pocket pair, everyone will probably fold. Even if the rock calls on the flop, he will probably fold if you bluff on the turn. Rocks do not chase because it will cost them several bets, not just the one bet it costs to call on the flop. The same general principle applies to third and fourth street in stud.

Adjustment No. 4: On early streets, don't play any pure drawing hands. A pure drawing hand is one that has little value unless you make the hand. For example,

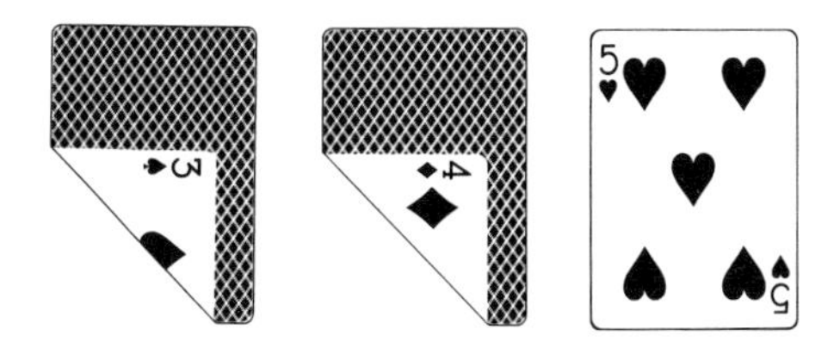

on third street in stud is almost worthless if you don't make a straight, while

is better because it can produce a bigger straight, trips, or a higher one or two pair.

Most people have no idea of how infrequently drawing hands are made. Othmer's computer simulations of third street stud hands found that only 19 percent of the three card open ended straights and 18 percent of the three flushes result in a flush or straight.

- [with a three card open-ended straight] "In all cases we finish with one pair the majority of the time and with two pair more often than we make a straight." (p. 127)
- [with three suited cards] "We end up with one pair or two pair the majority of the time. We must therefore play low suited cards more conservatively than high suited cards." (p. 93)

The same general pattern occurs with hold 'em drawing hands, but pairs and high cards have an even greater edge over the drawing hands because you start with only two cards rather than three toward the flush or straight. Even if you have both straight and flush possibilities with suited connectors such as

of hearts, you will make a straight or a flush less than 15 percent of the time. You are much more likely to end up with nothing, a pair, or two pair.

In a loose game, particularly a passive one, it pays to draw. You can play the hand cheaply; the pot odds justify taking the small risk; and the implied odds are good because you will get paid off if you make the hand. In a TPG the pot odds are low; you will almost never have the number of callers you need to justify calling with a small drawing hand. The implied odds are even worse; if you make the hand, you probably won't get paid off.

Unless the position and other conditions are good, just fold small drawing hands in stud and suited connectors lower than nine-eight in hold 'em.[18] Unless you are in late position, throw away that

---

[18] The exception would be in very tight games where a raise will often steal the blinds or get you heads-up. Against one rock you can often steal later on or win with a small pair. Combine this with the good chance of stealing the blind and a preflop raise may be in order if no one else is yet in. However, if the game is a bit looser or you are in early position, your small suited connectors may have to deal with two or three opponents which is much worse.

suited that you enjoy playing. You have little chance of making a flush and only one worthwhile card to pair. Even if you pair the ace, you can't bet it confidently because you can easily be outkicked. In this game hardly anyone would play ace-six or less. If you bet and get called, you may be beaten.

If You Are a Tight-Passive Player

You are a tight-passive player (TPP) if *both* of your scores are three or lower. In that case this chapter focuses directly on you. Before reading any further, write your styles grid scores from page 96.

My styles grid scores are: ____,____

Figure XIII: Tight-Passive Players

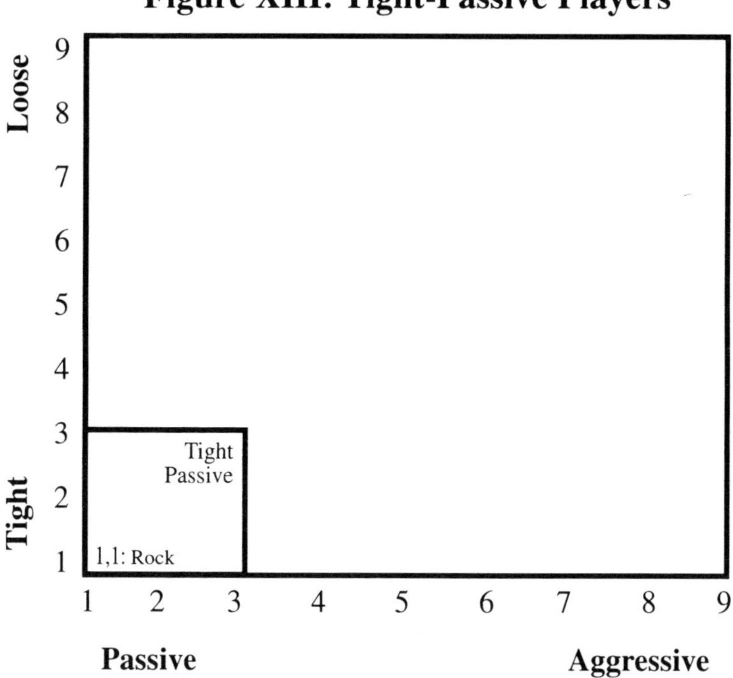

Place an X on Figure XIII at the point that matches your grid scores. The closer that X is to the bottom-left corner of the grid, the more tight-passive you are, and the more relevant this chapter is to you.

Although anyone with two scores of three or lower is a TPP, most of the examples and principles refer primarily to the *extremely* tight-passive player, the "Rock," 1,1. If either of your scores is more than one, everything here is off, maybe a little, maybe a lot.

If either of your scores is more than three, you are not a TPP, and much of this chapter does not directly relate to you. For example, if you are a 3,4, you are tight and slightly passive. Some of this chapter will fit you, while other parts may be quite inaccurate.

This chapter is divided into five sections.

1. Accepting the Consequences
2. Understanding Your Motives
3. Improving Your Play
4. Selecting the Right Game
5. Getting Your Act Together

We begin by discussing the general consequences because virtually all tight-passive players get the same overall results. The following four sections will help you to understand why *you* play that way and what you should do about it. Since this chapter is for tight-passive players, most remarks will be directed to "you" rather than "he" or "they."

Accepting the Consequences

If you are a TPP, particularly a 2,2 or lower, you may not like the next few lines, but you should take them seriously. The consequences of your style are fairly obvious.

- You will win a little money if you play in the right games.
- You will lose if you play in the wrong games.
- You may be frustrated by poor action.

- You will frequently get bluffed.
- You may be bored.
- You can relax and socialize at the poker table.
- You will not be very welcome in most games.
- You will often encounter hostility and contempt.

Winning and Losing

Your pattern of strengths and weaknesses works only in certain games. If you pick the right games, you will win a little. If you pick the wrong games, you will lose. Here are your major strengths.

1. Poker rewards patience above all, and you have lots of it. You can sit there all day, just folding hand after hand. You will be especially successful in the lowest limit stud games (such as $1-$5) because there is no ante or a tiny one, and the bring-in is trivial.
2. You will succeed in almost all low-limit games because so many people play so loosely. They will stay in with almost anything and chase you when you clearly have them beat. They also tend to be oblivious. Some of them will not even recognize your style, and lots of them will not adjust to it. They will give you much more action than you "deserve."
3. Many TPPs play primarily to pass the time and to supplement pensions or other small, fixed incomes. This style satisfies both needs very, very well. It gives you something to do and produces a steady stream of small wins with infrequent losses.

Here are your major weaknesses.

1. A complete rock is going to lose against fairly skilled players, but he probably will not lose much. You do not get enough value from your winners, are very vulnerable to bluffs, and do not steal enough (or perhaps any) pots. You also give too many free cards and some of them will beat you.

Frustration from Poor Action

You may be frustrated when you get no action on your good hands, and it will happen frequently. Lots of rocks complain: "I've had garbage all day. I finally get trip aces, and nobody stays!"

Of course, nobody stayed! They know that you don't raise without the nuts. When you raise, they run. As you have been told many times, "You can't get action if you don't give action."

Your problem is not that you play such a tight-passive style, but that many people know it. You are too predictable, a fatal error. You have to change your approach.

Being Bluffed

Your style is so obvious that even fairly weak players perceive that they can bluff you. In fact, you will be the target of more bluffs and steals than anyone else. You really do not want people to try to bluff you especially those who virtually never bluff, because some of their attempts will succeed and you are encouraging them to play better.

Boredom

This style would bore most people, and it may bore you, but the boredom is probably not that great. You do not seriously expect to win much, and you *like* a slow pace and steady wins with infrequent, small losses. Besides, like many patient people, you probably do not bore easily.

Relaxation and Socializing

Because your style demands so little from you, you can relax and socialize. Some TPPs even read the paper, watch TV, or try to pick a winner in the next race. They just look at their cards, throw away all but the best hands, then do something else.

The purely social side is mixed. Because of your style, you may not be or feel welcome. However, you may enjoy the card room's low key socializing and treat it essentially as a club. It is not a bad club. It is open all or nearly all the time, and there are no initiation fees or monthly dues. You can spend lots of time there and enjoy meeting other regulars.

These advantages are particularly valuable if you are retired. There are young people around, and you may get tired of seeing only other senior citizens. Poker is more fun than most senior center's activities, or watching the stock market. And you can actually make a few dollars.

Being Unwelcome

You may not be welcomed by anyone except your old friends. You don't give or get much action, making it boring and frustrating to play with you. Management and the dealers may not highly value your business because the pots are small, causing tiny rakes and tokes. They may not appreciate the fact that you help to start games and keep them going.

Hostility and Contempt

Many players are secretly or even openly hostile or contemptuous because they want action, and you don't give it, and they respect machismo, but you don't have it. Some of them openly express their feelings. You have probably been offended by nasty remarks about your "cowardice," "cheapness," etc.

Your reactions can easily create additional problems. You may angrily insist on your right to play the way you wish, but rude people do not respect that right. You may even get so upset that you try to prove your machismo by gambling more, which is exactly what they want. They play that game better than you do, and trying to beat them at their own game can put you at a serious disadvantage.

Just accept the reality that — no matter what you do — some people are going to be nasty because of who you are. Your best revenge is not to try to get their respect by acting foolishly; it is to exploit their perceptions to take their money. We will discuss ways to do it a little later.

Understanding Your Motives

The first question is: *Why do you play poker?* The next one is: *Why have you chosen the tight-passive style?* You certainly are not playing primarily to maximize your profits because you either win or lose a small amount. You definitely are not turned on by the excitement of risk or the competitive challenge because you minimize both. Since you obviously have other motives, you should understand them and their implications.

Let's find out why you *really* play poker. Go to the "Why Do You Play Poker?" chapter in "Part One: The Right Stuff." Quickly reread it, then copy your answers from page 35 into the "Self-ratings" column below.

The next few paragraphs may change the way you see your motives.

Table IX: My Motives for Playing

Make money	_______%
Socialize, meet people	_______%
Relax	_______%
Get excitement of risk	_______%
Test self against competitive challenges	_______%
Sense of accomplishment from winning	_______%
Pass time	_______%
Other (specify)	
_____________	_______%
_____________	_______%
_____________	_______%

Total (must be 100%) _______%

Every player should know why he has chosen his style, but this self-knowledge is somewhat less important for you than for loose players. Regardless of whether they are passive or aggressive, they lose lots of money, while you generally win or your losses are small. However, understanding your motives could increase both your winnings and your other satisfactions.

Your style clearly suggests that you are inherently conservative and cautious, preferring small, steady wins and occasional small losses to extreme swings from winning a bundle one day to taking a real bath the next. Other motives are relaxing and passing the time; in fact, they may be more important to you than making money (even if you rated them lower).

The social aspects may be important to you, even though you may not talk much or look very sociable. You may like their low key socializing and treat your cardroom as a club.

Take another look at the self-rating of your motives. If you did not assign at least 75 percent to a combination of making money, passing time, socializing, and relaxing, or similar motives in the "other" category, you are probably kidding yourself. You are definitely not playing to meet competitive challenges or to get excitement.

You deliberately avoid both. You rarely take chances, and you do not want to test your skill by challenging tougher players. In fact, your style is largely caused by your fears, not your desires. In the final section, "Getting Your Act Together," you may want to revise your ratings.

If you are a small loser, the cost of your recreation is quite low, probably less than you would spend for most hobbies. If you pick the right games, you will win, giving you a pretty good piece of both worlds. You have a hobby that makes you a few bucks.

Improving Your Play

The preceding chapters on loose players begin by stating that their styles cost them lots of money. That point is not true for you. Your style is a *minor* asset. *You can win with it, but you can't win much.*

You have the more important half of the best style, tight-aggressive. Your patience and discipline will enable you to win a little in many games, but you will lose in the wrong ones. We will discuss that subject in the next section.

General Stylistic Changes

Unless you want to continue to be bored, restricted to the smallest games, and forced to settle for tiny wins, you have to become more aggressive. Doing so will certainly cause your swings to be greater: You will win more on good days and lose more on bad days. But your long term net will be considerably higher, and you will get more excitement and respect from other players.

I apologize if I have offended you, but you were probably not surprised. You wouldn't be reading this book if you were not dissatisfied with some aspects of poker. You want to win more, and you may be somewhat bored and unhappy about other players' attitudes toward you.

You may have shrugged it off, but it bothered you. You wanted better results, more fun, and more respect, but you hoped to get them without really changing your style.

Unlike the loose players, you do not have to change your style to win. You can continue in the same old, comfortable rut. But, if you want to get out of that rut, make more money, be less bored, and get more respect, you have to change your style and take some chances.

You should move from the left bottom corner toward the right bottom corner of the styles grid, and the further you go, the better. You already have the more important half of a good game. You just have to get more aggressive.

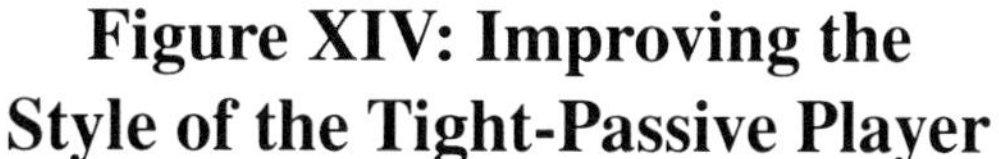

Figure XIV: Improving the Style of the Tight-Passive Player

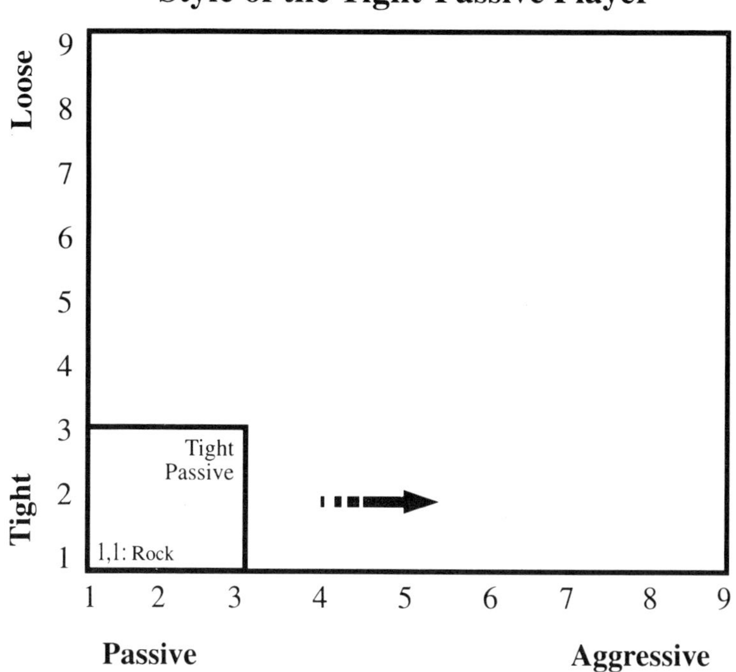

Specific Changes

To win more money, reduce boredom, and get more respect, you should take several steps: *Avoid playing "weak-tight," create a looser image, sit to the left of the aggressive players, don't give so many free cards, develop card reading skill, slow play big hands, check-raise selectively, invite people to bluff, call more frequently on the river, exploit your image, and select the right game.* Otherwise, you will stay in that same boring rut that caused you to read this book.

Specific Change No. 1: Avoid playing "weak-tight." In his *Poker Essays* (p. 108) Mason Malmuth wrote:

- "A weak-tight player exhibits four characteristics: (1) he clearly will play fairly tight, (2) he usually plays in very predictable patterns, (3) he has the ability to fold marginal hands, and (4) he bluffs very little...
- "they often look for excuses to fold their hands...
- "one of the reasons to play tight is that it makes your bluffs more effective. The weak-tight player does not take advantage of this. In fact, when he bets or checks, he is giving away too much information...
- "Although weak-tight players are great opponents because you can win lots of chips from them, I believe this type of play is the first step toward winning."

The good players soon recognize and adjust to the pattern. They avoid getting involved unless they have premium cards, and they bluff or semi-bluff frequently. If you are seen as "weak-tight," you will not get the action you want, but you will get exactly the action you don't want: Good players will bluff you out of some of your pots. You have taken "the first step toward winning." Now take the second step: Get much more aggressive.

Specific Change No. 2: Create a looser image. Your image is a major liability. You don't get as much action as you like, and lots of people bluff and generally run over you. You should therefore mix up your play by *occasionally* bluffing or even raising with a weaker hand than normal. If you have to show your hand, you should sometimes let everyone know what you did. You will not fool the better players, but many weak, gullible players can be convinced that you are looser than you really are.[19]

Specific Change No. 3: Sit to the left of the aggressive players. This advice applies to almost everyone, but it is especially important for you. You do not want to take the risk of calling before the LAP, then having to call a raise. If you sit behind them, their raises occur in front of you.

There is another reason for sitting behind them. If you call ahead of them, they will not raise nearly as often. In fact, they may fold a hand that they had originally planned to raise. Your tightness is an "action-killer." When you call, some players slow down or run away.

However, if an LAP raises ahead of you, most people will focus on the raiser. They may hardly notice that you have cold-called the raise (which you would not do without an excellent hand). You can win huge pots by just waiting for the right hand behind the action player. Of course, you should often reraise, but, when you want *both* a raise and multiway action because you have a great hand, slow playing behind an LAP's raise can be extremely profitable.

It will be quite easy for you to sit to an LAP's left. In fact, he probably wants you there because you raise so rarely, and he knows he can steal your blinds and bring-ins.

Specific Change No. 4: Don't give so many free cards. Your conservatism makes you check with hands most players, especially good ones, would bet. You do so to "save money," but

---

[19] It actually might be better if you never show your hand. This way you may get away with some steals and no one will ever know, allowing you to steal again sometime in the future.

it is a very expensive habit. Checking gives your opponents free cards, and some of those cards will beat you. You *must* bet (and raise) more often.

Specific Change No. 5: Develop card reading skill. Some TPPs are poor card readers for two reasons:

1. They focus on their own cards, not those of the other players. They may base their decisions on a formula. These types of hands are worth playing; those types should be folded; a few types should be raised. These formulas ignore a central poker principle: *Hands have only relative value.* The question is not whether a hand is "good" or "bad." It is whether it is better than the other hands. You must also relate your hand to your own and your opponents' positions because position has a huge effect upon its value and the way it should be played.
2. They tend to be too pessimistic. They tend to think of the worst case. For example, they might not raise with a near nut straight because they are afraid of a nut straight. This tendency is just another example of allowing one's natural attitudes to override the important evidence: What does the pattern of betting suggest the other players *really* have?

If either of these points describes you, you should work on your card reading skill. The techniques for developing card reading skill are described in Part Two. Unlike the loose players, your style makes it easy and enjoyable to develop this skill. You fold so many hands that you are bored. Instead of daydreaming, watching TV, or chatting, try to put players on hands. You will be surprised by how much you learn, and it will make you a much better player (if you have the courage to use that skill).

Specific Change No. 6: Slow play big hands. Although you should become generally more aggressive, you should become more passive with big hands. If you raise, you will frequently lose "customers." Only a fool or a stranger will call your raises without very good cards.

Consider slow-playing really big starting hands such as aces, kings, or ace-king suited in hold 'em or a hidden set on fourth or fifth street in stud. Right now you probably raise because you want to "protect your hand." You can remember not raising and having somebody draw out on you.

Of course, they will occasionally do that, but over time you will make much more money than just picking up the blinds/antes or winning a small pot on an early street. The larger pots you win will more than compensate you for the times you get drawn out on. For example, page 171 reports that against only one hold 'em player a pair of aces will win 80 percent of the time, but it will beat nine players only 30 percent of the time. However, it will win over three times as much money because the pots will be so much larger. Remember, the idea is to win money, not a lot of pots.[20]

You apply that principle when you fold a hand that might win, but would cost you more than it is worth. The same general logic requires slow playing to maximize your profits on really big hands.

Specific Change No. 7: Check-raise selectively. For most people the reasons for a check-raise are similar to those for slow-playing, but not for you. You have to pick your spots carefully.

Let's say that an LAP is on your immediate right (which is where you want him). If you are playing hold 'em and are the small blind, then he is the button. If you flop a powerhouse and check, everyone else checks, he bets and you raise, everybody else will fold. People rarely check and cold call for two bets, and no sensible player will do it if you raise. Raises are much more noticed than bets. If you bet out, some people will call, but they will not call your raises.

With an extremely strong hand you will usually get better results by betting out, getting a call or two, then having the LAP

---

[20] Also keep in mind that this example was based on some unusual conditions. Your real world game may be somewhat different.

raise. If you just call, so will they. They are not afraid of the LAP's raise, and they have already put in one bet. If you bet and they call, and the LAP raises, you can reraise. They may call because the pot is bigger and they have more invested. If they fold, you have still gotten one more bet from each of them than you would by check-raising. Therefore, you should check-raise with the LAP on your right *only* if you want to reduce the field (e.g., if the pot is big and your hand is vulnerable). Otherwise, bet out.

If the LAP is on your left, a check-raise is the way to go. Let's say you are in the worst possible seat, to the immediate right of a maniac; you don't want that seat, but you are stuck with it for the moment. With a great hand, a check-raise is the ideal play.

If you bet, and he raises, most people will fold. If you check and he bets, lots of people call because they don't respect his bets. Then you can raise. If he just calls, most of the others will call because the pot is so big. You can also make this play with a good draw unless you feel the maniac will raise again.

He might reraise, but they may call two bets now because the pot is bigger, and they have more invested in it. Even if they fold now, you have gotten one more bet from each of them than you would have gotten by betting out and being raised.

Specific Change No. 8: Invite people to bluff. Since many people will see you as weak-tight, invite them to bluff on the river. Let's say you have a good, but not great hand such as top pair on the flop, and you put the only other player on a weak hand. The turn is a small card that puts a second suited card on board, and you bet and get called. The river is another one that completes the backdoor flush. If you bet, he will not call (unless you have misread the hand or he has made the flush). Check to invite him to bluff, then call.

Specific Change No. 9: Call more frequently on the river. Even when you do not invite a bluff, you *must* call more frequently on the river. Simple economics demand it. If you win just one hand that you would have folded and lose one bet on each of six hands that you wanted to fold, you will be ahead of the game. Sometimes you will catch someone bluffing; sometimes they will think their hand is worth a bet, but be wrong.

One of virtually everyone's faults is the "egoistic fallacy." We tend to think that everyone is like us (or should be like us). This fallacy frequently causes you to think they have you beat because you would not bet without a better hand than you have now.

But *they aren't you.* They start with hands you wouldn't even think of playing, stay in with weak draws and no pot odds, raise with junk. The primary reason you win is that they are so much looser than you. *Why do you think that they suddenly get smarter and tighter on the river?*

The same motives and perceptions that caused them to be too loose and aggressive (by your standards) in the early rounds will make them bet on the river. So call them and take the money. You won't take it often, but the pots you win will more than compensate for the losing calls.

Specific Change No. 10: Exploit your image. You are almost certainly seen as what you are, a rock or close to it. In fact, you might be just a 3,3, but still be called "The Rock." It is *not* a compliment, but you can take advantage of it.

You have already seen that people avoid you. Exploit their fear by *selectively* acting out of character. Since you are seen as a rock, you can more easily bluff, semi-bluff, and steal blinds and antes. They are all aggressive actions, which is exactly the right direction for you to go.

Specific Change No. 11: Check-raise often. Many TPPs do not check-raise often enough, and a few don't do it at all. They may regard it as illegitimate or dislike risking a reraise. But check-raising is not just a legitimate act; it is an *essential* one.

If the other players know that you will not check-raise, every time you check you give away too much information. The other players know they can bet or bluff without fear of being raised, and they will do it to squeeze out another bet or, worse yet, to steal your pot.

Remember, you are much more vulnerable to bluffs than any other style. If you don't check-raise often enough, you will encourage people to do exactly what you don't want them to do. You have to punish their attempts to take advantage of your passivity.

There are two reasons to check-raise more often. First, it will increase your profits on some of your winners. Second, it will protect your marginal hands and reduce the number of times people try to bluff you.

Specific Change No. 12: Bluff much more frequently. You have less chance of being called than anyone at the table. The return on a bluff is often spectacularly high, five, ten, or even more times the amount invested. Of course, you should pick your spots; don't bluff when they look strong and confident because somebody will probably call. Wait until you see weakness or the proper strategic situation develops, then pounce!

Incidentally, your bluffs are sometimes more likely to succeed when you are first to act. You may not bluff unless everyone has checked to you. But they know they have shown weakness by checking, and are likely to suspect a bluff. However, a combination of their perception of you and your betting first will scare almost anybody.

Specific Change No. 13: Steal blinds much more frequently. The psychology is the same as for bluffing, and the returns are almost as good. You will not win as much each time, but you will frequently win because the blinds will often fold.

Let's say you are the button; everyone has passed; and the blinds are average players. Raise with any two half-way reasonable cards. Given your image, they won't call without a solid hand. If they do call, they will probably check to you on the flop. Go ahead and bet again. Unless the flop hit them they will have trouble calling.

Here's an example of the above concept. You are on the button; no one has called, and you raise with

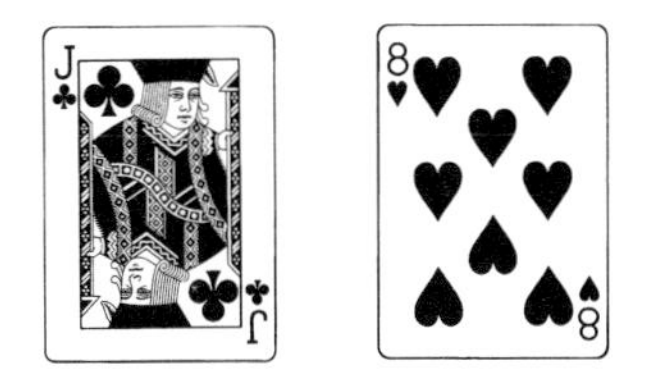

Many good players would raise with it, but you would normally not do it. The big blind calls with

The flop is

When you bet he will almost always fold the better hand.

When you finally show your hand, you get the second benefit of stealing the blinds: You drastically alter your image. The better players will know what you were doing, but many people — especially the weaker players — will become confused and begin to make mistakes against you. That raise will stick in their minds long after they have forgotten the dozens of times you folded.

People remember aggressive raises much better than the number of times you folded.

Selecting the Right Game

Select games that allow you to play your way, but give you the best chance to win.

- The lowest limits you can tolerate.
- The smallest antes or blinds.
- Lots of loose-passive players.
- No more than one loose-aggressive player.
- A large pool of players.
- A full table.

Low Limits and Small Antes or Blinds

Generally, the lower the limits, the weaker the players. In the smallest games many players are loose and passive. In addition, most of them will not recognize your style or exploit your predictability, but the better players in the larger games will quickly identify and adjust to your style, turning you from a winner into a loser.

The ratio of antes to bets also favors you in the smallest stud games, but works against you in the larger ones. You are virtually unbeatable at the smallest stud games because there are no antes (or trivial ones), and the players are so loose. The one negative in the smaller games is that the rake is relatively high, but you still have the edge in them.

As the game gets larger, the antes become a larger fraction of the bets, and the players get tighter and better. These changes cause your style to shift slowly from an asset, to neutral, to a liability.

The same process occurs more slowly in hold 'em because the blinds are always about the same percentages of the bets.

Therefore, your only edge is the other players' looseness and weakness.

A few hold 'em games such as $1-$4-$4-$8 have blinds that are a much smaller fraction of the bets. You can beat those games by just playing tightly. However, that structure favors drawing hands over big cards because people can draw for $1 (or $2 depending on the size of the blind), but bet $8 if they make a hand. It also favors bluffers because they can bet a larger fraction of the total pot. You must therefore change your starting hand requirements, raise more frequently to protect your hand, and beware of bluffers.

Lots of Loose-Passive Players and No More than One Loose-Aggressive Player

Loose-passive players are the easiest to beat for everybody, but they are your "natural prey." You win, not by making good plays, but by taking advantage of other people's mistakes, and nobody makes more of them than loose-passive players. In fact, if you play long enough in a loose-passive game, you are almost guaranteed to win.

You may be tempted to play with several loose-aggressive players because they play so foolishly, but beware. They will, of course, give you much more action on your good hands, but they will also run over you. They will bluff and semi-bluff you, steal your blinds, make you put in more than you like on many hands, and generally force you to do what you most dislike — if you want to win — call with weak hands.

A Large Pool of Players

The larger the pool, the more strangers you will encounter, and it is much easier for you to beat strangers. With only a few regulars, you will soon be identified as "The Rock," get no action on your good hands, be bluffed, etc. The pool of players expands rapidly as the limits get smaller, giving you another reason to play in the smaller games. In fact, as the games get bigger, the percentage of regulars very rapidly increases, making your competition tougher on many dimensions.

A Full Table

You can't beat short-handed games. In hold 'em, you can't wait for the hands you like because someone who bets every time will show a profit against you. In stud, you will play your weak hands poorly and give too many free cards.

Your tightness and passivity may go unnoticed for quite some time at a full table, but will soon be recognized in a short-handed game. And these games require much more stealing of blinds and antes, bluffing, and generally loose-aggressive play, which is exactly the opposite of your style. Since you don't have a chance, don't play.

Getting Your Act Together

If you are a tight-passive player, this chapter has told you a lot about yourself and your playing style. Let's relate it to the questions you answered earlier.

Whenever it says to review and copy scores from a previous chapter, you might find it useful to skim that chapter to remind yourself of the content.

This exercise will take some time, and the answers you write today may be revised as you develop yourself. It may be boring or irritating to spend so much time, but it could pay huge dividends.

Your Right Stuff Ratings

Go to "The Right Stuff Questionnaire" on page 294. It should be dog-eared or paper-clipped. The next few lines are identical to that page. Look at the answers you wrote some time ago. Do they still seem correct? If not, revise them and write your answers here.

Which right stuff dimensions are assets, liabilities, or neutral for you?

Assets *Liabilities* *Neutral*

How can you take advantage of your assets?

How can you reduce the effects of your weaknesses?

Your Card Reading Grid Scores

Go to page 47. It should be dog-eared or paper-clipped. Answer the following questions.

My score is closest to the corner named _____

I have the following similarities and differences from that sort of player

Similarities:

Differences:

How do these similarities and differences affect your poker playing?

What are you going to do about it?

Your Styles Ratings

Look at the styles rating that you wrote on the first page of this chapter. Write it here.

My styles grid scores are: ____,____

Now that you have read this chapter, does that rating seem accurate? Circle the appropriate answer. Yes No. If you circled "No," write a more appropriate set of scores here ____,____

If you changed either or both scores, briefly state why you did it. The more you write, the more benefit you will get.

Your Motives for Playing

Look at your self-ratings on motives from page 227 of this chapter. Copy them into the "Self-ratings" column of the table below. Use pencil and make sure they add to 100 percent.

Table X: My Motives for Playing

My Motives	Self-Rating	Revised Rating
Make money	____%	____%
Socialize, meet people	____%	____%
Relax	____%	____%
Get excitement of risk	____%	____%
Test self against competitive challenges	____%	____%
Sense of accomplishment from winning	____%	____%
Pass time	____%	____%
Other (specify)		
____________	____%	____%
____________	____%	____%
____________	____%	____%
Total (must be 100%)	____%	____%

Based on all you have read, do those percentages seem accurate? If not, insert better numbers in the "Revised Ratings" column. Use pencil and make sure that they add up to 100 percent.

General Questions

Write the answers to these very general questions:
My current style *satisfies* these motives:

My current style *frustrates* these motives:

I should *change* my general style *from:* __ , __ *to* ____,____ because I want to:

Specific Actions

Review the entire chapter and write down *specific actions* you will take.

I should *play in* the following kinds of *games:* ___________
because they ______________________________

I should *avoid* the following kind of *games:* ________________
because they ______________________________

I should make the following *specific changes in my strategy:*

1.

2.

3.

4.

Dog ear or paperclip these pages. From time to time review your plans, note how well you have implemented them, and, if appropriate, revise them.

Good luck!

Part Seven

The Tight-Aggressive Player

The Tight-Aggressive Player

Introduction

Tight-aggressive players (TAPs) will be discussed last because they have the ideal style, the one you should try to copy. Virtually all top professionals, and the best players in your game are TAPs.

This style is *not* natural. It has almost always been carefully chosen, then deliberately developed. Instead of yielding to the natural desires and fears that most people have (such as a love of action, desire for acceptance, or fears of conflict or risk), TAPs have controlled these feelings and chosen and developed the style that matches poker's demand for controlled, selective aggression.

They wait until they have the right cards and the right situation, then attack mercilessly. If the situation changes, or they get new information, they back off or even fold. Their entire style exemplifies poker's most basic rule: *Never do anything without an edge, then take maximum advantage of that edge.*

Tight-Aggressive Opponents

"Tight-aggressive players" (TAPs) include anyone with scores of 1-3 on the tight/loose dimension, and 7-9 on the passive/aggressive dimension. Many of these principles and examples refer primarily to stone killers (1,9). The closer a player's scores are to that pattern, the more likely he is to act, think, and feel like a stone killer.

If either score is outside of the pattern (above 3 on tightness or below 7 on aggression), a player is outside of the corner labeled "tight-aggressive," and some of the principles may not apply to him.

Since TAPs share aggressiveness and tightness with the adjacent "corners," some parts of this chapter will overlap with the chapters on loose-aggressive and tight-passive players.

Figure XV: Tight-Aggressive Players

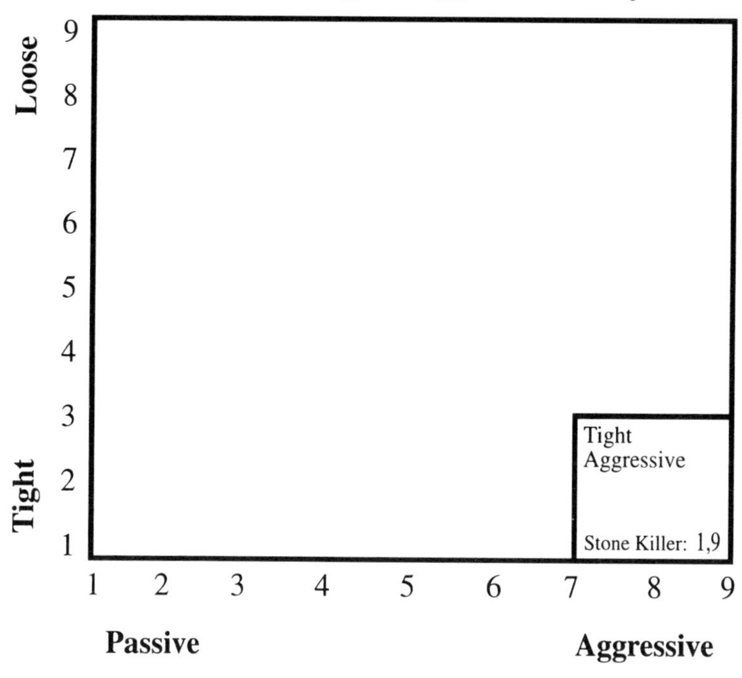

The TAP is the most dangerous player. Nearly all the best professionals are TAPs, as are the best players in most games. They do *not* come to play. They come to *win.* Poker is not a game for them, at least not in the sense of relaxing recreation.

They do almost anything to win, perhaps for economic reasons, perhaps for the sheer love of winning for its own sake, often for both. They make money at poker. It is the only significant source of revenue for a few of them. For others it is a "second job," a welcome supplement to their salaries or pensions. For all of them poker provides the pleasure of competing successfully and making money.

The tight-aggressive style is not at all natural because tight control and aggression do not naturally go together. Tight people tend to be cautious, while aggressive people often lack self-control. Almost the only other place you ever see that tightly controlled, aggressive people is in professions such as fighter pilots and police officers.

Because it is unnatural, the tight-aggressive playing style rarely occurs without lots of work. Maniacs, calling stations, and rocks are just acting out their natural tendencies, but *"Stone Killers" are made, not born.* They have *worked* to hone their skills and develop the right attitudes and habits.

Quick Recognition Signals

TAPs are not just the hardest players to beat. They are also the hardest ones to identify. The other styles reveal and express players' basic personality; what you see is usually what you get. But since TAPs have worked to develop an unnatural style, they often have the motivation and discipline to create a false image.

Some of them "talk loose and play tight." Many of them appear charming and sociable. Others are deliberately obnoxious because they want you to get angry and eager to beat them. A few even act like fools or drunks.

Why would anyone be willing to be disliked or regarded as a fool or a drunk? Because the weak players' respect is less important to them than winning. As Roy Cooke put it:

> "Take [your] image ... manipulate it as best you can, and work with it to get the results that you want. It's not about winning respect. It's about winning chips."

If they decide to project a false image, they may apply three principles.

1. *They project the image that gives them the biggest edge, not the one that makes them most comfortable.* They deliberately sacrifice comfort, respect, and affection for money. The goal is always to increase their edge by confusing the opposition.
2. *That image is false, but credible.* An incredible image is worthless, but a true image allows people to read them and counter their strategies. TAPs balance revealing too much about themselves and acting so out of character that nobody buys their act.
3. *Their image is based upon a realistic assessment of themselves and their situation.* They can then balance the conflicting demands between the ideal image and their own limitations. The most profitable image may not be credible, while the most credible one may not be profitable.

Since any facade can conceal a TAP, you have to interpret *all* signals cautiously. Make sure you are dealing with the reality, not the deliberately false image. Minimize what they say, a careless or lighthearted manner, or any apparently loose plays they may advertise, and count how many hands they play, how often they stay to the river, and especially how often they raise and do *not* win the pot.

If someone frequently folds, but plays a few pots very aggressively, raises early, but folds if the cards go against him, and rarely goes all the way to a showdown without winning — sometimes with mediocre hands — he is almost certainly a TAP.

That pattern strongly suggests that an apparently different sort of player is really a stone killer.

Remember, they are *selectively* aggressive. They do not want a fair fight or an even gamble. They give lots of action, but *only* when they have an edge. It is *not* wild gambling to raise and reraise with a hand that is just slightly better than the others. It's great poker.

Of course, not every TAP is a good actor. They may try to deceive you, but you can identify some of them if you work at it. Look for the following signals.

Signal No. 1: Discipline. The word that best describes them is "disciplined." It takes extreme discipline to do all the unnatural things this style demands. They have to control their desire to gamble, socialize, relax, and do all the other things that most of us do at a poker table. Their discipline affects everything they do.

Signal No. 2: Alertness. They are almost always alert. They rarely fumble for their chips, ask what the bet is, or whose turn it is to act. They *know* what is going on.

Signal No. 3: Concentration, even when they have folded. After folding, most players relax, but the TAP usually keep "working," studying the action, learning how people play, planning their future strategy.

Signal No. 4: Intensity. Some TAPs cannot conceal their hunger to win. For example, if you try to talk to them, they shrug you off, and they may even be rude about it. Their intensity is so great that you can almost hear their brains working.

Nearly all TAPs are obsessed with winning, and some of them are too obvious about it. They shoot angles, complain about minor rules violations, get nasty when someone acts out of turn, deliberately take the last chip from a big loser, and generally make the game too intense and serious for some people.

They should know better, but their hunger to win overwhelms their judgment. In fact, if you told them their intensity turns off other players, they might not understand. They are proud of their intensity and cannot understand why anyone would object to it.

Signal No. 5: Concealed contempt. They know they are good, and part of them looks down on weaker players. Their control usually helps them hide that contempt. For example, they rarely criticize stupid plays because they don't want to educate the weaker players or chase them away. However, a few of them do make that mistake, and even more of them reveal their contempt by the way they look at or discuss bad players.

As always, *observe the way others react to them.*

Recognition Signal No. 1: Coldness. If nobody welcomes someone they clearly know, he is probably tight; hardly anyone likes to play with tight players. However, coldness alone does not tell you whether he is passive or aggressive. Look for the following signals *combined with coldness.*

Recognition Signal No. 2: Respect and fear, especially from good players. This suggests tightness-aggression. For example, if a strong player wants to change seats to the newcomer's left, the newcomer is probably aggressive. If you also sense coldness, he is probably tight-aggressive. If a good player wants to change games, the stranger may be tight-aggressive.

Recognition Signal No. 3: Hostility, fear, and even contempt from weaker players. If the weaker players, especially the loose-passive ones, seem frightened or want to change tables, and you also sense coldness, he is probably tight-aggressive. They don't just fear his ability; they also dislike his intensity and ruthlessness.

Recognition Signal No. 4: Remarks about toughness, intensity, or ruthlessness. These feelings are sometimes expressed directly.

Listen for remarks such as: "He plays too hard." "He never loses." "It's not a game to him." "I love it when he loses."

Unfortunately, these feelings are not often expressed directly. Since the TAPs are so hard to beat, you have to work hard to pick up subtle signals. But, since they are so dangerous, you should work hard to identify them.

Strengths

Competitively, this style is nothing but strengths. Poker rewards discipline, tightness, and selective aggression, and TAPs have all of them.

TAPs are usually good to excellent card readers. They have to focus on other players to play that style, and they have the time and personal qualities to develop their skill. Their folding so often gives them time to learn how other people play; and their discipline, intensity, and concentration help them to use that time productively.

They have lots of confidence in their judgment. They could not play this way without it. It takes great confidence to throw away a good hand because you think it is beaten or to raise with a mediocre one because you think it is a winner.

Weaknesses

Competitively, the TAP style does not have any significant weaknesses, except the tendency to turn off some weaker players.

Their obsession with winning may indicate some serious *personal* weaknesses. They may agree with Jack Straus' position: "I'd bust my own grandmother if she was playing poker with me." That obsession made him a great champion, but it would scare most people and drive away some good "customers." It may have also affected his personal life, but it is none of our business.

TAPs do not satisfy other needs. They certainly do not relax or socialize, nor do they get the pure pleasure of gambling for the hell of it. Poker is serious "business" to them, even if they don't need the money.

The name of the game is "win," and they may pay a psychological price for it. However, most of them probably don't really care. They play to win, and they win, end of story.

Reading Their Cards

The TAP's cards are exceptionally hard to read. Besides being deceptive, they think and act differently from most players. They control themselves, while other players often yield to their impulses.

For example, many players focus on their hands' absolute value, not how it compares to the other hands. They may even "fall in love" with their big hands and ignore signals that they are beaten, betting more aggressively with a losing full house than with a winning pair. Instead, TAPs bet according to their reading of their hands' *relative* strength. They will fold "good" hands that seem beaten and raise with "mediocre" or even "poor" hands that they expect to win, or they make these raises in an effort to improve their chances of winning. In addition, they always consider the size of the pot when making their decisions.

To read their cards you have to learn what they think other people have. Of course, you should do it with everyone, but it is much harder with them. You must decide what they think the other people are doing and interpret their actions in terms of their perceptions and motives, not the ones you would have in that situation.

Incidentally, TAPs rarely have tells or telegraphs. Their entire approach emphasizes control, and they are not going to give away any information.

They act for a deliberate purpose, not to express a desire or fear. Other styles often reverse that principle, yielding to their impulses instead of making thoughtful decisions. LAPs raise because they crave action; LPPs call because they want to be included; TPPs fold because they fear risk. The TAPs minimize these impulses and act deliberately. They know what they are doing and why they are doing it. The key to reading them is: *Look for the purpose of their actions.*

Their purposes are considerably more varied and complex than those of other players. When a rock raises, he is confident he has you beat. A maniac may raise for the hell of it, but a TAP can raise for several reasons:

1. He thinks he has the best hand.
2. He thinks the expected value (EV) of his draw justifies a raise.
3. He wants to limit the field so that his hand — which may not be the best at the moment — has a better chance of winning.
4. He wants a free card on the next round.
5. He is bluffing.
6. He is semi-bluffing.

Obviously, reading his cards is considerably more complicated than reading those of anyone else. Let me describe two excellent plays by TAPs. Both show a great deal of card reading skill and extreme confidence in that skill.

1. A hold 'em player raised in a late position before the flop with

The flop was

giving him two top pair, an excellent hand. One player bet, a second player called, he raised, and they all called. The turn was the J♥. They checked, he bet and got two callers. The river was a second jack, one player checked, and a loose-passive player bet. There were about 12 big bets in the pot. He thought carefully, then folded. She had

had been hoping for a gut straight, and backed into three jacks. He believed that she would not bet without trips, and he was dead right.

2. In another hold 'em game a player reraised a rock with ace-trey at the river when the board was

because he correctly concluded that the tight passive raiser had an ace-deuce making his aces full of deuces a tiny notch smaller than his own aces full of treys. He reviewed the entire betting pattern, related it to the raiser's style, decided he had a winner, and backed his judgement.

These examples show the essence of the TAP style. One of them bet aggressively, then folded for just one bet when he thought he was beaten. The other one made a good reraise because of his card reading skills. It would be extremely difficult for anyone who did not know both players to put them on those hands.

Their complexity and unemotional, analytic approach forces you to work much harder to read their cards. General principles such as we used with the other styles just don't work very well with them. You have to get into their heads and *learn how this particular TAP thinks and plays.*

One useful step in that direction is to *focus your attention only on the TAP* whenever you are out of the pot. Make understanding him "your project." Watch when he folds, raises, etc. Keep asking why he has taken certain actions. Predict what he will do next, then try to figure out why he did or didn't do it.

Look for patterns. They are certainly there; you just have to work harder to see them. Make notes. If you study well, you may not only learn how to read him, you may also improve your overall game. One of the best ways to learn a skill is to copy a master.

Playing Against Them

As always, this section concerns three decisions: Should you play with them? Where should you sit? How should you adjust your strategy?

Should You Play with Them?

What should you do when a TAP sits down? That's easy: *avoid him.* If the rest of the game is good, keep playing, but minimize confrontations with him, and be much tighter and more careful whenever he is in the pot.

He is probably too tough for you. He may look like fun to play with, but he's got the edge, and it is probably going to cost you, perhaps a few dollars, perhaps a lot of them. If you get lucky, you may win, but it probably won't be much. There are only three reasons to play with a TAP. They are:

1. *The rest of the game is easy.* If there are several weak players, of course, you should play. The TAP is not going to be in many pots, and you can beat the others.
2. *You want to test or challenge yourself*. You can do it for the sheer fun of it, to see how well you do against the toughest style. If the money is not important to you, and you love challenges, do it.

   You might also be thinking of moving up, say, from $10-$20 to $20-$40 or higher. In general, games get tougher as you move up: The players are more skilled, tighter, and more aggressive. The higher you go, the fewer people stay for the flop or fourth street, the fewer hands go to the showdown, and the more raises occur on every street.

   Playing with a TAP or two at your current level is a fairly inexpensive way to learn whether you are ready to move up. If you can't win with the advantage of having several weaker players in the game, stay where you are.
3. *You want to learn from them.* It costs money to learn any game, and you may have paid high fees for tennis or golf lessons. Poker players rarely hire coaches, but we pay for our lessons. If you want to improve, you pay "tuition" to the tougher players.

Watch them closely. When do they bet, call, raise, or fold? Where do they sit? How do they talk? What do they do when they are out of the pot? Ask questions: Why did you raise? What hand did you expect from Charlie? What did you think of Sheryl's play a few hands ago? Don't interrogate or cross-examine them, and ask mostly about other people's play. You can learn a lot by talking to them, both at the table and while you are waiting to play. Some TAPs will rebuff your attempts to pick their brains, but some of them will give you useful insights. Lots of people enjoy the guru role.

If you want to learn by playing with them, do it in games where you have a chance to win, ones with several weak players.

Don't sit down if the game is full of sharks, unless you are willing to pay a high price for your lessons.

Regardless of how easy the other players are, be very cautious with the TAP. Avoid him whenever you can. If he is in, don't play without a better hand than usual. Avoid one-on-one confrontations. If in doubt, run. Learn by playing with a winner, but keep your tuition down by staying out of his pots.

Where Should You Sit?

You are better off on his left than his right. That rule applies whether an aggressive player is loose, tight, or in between. If there are two aggressive players in the game, one loose and one tight, choosing a seat is a tough decision, one we could argue indefinitely. I'll just describe the effects of having them to your left and let you make your own decision. Let's assume that you have not spotted a telegraph about their intentions.

If the loose-*aggressive player is to your left:*

- You will be raised much more often because he raises with weak cards.
- You will be much more tempted to call the raises because you have less to fear. You may call raises with marginal hands (which you should not have played at all with an LAP to your left). You may then lose lots of money on hands you never should have played.
- You can slow play and check-raise much more easily because the LAP will bet and raise with much weaker hands.
- You will be bluffed much more often, but less skillfully, making the decision to call more frequent, but less difficult.
- Your swings will be much larger. You will win more when you are lucky, and lose more when the cards go against you.

However, if the tight-*aggressive player is to your left:*

- You will be raised much less frequently because he won't raise without a good hand for that situation.

- You will be less tempted to call the raises because you know they are based on good cards. You may fold marginal hands, reducing your loses on them.
- You cannot slow play and check-raise as easily or as often because the TAP will be more aware of your hand strength.
- You will be bluffed less often, but more skillfully, which makes your decisions less frequent, but more difficult.
- Your swings will be somewhat smaller, but you will probably lose more over time. Since LAPs are losers, while TAPs are winners, you are giving the toughest player the added edge of position over you. You can probably beat the LAP even when he has position on you, but the TAP is going to beat you, and he will beat you more with good position.

You really don't want either of them on your left. If you have to choose, think carefully, but get a seat change button. As soon as possible, get a better seat.

How Should You Adjust Your Play?

These concepts are both difficult and essential because they are such tough opponents.

Concept No. 1: Don't play unless you are at your best. This point is related to the general advice to avoid the TAP. Since they are so tough, don't play against them if you are the slightest bit on tilt, distracted, short of money, or anything that harms your game. You would not play golf for money against the club champion when you've got the flu or your back hurts; just apply the same principle to poker.

Concept No. 2: Mix up your game. Being predictable is always a weakness, but it can be deadly with them. They read cards well and will push whenever they can. If you don't mix up your game, they will soon learn how to read you, then beat you mercilessly. And mix up your game *randomly* rather than try to use your judgement against someone with greater judgement than you. (See the chapters on game theory in *Getting The Best of It* and *The Theory of Poker* both by David Sklansky.)

Concept No. 3: Make fewer pure bluffs, but be willing to semi-bluff. It is usually easier to bluff good players than bad ones, but TAPs study players intensely. They read tells well, and they have enough confidence in their skill to call with weak hands. Of course, that is just a general principle. Perhaps *this* TAP can't read you. Try him out a couple of times, and follow the guidelines for bluffing the TPP. For example, bluff early if the board is all small cards since they are not apt to play them. If your bluffs work, fine. If not, you've been warned.

Concept No. 4: Don't bet marginal hands for value. There are four reasons. First, a TAP would not be in there without good cards; he may well have you beat. Second, if he has a better hand, he will probably raise. Third, if you have him beat, he will probably fold. Fourth, TAPs can make plays that cause you to make mistakes. You'll save money over time by checking marginal hands.

Concept No. 5: Don't raise without a great hand. The same logic applies to raises. He may have you beat and reraise. If you have him beat, he will often fold. Follow the same rule you applied to a rock, but be even more careful because of the danger of a reraise.

Concept No. 6: Check-raise less often, especially on the last round. Since they are tight, they may check behind you. If they do bet, they may have you beat. Worse yet, if they bet, and you raise, they may reraise if they have you beat and fold otherwise.

Thus it is usually better to just come out betting with most of your good hands on the end.[21]

Concept No. 7: Don't try to steal their blinds. Since TAPs do not over-protect their blinds, your attempts to steal will often succeed. However, when they fail, they can be quite costly, particularly if you are in the small blind (because the big blind has position on you). If he calls, you are one on one with the toughest player; your cards are weak; and he has position on you. That's the last place you want to be. Furthermore, he will recognize your late position and be willing to reraise with some "marginal" hands.

If the TAP is to your immediate left, suggest to him that you "chop the blinds," (each player takes back his money). Chopping is particularly desirable — and quite customary — in games with a rake. Don't wait until the situation arises; agree in advance.

You don't want to fight anyone to your left, but provoking a very tough player there is really asking for trouble. What do you do for an encore, challenge Mike Tyson to a biting contest?

Playing in a Tight Aggressive Game

A tight-aggressive game (TAG) has two or more TAPs, no more than one loose player, and the rest of the players are average or tight. Relatively few people contest most pots; raises and reraises occur frequently; and many hands end before the showdown.

The chapters for the other style opponents contained a section titled "Accept that the Rules are Different." That section does not fit here because most of the good poker writers play in and write about tight-aggressive games.

---

[21] This idea applies mainly to those situations where you are heads-up with the TAP. If many players are in, you will need to use the concepts that apply to multiway pots.

The rules for playing in these games are derived from the ones for playing against one TAP, but there are some additional implications, and you absolutely *must* adjust your game. A TAG is the toughest game. If you do not accept and adjust to that fact, you can get hurt badly.

The first question is, of course, *should you play at all?* The answer is almost always: *No!* In fact, if the game is at all short-handed, the answer is almost certainly: *No!*

There are lots of reasons not to play, and hardly any reasons for playing. You are probably going to lose, and you may lose much more than you can afford. If you win, you won't win much. The game can be so stressful and demanding that you can't relax. If you do not play your very best, you have no chance at all, and, even then, you may easily lose. So, why bother?

There were three reasons for playing against an individual TAP, but the one about the other players' weakness does not apply. Unless you have strong desires to test yourself against the best or to learn from playing with them, don't play. If those motives are really important to you, and you are willing to take the unavoidable risks, go for it.

However, before you decide to sit in, think carefully about what it might cost you both financially and psychologically. Let's assume for the moment that you can afford the money. The more important question may be: How will it affect your ego? If you get a lot of pleasure from thinking you are one of the best players, you may not want to learn that you are not that good.

Here are some adjustments you may need to make.

Adjustment No. 1: Don't play unless you are at your best. That warning is much more important now. Before you were warned about a tough player. Now the whole game is tough. If you are even a little off, you can get hurt badly.

Adjustment No. 2: Decide in advance how much you will risk. Nearly everybody plays badly when they are desperate to get even, and that risk is greater than usual here. You are more likely to lose than in any other game, and it will be harder than ever to get even. In addition, you may not want to admit to yourself that they play better than you do. You may make all the rationalizations about bad luck, etc., then buy more chips.

If you do not set a limit and stick to it, you can get stuck, buy more chips, lose them, get desperate, and go for your bankroll. So think carefully before you sit down, and immediately buy *all* the chips you intend to risk.

However, setting this stop loss limit does have a major downside. As you get close to your loss limit, you may go into "tournament mode" and fold some marginally profitable hands to conserve your chips. Conversely, you may play a hand you should fold because you are short-stacked and the blinds are coming.

Adjustment No. 3: Tighten up on the early streets. Since the game is both tight and aggressive, you have to be *more selective* on third street in stud and before the flop in hold 'em. You have to be even tighter than in a TPG, especially in early position.

People are playing premium cards, and some of them are playing them aggressively. If you call with marginal or worse cards, you don't have a chance. You will get beaten by their better hands, and their raises may force you to risk much more on them than you had intended. *This problem is particularly serious if you are in early position; you may find yourself isolated against a tough player who has position on you.*

Adjustment No. 4: Pick your seat with exceptional care. Since the game is so tough, you need every edge you can get. Study the players, watch the action, and change to the best seat you can get. (Note: You also do this for defensive reasons. Having the wrong players acting behind you can cause you to make unnecessary mistakes.)

Adjustment No. 5: Follow the rules for playing against TAPs even when they are not in the pot. Because the overall game is tight-aggressive, you have to treat *everyone* more cautiously than usual. This kind of game changes many players, making them tighten up and become more aggressive. If you study the action, you will see that all but the weakest players move in that direction. You had better move that way too.

If You Are a Tight-Aggressive Player

You are a tight-aggressive player (TAP) if your tight/loose score is three or less, and your passive/aggressive score is seven or more. In that case this chapter focuses directly on you. Before reading any further, write your styles grid scores from page 96.

My styles grid scores are: ____,____

Figure XVI: Tight-Aggressive Players

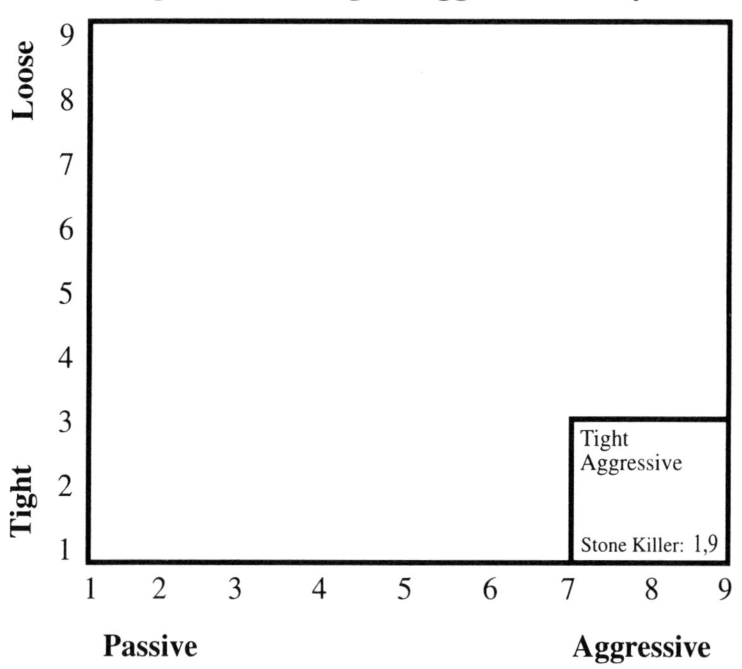

Place an X on Figure XVI at the point that matches your grid scores. The closer that X is to the bottom-right corner of the grid, the more tight-aggressive you are, and the more relevant this chapter is to you.

Although anyone with this pattern of scores is a TAP, most of the examples and principles refer primarily to the *extremely* tight-aggressive player, the "Stone Killer," 1,9.[22] If your tightness score is higher than one, or your aggression score is lower than nine, everything here is off, maybe a little, maybe a lot.

If either of your scores is outside of the pattern, you are not a TAP, and much of this chapter does not directly relate to you. For example, if you are a 3,6, you are tight and slightly aggressive. Some of this chapter will fit you, while other parts may be quite inaccurate.

This chapter is divided into five sections.

1. Accepting the Consequences
2. Understanding Your Motives
3. Improving Your Play
4. Selecting the Right Game
5. Getting Your Act Together

We begin by discussing the general consequences because virtually all tight-aggressive players get the same overall results. The next four sections will help you to understand why *you* play that way and what you should do about it. Since this chapter is for tight-aggressive players, most remarks will be directed to "you" rather than "he" or "they."

---

[22] Again remember that the best players are not quite this extreme.

Accepting the Consequences

If you are a TAP, particularly an extreme one, you may not like the next few lines, but you should take them seriously. The consequences of your style are fairly obvious.

- You will win consistently as long as you play within your limitations.
- You may lose your bankroll if you move up to much bigger games.
- You may damage your health.
- You will not be welcome in most games.
- Many people, especially the good players, will respect you.
- Many players will be envious, and some of them will dislike you.

Winning Consistently Within Your Limits

You will beat almost everyone, even players with better card reading and other skills, because your style gives you an enormous edge. Because they are looser, they will have more losers, and your well developed killer instinct will produce a larger profit on your winners. As long as you stay at the right level, you're golden.

Losing Your Bankroll in Much Bigger Games

Your greed and love of competition may make you move up too fast or too high. You have beaten most games *because* you have the best style. However, the higher you go, the less edge your style will provide because more players will be tight-aggressive, and they will also be highly skilled. You will *not* be able to win on style alone.

The higher you go, the more skilled the competition will usually be. Of course, there are weak players at every level, but the general style and skill level become tougher and tougher.

Athletes have the same problem. Lots of great high school players can't make the team in college, and countless college stars never make it into the professional leagues. You should think carefully before trying to move up. You're good, but you are probably not good enough for much bigger games.

Damaging Your Health

You would not have worked so hard to develop the best style if you were not committed to the game, but you may play so often and so intently that you damage your health. Of course, lots of other kinds of players play too much, but tight-aggressive players are particularly likely to overdo it. The others' losses may keep them from playing too much, while you have an extra incentive to play lots of hours: You win.

Cardrooms should have a sign similar to the surgeon's general's statement on cigarettes: "Warning, too much poker can be dangerous to your health." The lifestyle is almost a "prescription" for a heart attack and other nasty problems. Lots of players spend far too many hours on back-destroying chairs, in smokey rooms, with hardly any exercise, and a steady diet of unhealthy food. It is a deadly combination.

Of course, you could follow in the footsteps of Johnny Moss who lived and played competitively into his late eighties, but many top players die in their sixties.

Not Being Welcome in Most Games

The reason is obvious: You're a winner, and losers are much more welcome than winners. On this point poker is extremely different from most games. Most people like to play with experts.

For example, some tennis players pay large fees to play in Pro-Am tournaments.

But poker is different. Since we know we haven't got a chance, we don't mind losing to a tennis professional. We would forget the final score and remember when we hit a winner or heard him say, "Nice shot." When a rich executive blew one by a great player, the TV announcer said: "He's just had the dream of every hacker, acing a top pro."

In poker hardly anyone wants to pay for the privilege of competing with better players. They might be willing if you were famous, but you're not. You play better than most people, but losing to you is not like losing to Doyle Brunson. Some people lose serious money to him just to say they did it. If you kick somebody's butt, he doesn't get a memorable experience to brag about; all he gets is a sore butt and a thinner wallet.

Respect, Especially from Good Players

The poker culture is very macho, and the best players get lots of respect, not just for their skills, but for their ruthlessness. We give respect — sometimes reluctantly — to people who are good at doing things that many cultures see as improper, even illegitimate, such as stealing pots, deceiving, squeezing the maximum profit from a hand, and even taking another player's last dollar.

Envy and Hostility

These feelings are closely related to not being welcomed, plus another factor. Poker players are so competitive that we compete about nearly everything. The status hierarchy is not as clearly defined as a tennis club's ladder, but we all know about where we stand. Lots of people are going to envy you, not just for the money you win — although it is certainly important — but also because you rank higher than they do.

What can you do about it? Not much. It's human nature to envy and dislike the people above us. As long as you are there, some people are going to try to pull you down. They may, for example, talk behind your back, accuse you of shooting angles or even cheating, and do other nasty things to prevent them from accepting that you play better than they do. You can reduce their hostility by being gracious and courteous, but you will just have to learn to live with those feelings.

Which brings us to the major weakness of lots of TAPs: Open contempt and rudeness toward weaker players. You know it is dumb to criticize your "customers," flaunt your winnings, and do the other adolescent things that some good players do.[23] So, if you have this problem, grow up. You're too good to lower yourself. You can be a tiger at the table, but still be a gentleman or lady.

Understanding Your Motives

The first question is: *Why do you play poker?* For the other styles the second question was: *Why have you chosen your* style? However, you did not just *choose* the tight-aggressive style. You had to work hard to develop it. Therefore, for you the second question is: *Why did you work so hard to develop your style*?

The answers to both questions are obvious. You play poker to win, and you developed this style because it gets the best results. However, you may have minimized your other motives.

Understanding *all* your motives could help you to make two extremely important decisions: The level and types of games you select, and whether you try to become a full-time professional. We

---

[23] One former winner of the $10,000 WSOP No Limit Hold 'em Championship had a temper tantrum on national television. He walked around yelling about a player's bad play, completely oblivious to the cameras. That sort of action should never occur.

saw that Nick "The Greek's" ego and love for challenges made him blow his bankroll against Johnny Moss, a much better player.

The same sort of thing happens all the time. Countless young men and a few women try to beat players who are too tough for them. Usually, they just lose their bankrolls, but some of them destroy their lives.

They are usually the best player in their little world, and they want to try the big leagues. They save for months or years and may even borrow to get a bankroll. They quit their jobs, move to Las Vegas or another poker town, play in bigger games, and go broke. If you are thinking of trying it, read the appendix, "Don't Quit Your Day Job."

Your style has both economic and psychological causes, and the psychological drives may be stronger (but you probably did not rate them as highly). You may have underrated these other drives because poker players talk much more about winning money than all other motives combined.

This over-emphasis is caused primarily by the poker culture. We talk about money the way Wall Street traders talk about it: It's the way we keep score.

You are almost certainly competitive in many other areas. For example, you probably enjoy other games and play them well. You may also be very competitive for status and other psychological satisfactions.

If I wanted to get psychoanalytic, I would say that you are close to being obsessive-compulsive, but that's not my purpose here. Let's just see *which other* motives influence your poker playing.

Let's start by looking at the self-ratings of your motives from the "Why Do You Play Poker?" chapter in "Part One: The Right Stuff."(p. 35). Copy your scores from there into the "self-ratings" column. The next few paragraphs may change those ratings.

Table XI: My Motives for Playing

Motive	
Make money	_______%
Socialize, meet people	_______%
Relax	_______%
Get excitement of risk	_______%
Test self against competitive challenges	_______%
Sense of accomplishment from winning	_______%
Pass time	_______%
Other (specify)	
_____________	_______%
_____________	_______%
_____________	_______%
Total (must be 100%)	_______%

Every player should know why he has chosen his style, but this self-knowledge is much less important for you. Regardless of your reasons, you have developed the best style (from a win-lose perspective).

If you did not assign at least 20 percent to "Test self against competitive challenges" and/or "Sense of accomplishment from winning," I think you are kidding yourself. You are *not* playing just to make money. Anyone with the brains and discipline to win consistently could probably make much more money doing other things.

If your total scores for "Make money," "competitive challenges," and "sense of accomplishment from winning" did not total at least 75 percent, I would be quite surprised, and something is very wrong. Either there are unsuspected factors operating, or you are kidding yourself.

If your scores fit that pattern, *you have developed exactly the right style for your motives*. No other style will produce remotely as great profits and feelings of competing successfully. The only negative could be frustration of your other motives.

For example, do you regret not being able to relax and enjoy the game? Would you like to be friendlier with the other players rather than regarding them just as opponents to beat? Do you sometimes wish you could yield to foolish impulses and chase better hands or gamble just for the hell of it? If these things *seriously* bother you, soften your style a *little*: Lighten up, loosen up, and be a little less aggressive. In other words, remember it's a game, and it's played for pleasure.

If these things don't bother you, don't change your style, not one little bit. You're doing fine. In this part of the chapters on every other style I emphasize the importance of changing their style. There is a grid with arrows from where they are now toward your corner. You are already where they should go, and they probably can't get there. You've found the right home; enjoy it.

Improving Your Play

You have the ideal style.[24] However, there are other ways to improve your game.

Work on Your Image

Many TAPs have a personality problem. A few of them are nasty, but most of them are just too intent and serious. They take the game so seriously that some of their best "customers" avoid them. They would rather play with people who make the game more fun.

---

[24] As already mentioned, even though tight-aggressive is clearly the best style, the extreme TAP, the stone killer, (1,9), will not do as well as someone who plays a few more hands and who plays a little less aggressively. Extreme tightness will cause stone killers to miss some profitable opportunities, and extreme aggressiveness will cause them to put more money into the pot than they should given the correct value of their hands.

You may say, "So what?" but that's dumb. You do not want soft players to avoid you, and the softer they are, the more turned off they will be by an overly serious manner and attitude. Let me put it in the simplest possible words: *The harsher you appear, the less money you will make.*

For example, one high stakes player seems to be a rich, charming playboy. He dresses expensively, wears gold chains and a Rolex, spends freely, and always smiles and laughs. When he wins, he says it is all luck. When he loses, he congratulates the winner, even laughs at his mistakes (and most of them never happened). While playing, he seems almost uninterested in the game: He chats away about nothing, watches and comments on the televised games and races, or points out and smiles at a passing pretty girl.

He may look like a rich playboy, but he lives entirely on his poker winnings. His relaxed, pleasant manner relaxes his "customers," while increasing his edge. They get distracted, but he knows exactly what is going on. He can operate at two levels: While apparently ignoring the game, his mental computer is recording and evaluating *everything*. His play seems relaxed and careless, but he knows exactly what he is doing.

Several live ones love to play with him. They play for fun, and he is fun to play with. The best move a stone killer can make is to be such a pleasure to play with that live ones ask to join his game.

Don't Try to Win Every Last Dollar

You might want to go a bit further than just *appearing* gentler and less serious. Sometimes it pays to *be* that way. Let me tell you about the richest man I've ever known well, Ed Ryan, the founder of Ryan Homes. He started as a carpenter and made over $100 million building houses. His hand-picked successor was extraordinarily competitive: He had to win at everything — even trivial arguments.

While grooming him to take over, Ed repeatedly said: "Don't try to win them all. Pick your spots. Let somebody else win once in a while." His successor learned that and other lessons, took the company to greater heights, and ended up on the cover of *Business Week.* Ed didn't make $100 million by being a dummy; so follow his advice: Once in a while let the other guy win.

Selecting the Right Game

For every other style I recommended playing in the smallest game they could tolerate. My advice to you is to play in the biggest game you can handle.

Before trying to move up, you should recognize that your style is the major reason you have succeeded, but that style will not give you such an edge in bigger games. At your current level you are probably much more tight-aggressive than the opposition. Since larger games are usually tighter and more aggressive, your current style will become closer to average.

For example, the style that is 3,7 in $10-$20 games, might be 5,5 in $30-$60 games. The same sort of thing happens to football players. A 240 pound defensive end might star at most colleges, but he is too small for that position in the NFL.

As you move up, you may have to become even tighter and more aggressive, and you will almost certainly have to develop other qualities as well. You will not be able to win on style alone. A complete knowledge of the game becomes mandatory.

Since you will not know whether you can handle a game until you try it, experiment in a carefully planned way. Don't move up more than one level at a time, and spend some time at each level, making sure that you can beat it, before trying to move further. If your results are poor, be willing to move back down. You can always study some more and try again.

At each level be very cautious at first. Move up only when you are playing your best. Select the softest games. Don't risk your entire bankroll; set aside an amount you can afford to risk; if you lose it, drop down a level or two. Take frequent walks during the game to review the game and your strategy. After the session discuss it with other strong players to learn how to improve your game.

Sooner or later you will hit your limit, the biggest game you can handle. Stay there and enjoy yourself. It is far better to win consistently at $20-$40 than to struggle to survive at $50-$100.

Getting Your Act Together

If you are a tight-aggressive player, this chapter has told you a lot about yourself and your playing style. Let's relate it to the questions you answered earlier.

Whenever it says to review and copy scores from a previous chapter, you might find it useful to skim that chapter to remind yourself of the content.

This exercise will take some time, and the answers you write today may be revised as you develop yourself. It may be boring or irritating to spend so much time, but it could pay huge dividends.

Your Right Stuff Ratings

Go to "The Right Stuff Questionnaire" on page 294. It should be dog-eared or paper-clipped. The next few lines are identical to that page. Look at the answers you wrote some time ago. Do they still seem correct? If not, revise them and write your answers here.

Which right stuff dimensions are assets, liabilities, or neutral for you?

Assets	*Liabilities*	*Neutral*

How can you take advantage of your assets?

How can you reduce the effects of your weaknesses?

Your Card Reading Grid Scores

Go to page 277. It should be dog-eared or paper-clipped. Answer the following questions.

My score is closest to the corner named _____

I have the following similarities and differences from that sort of player

Similarities:

Differences:

How do these similarities and differences affect your poker playing?

What are you going to do about it?

Your Styles Ratings

Look at the styles rating that you wrote on the first page of this chapter. Write it here.

My styles grid scores are: ____,____

Now that you have read this chapter, does that rating seem accurate? Circle the appropriate answer. Yes No. If you circled "No," write a more appropriate set of scores here ____,____

If you changed either or both scores, briefly state why you did it. The more you write, the more benefit you will get.

Your Motives for Playing

Look at your self-ratings on motives from page 272 of this chapter. Copy them into the "Self-ratings" column of the table below. Use pencil and make sure they add to 100 percent.

Table XII: My Motives for Playing

My Motives	Self-Rating	Revised Rating
Make money	____%	____%
Socialize, meet people	____%	____%
Relax	____%	____%
Get excitement of risk	____%	____%
Test self against competitive challenges	____%	____%
Sense of accomplishment from winning	____%	____%
Pass time	____%	____%
Other (specify)		
____________	____%	____%
____________	____%	____%
____________	____%	____%
Total (must be 100%)	____%	____%

Based on all you have read, do those percentages seem accurate? If not, insert better numbers in the "Revised Ratings" column. Use pencil and make sure that they add up to 100 percent.

General Questions

Write the answers to these very general questions:

My current style *satisfies* these motives:

My current style *frustrates* these motives:

I should *change* my general style *from:* __ , __ *to* ____,____ because I want to:

Specific Actions

Review the entire chapter and write down *specific actions* you will take.

I should *play in* the following kinds of *games:* __________
because they ______________________________

I should *avoid* the following kind of *games:* _______________
because they ______________________________

I should make the following *specific changes in my strategy:*

1.

2.

3.

4.

Dog ear or paperclip these pages. From time to time review your plans, note how well you have implemented them, and, if appropriate, revise them.

Good luck!

Part Eight

Our Deadly Sins

Our Deadly Sins

Introduction

We have spent a lot of time discussing the major types of players. Let's close by considering something that all of us share, our deadly sins. Some of us have all of them; a few champions have only one or two of them; but none of us is free of them.

Of course, some people try to deny that fact, to pretend that they are better than they really are, but denial is one of the worst sins. It prevents us from doing anything about our own sins and weaknesses. The first step in improving ourselves is to see how we are beating ourselves. Only when we understand how our own drives and attitudes and thinking patterns prevent us from playing our best can we become the players we want to be.

Our Deadly Sins

Near the start of the book we considered the "Right Stuff," the something extra that separates the winners from the rest of us. Let's end by something that all players share — even the winners — our deadly sins. Traditionally, there are seven deadly sins, but — since we are a sinful bunch — we have ten of them. They are as follows:

Deadly Sin No. 1: Poor self-control. It is the deadliest sin and the underlying cause of all the others. We'd rather "do what comes naturally," but *it is natural to lose*.

Even consistent winners take self-defeating actions that make us comfortable, but we often rationalize that they improve our game. Nothing about winning poker is natural; to win we need enough self-control to do the unnatural things it takes to win.

Deadly Sin No. 2: Denying reality. It is the second most deadly sin, and nearly all of us do it occasionally. We deny that this particular bet is foolish or that we are playing poorly because we are tired, bored, or losing. We deny that this game is too tough for us because we do not want to admit our own limitations. Any type of denial can quickly destroy our game and our bankroll.

Deadly Sin No. 3: Impatience. Even the tightest rock occasionally yields to it. Waiting for the right hand or game gets so boring, especially when we are running badly. So we "take a shot." Sometimes it pays off; usually it costs a few chips; and it occasionally costs us a bundle.

Deadly Sin No. 4: Focusing on ourselves, not the other players. We are so concerned with our own cards, our own stack, our own strategy, that we forget that the critical information comes from the other players. For example, we have all fallen in love with a hand and ignored obvious signals that it was beaten.

Lots of us take our favorite or "lucky" seat instead of choosing one that will give us the best position, and nearly all of us have lost lots of money by "studying" our hand. Those cards will not change — no matter how we squeeze and study them — and while we are studying them, we miss signals and can't review the play of the hand, reducing our ability to read the opponents' cards and choose the right strategy.

Deadly Sin No. 5: Yielding to our emotions. Anger and machismo can make us take foolish chances — by overplaying hands, challenging tougher players, playing for higher stakes than we can afford, and continuing to play long after we run out of gas. A desire to look generous can make us give up a bet here and there that add up to big money over time.

Deadly Sin No. 6: Poor concentration. Sometimes we watch a game on TV, or talk to our neighbor, or even try to pick thc winner of the next race. Usually it is more subtle, but equally destructive: For example, we have all fallen into the trap of thinking about earlier hands — especially bad beats, huge pots we won, or bad plays we regretted.

But poker is a very "now" game, and it waits for no one. When the action is to us, we have to do something *immediately,* and we are stuck with whatever we do. If we fold a winner, call with a loser, or just miss a bet because of poor concentration, that money is gone forever.

Deadly Sin No. 7: Rigidity. Most of us all follow a comfortable routine which makes us predictable and easy to read. Rigidity also prevents us from adjusting to different players and changed conditions. We play our hands pretty much the same way regardless of the circumstances.

For example, hardly anyone adjusts quickly when two or three players take a short break. The game changes completely when a rock gets up and is replaced by a maniac, but we may not change quickly enough or at all.

Deadly Sin No. 8: Educating the opposition. We show our cards, especially when we get bad beats, or we explain why we made a certain play, or we criticize or even lecture other players. We do it because we want respect or sympathy, or we just have to express our frustration, but poker is about winning money, not making ourselves feel good. Every time we show our cards, or tell a story, or criticize a player it can cost us money. A weak player may get stronger or quit, and a strong player may learn how to beat us.

Deadly Sin No. 9: Aching to Get Even. The dumbest words in poker are, "I've got to get even," and most of us say them occasionally. Worse yet, we take foolish risks, which often put us deeper into the hole, making us more desperate and more foolish. The fact that we are losing indicates that *something* is wrong. Maybe the game is tougher than we think, or we are playing poorly, or perhaps the poker gods just don't like us today.

Losing should make us more conservative, but we call or even raise with hands we would normally fold. We may even move up to higher limits, despite knowing that the game is tougher. After all, our luck *has* to change, doesn't it?

Wrong! In fact, if we ignore the fact that *something* is wrong, get more aggressive, and play for higher limits, we can easily destroy ourselves and our bankrolls.

Deadly Sin No. 10: Blaming bad luck. We all do it. Blaming bad beats, unlucky streaks, and the stupid plays that beat us, help us to protect our egos by justifying poor results.

Blaming bad luck is a form of denial; we deny that only *we* are responsible for our (long term) results. It makes us feel better, but prevents us from working on our own weaknesses. To play our best we have to accept that responsibility, increase our self-control, and sin less frequently.

Conclusion

This book has covered a wide range of subjects, from "The Right Stuff," to "Our Deadly Sins," to the motives and strategies of different players. Did it cover everything about poker psychology? Of course not.

After studying and teaching psychology for over forty years and playing poker for even longer, I am still concerned about how little I know, how often I get surprised, and the foolish mistakes I make. Sometimes I *know* better, but let my own weaknesses damage my play; sometimes I just don't know why someone made a certain play or what he will do the next time. All practicing psychologists — regardless of their specialty — often feel the same way.

Psychology is not an exact science, and nobody ever masters it. In fact, to keep our licenses and do our jobs, psychologists have to take continuing education courses. If we add in the fact that poker is a game of deception, in which we play "head games" with each other, all we can do is become a little sharper, a little more insightful, a little better at understanding ourselves and other players, and a little more confusing to our opponents.

You should therefore make learning poker psychology one of your priorities, right up there with strategy, game selection, and the other critical skills. In his "Foreword" Mason Malmuth wrote: "Many of the tactics that appear in our books are based on the psychology of your opponents." The authors of many other excellent poker books could say the same thing.

That statement is particularly true for *The Theory of Poker,* and Two Plus Two's books for advanced players. The Fundamental Theorem of Poker is essentially psychological:

> **Every time you play a hand differently from the way you would have played it if you could see all your opponents' cards, they gain; and every time you play your hand the**

same way you would have played it if you could see all their cards, they lose. Conversely, every time opponents play their hands differently from the way they would have if they could see all your cards, you gain; and every time they play their hands the same way they would have played if they could see all your cards, you lose.

Sklansky and Malmuth know that you cannot be an advanced player unless you understand poker psychology, and they constantly try to help readers to understand it. All this book has done is provide a more formal framework for their own and other authors' insights.

So study the books again, but look at them a little differently. Try to relate the specific strategies and tactics to a psychological framework. Whenever you play, keep trying to identify players' styles, and see how they match and differ from the grid groups. I would never claim that my grid — or any other system — can completely describe *anybody*. Then think of exactly how you can use that information.

This study and planning will help you to continue to develop your game. And that is what life is all about, continuing to grow. When you stop growing and lose that love of learning, you inevitably start decaying. Poker — and just about everything else — becomes a boring routine, a grind, not a source of stimulation and excitement. You play the same old cards, in the same old way, with the same old people.

If you consider developing your game as a continuing priority, it is always new, exciting, and challenging. You may never become a master (I certainly won't), but it is a wonderful kick to know that you won a pot, squeezed out an extra bet, or made a great lay-down just because you read the other players better than they read you.

Good luck!

Appendix A

The Right Stuff Questionnaire

This questionnaire asks you to rate yourself on each of the dimensions from Part One: "The Right Stuff." Rate yourself *only* on the way you think and act at a poker table. If, for example, you are extremely controlled at work, but impulsive while playing, give yourself a low rating for self-control.

It can be difficult and frustrating to rate yourself, and you will probably change your mind about some ratings. Use pencil to make those changes easier.

To simplify the process there are descriptions of only the lowest (#1), average (#5) and highest (#9) scores. Just circle the number that seems to fit you best. If, for example, you lean a little toward wanting an edge rather than having a desire to gamble, you might rate yourself as a 6 on the first scale, "Demanding an Edge."

Demanding an Edge

1. I don't want an edge. I deliberately gamble by playing with weak hands and against strong players.
2.
3.
4.
5. I am evenly balanced between my desire to gamble and to have an edge.
6.
7.
8.
9. I always demand an edge. I won't play a hand or sit down in a game unless I have the largest possible edge.

Obsession with Winning

1. I play for fun, and I don't really care whether I win or lose.
2.
3.
4.
5. I am evenly balanced between playing to win and playing for fun.
6.
7.
8.
9. I'd bust my grandmother if she played poker with me.

Self-control

1. I have hardly any self-control. I yield to my impulses all the time.
2.
3.
4.
5. I am evenly balanced between yielding to impulses and extreme self-control.
6.
7.
8.
9. I have extreme self-control. I almost always think carefully before acting, and I hardly ever yield to impulses.

Realism

1. I am not at all realistic. My hopes and fears have a huge impact on how I see things.
2.
3.
4.
5. I am evenly balanced between realism and letting my hopes and fears affect how I see things.
6.
7.

8.
9. I am brutally realistic. I refuse to let my emotions affect how I see things.

Concentration

1. I don't concentrate on the game. I let my mind wander all the time.
2.
3.
4.
5. My concentration is about average.
6.
7.
8.
9. I concentrate all my attention on the game.

Thinking Visibly

1. My thinking is not at all visible to me. I often do not know how or why I made a decision.
2.
3.
4.
5. I am average about thinking visibly.
6.
7.
8.
9. I think very visibly. I know exactly how and why I make nearly all decisions.

Admitting Mistakes Quickly

1. I am extremely slow to admit mistakes. I ignore very clear evidence that my hand is beaten, or I am playing poorly, or a game is too tough.
2.
3.
4.

5. I am average about admitting mistakes, neither quick nor slow.
6.
7.
8.
9. I am extremely quick to admit mistakes. As soon as the evidence suggests that my hand is beaten, or I am playing poorly, or the game is too tough, I admit it and take corrective action.

Learning From Mistakes

1. I am extremely poor about leaning from my mistakes. I make the same ones again and again.
2.
3.
4.
5. I am average about learning from my mistakes.
6.
7.
8.
9. I am extremely good about learning from mistakes. I hardly ever make the same mistake twice.

Accepting Responsibility

1. I am extremely poor about accepting responsibility. I blame bad luck and other players for my problems.
2.
3.
4.
5. I am average about accepting responsibility.
6.
7.
8.
9. I am extremely good about accepting responsibility. I believe that I make my own luck and cause my own problems.

Depersonalizing Conflict

1. I take conflicts very personally. I often get angry or upset and let my feelings affect my play.
2.
3.
4.
5. I am average about personalizing conflict.
6.
7.
8.
9. I almost never take conflicts personally. They are just part of the game.

Adjusting to Change

1. I adjust to change extremely slowly. I keep playing the same old way long after I should have adjusted.
2.
3.
4.
5. I am average in the ability to adjust to changes.
6.
7.
8.
9. I adjust to change extremely quickly. I am very aware of how the game is changing, and I change along with it.

Selective Aggression

1. I am not at all selectively aggressive. I either do not attack at all, or I attack almost everybody, even when I'm at a disadvantage.
2.
3.
4.
5. I am average in selective aggression.
6.
7.

8.
9. I am extremely selectively aggressive. I don't attack unless I feel it is to my advantage to do so.

Please note that nothing in this chapter or questionnaire was related to your skill. Stu Ungar had the greatest skills, but ended up as a loser because he lacked some elements of the "right stuff." He may never have even thought about it, but you should.

Ignore for the moment how skilled you are. Consider *only* the right stuff dimensions. Take a minute and write down your answers to some basic questions.

Which right stuff dimensions are assets, liabilities, or neutral for you?

Assets	*Liabilities*	*Neutral*

How can you take advantage of your assets?

How can you reduce the effects of your weaknesses?

Dog-ear or put a paperclip on this page. We will refer to it again and again.

Appendix B

Don't Quit Your Day Job

If you are thinking of becoming a full-time professional, forget it. Keep your day job because:

1. You probably won't make it.
2. There is little money and no future.
3. It's extremely unhealthy.
4. It's a dreary life.
5. It's a great "second job."

Reason No. 1: You probably won't make it. Most wannabees fail because they don't have *all* the qualifications. Unless you are an *excellent* player, with a big bankroll, and extreme discipline, you haven't got a chance. Then you need the inner strength to cope with the inevitable losing periods, the public's scorn for professionals, and the inescapable loneliness. Even if you have the skill and the bankroll, you probably won't make it.

Many big names have other sources of income or supplement their poker winnings through other means. If *they* have to supplement their winnings, do you seriously believe *you* can make it full-time?

Reason No. 2: There is little money and no future. Professionals have great nights or weeks, but their annual incomes and hourly "wages" are not at all exciting. Hayano, Sklansky, and Malmuth found that an excellent professional can average approximately 1 big bet an hour in middle sized games, less at larger limits. The unavoidable losing sessions keep the average down.

That $20 or more per hour is a nice bit of change for just having fun, but it is much less than you can make at most highly skilled jobs. If you are smart and disciplined enough to be an *excellent* player, you can probably make more money doing something else.

But what about the top players, the ones who win the big tournaments? First, they rarely get all those highly publicized dollars. They have to sell or trade shares in each other or make deals with backers because they can't stockpile enough money to bankroll themselves.

Second, they are the best in the world, and their incomes are trivial compared to their equals in other games. A mediocre player in the NBA or on the PGA circuit makes more than the greatest poker players, and Tiger Woods makes more money than the top twenty poker players *combined.*

The best players in most cardrooms make much less than a mediocre doctor, lawyer, or executive. They may win thousands or even tens of thousands of dollars some nights, but they also have nights or weeks when they lose money. The net is usually little more than chump change, and hardly any full-timers can afford to retire.

Hayano's research found that none of the full-timers was over 43 years old. At just the age that people become well-established in most careers, they had to start a new one. Sure, Doyle Brunson and a few others made it big and kept it, but for every one of them there are hundreds who played big and ended up broke. If you doubt it, just look around your cardroom. You'll see former high stakes players hustling the tiny games or working at menial jobs to get another stake.

Reason No. 3: It's extremely unhealthy. The lifestyle is almost a "prescription" for a heart attack and other nasty problems. Nearly every full-timer spends far too many hours on uncomfortable chairs, in smokey rooms, with hardly any exercise, and a steady diet of unhealthy food.

Reason No. 4: It's a dreary life. Sure it sounds attractive — play when you like, don't worry about a boss, and sleep until noon —

but the reality is much grimmer. Prof. Hayano found that most professionals needed an income from either work, a pension, trust fund, alimony, or some other source. They could not cope with the unpredictable income of full-time poker.

Hayano's book was based upon Southern California cardrooms in the 1970's. Then cardroom poker was legal only in California and Nevada, and only forms of draw poker were allowed in California. Today you can play many types of poker in dozens of states, and it is probably easier to make a living. But the financial realities are still tougher than you might think.

It's not just the finances that are dreary; it's the entire life. Alvarez wrote about the highest rollers of all, the ones who play in The World Series of Poker. A few of them have nice homes, fancy cars, and other expensive toys, but even the big winners live pathetic lives.

They play poker, eat (often right at the table), sleep, and then play poker again. They may play for more than 24 hours, and 16 hours is quite common. If any boss insisted you work such hours, eat lousy food, sit in an uncomfortable chair, in a smoke filled room, with no financial security or benefits, you would go on strike against the "unfair working conditions."

And you won't even enjoy the poker that much! One former full-timer said:

> "When I *had* to win to pay my bills, I was forced to play whether I liked it or not, even when I wanted to do something with my family, or didn't like the game, or just did not feel like playing. I love poker, but as a full-time job, it's boring and dreary."

Reason No. 5: But it's a great "second job." Lots of people supplement their incomes by playing poker. They play in all size games and can be almost any age. For example, keeping busy is a problem for many retirees. If they play 40 hours a week and make $300, they don't complain about making such low "wages." They are happy to get through the week and make a little profit.

Others play in much bigger games and win lots more money. Their hourly win rate is often higher than that of better players because they can be selective. A selective player can win much more per hour than a non-selective player with superior skills. In fact, the freedom to be selective allows some of them to survive. As Malmuth put it: "Ironically, many people who think they play great actually play reasonably well. If they would seek out the best games, they would be successful."

Part-timers can be dealers, barbers, lawyers, waiters, or whatever. They play well, but not well enough to make it as full-timers, or they want more security or a more balanced life. They have regular jobs and may even be committed to their careers. They play when they feel like it, in whatever games they like, and can spend their winnings however they wish. Sounds good to me.

Appendix C

Quick Summaries

Before playing poker, get in the habit of reviewing a couple of these quick summaries. It will help you to cope with difficult situations. For example, if a maniac puts your game on tilt, you will be ready because you recently read the suggestions for adjusting to loose-aggressive players and games.

Refer frequently to the quick summaries on your own style. They will remind you of how good players adapt to you, and of how you have to change your own game.

There are eight quick summaries, two for each style. The first one is for that type of opponent, and the second is for players with that style. For example, there is one for loose-passive opponents and another one titled: "If you are loose-passive." Each quick summary is printed on a separate page, and some ungrammatical shortcuts were made to save reading time.

Loose-Aggressive Opponents

Beware! They can destroy you very quickly.

Don't gamble with them; they can beat you at their own game.

Play with them? If you like action and play well, yes. If you are cautious, rigid, short of money, or unsure of your skills, no. If the game is short-handed, no.

Where to sit? Usually to their immediate left, but, if you see a telegraph, to their immediate right.

Read their cards: Look for the *absence* of raises, then exclude hands they would have raised in earlier rounds.

Strategic objective: Reduce your losses on weak and marginal hands, but raise and reraise with your better ones to isolate the LAP.

Strategic adjustments: Tighten up on early streets and always be more selectively aggressive.

Specific changes: Don't bluff or steal blinds and bring-ins. Don't bet positional hands. Raise or reraise to isolate them. Bet, raise, and check-raise more frequently. Invite them to bluff. Call on the river with questionable hands; raise with the right pot odds to prevent an overcall. Bet or raise with good draws and pot odds. *Always* look for telegraphs (they often signal their intentions, especially when they will fold).

Loose-aggressive games: Exciting and potentially lucrative, but dangerous. *Be careful.*

Accept that the rules are different. Most players' games have changed, including yours. Pot odds and implied odds have changed drastically. Somebody will draw out on you much more often than usual. The relationship between pot size and hand strength becomes unpredictable. Luck becomes more important. The tension is much greater.

Adjusting to these different rules: Apply LAP concepts, but take them more seriously. Look for changes in *everybody,* especially yourself. Revise your game plan. Select your seat very carefully. Tighten up on early streets. Slow play and check-raise more often. Don't over-focus on LAPs. Bet or raise with good draws and pot odds. Minimize bluffing, deception, and fancy plays. Bet for value more often on the river. Call on the river unless you are *certain* you are beaten. Hesitate and look for telegraphs *every* time; people will signal their intentions, but you may be too excited to notice.

If You are Loose-Aggressive

Consequences: Lose lots of money because this is the riskiest style, and good players study and get position on you. Usually welcome because you "make the game." Some people are hostile or contemptuous.

Strengths: With good cards you will win more than anyone (in the short run).

Weaknesses: With average or worse cards you will lose, perhaps very heavily. Over the long term, you *must* lose. In addition to losing lots of money from overplaying hands you should fold, you become everybody's target. Good players will recognize your weaknesses and identify your tells and telegraphs (and you may have more of them than most people). They will also get position on you by changing their seats. Even weaker players will learn to exploit your vulnerability to check-raising, slow playing, and inviting you to bluff.

Your motives: You don't play to win, but may pretend you do. You are addicted to action, love attention, and can't resist challenges. These motives cause you to take foolish chances and to deny reality, including your losses and the effects of your style.

Stylistic changes: You can't win without becoming tighter and more *selectively* aggressive.

Specific changes needed:

- *Calm down.* Listen to your head, not your heart.
- *Tighten up.* Play fewer hands and stop chasing so much.

- *Attack weaker players and avoid stronger ones*. Good ones won't play without an edge. Gamble *only* with other gamblers.
- *Develop card reading skill* by observing after folding or while waiting to play.
- *Exploit your image:* Mix up your game. Make people think you are still loose-aggressive while becoming more tight-aggressive.

Right games: Lowest limits you can stand. Many LAPs. Short-handed.

Loose-Passive Opponents

Look for them if you want to win easily, but beware of the frustrations and boredom.

Play with them? Yes. Easiest to beat, but so easy it can be boring, and you will be frustrated when they play terrible cards, then draw out on you.

Where to sit? On their immediate right because they don't raise often, or on their immediate left to raise and isolate them with their weak hands.

Read their cards: You can't understand their calls because they play almost anything. They don't bet weak or marginal hands; they may not even bet some good ones; and they don't raise without excellent ones. A reraise signals "the nuts." They rarely bluff (and a few of them never do).

Strategic objective: Maximize profits, but accept that they will repeatedly draw out on you.

Strategic adjustments: Be nice. Don't try for every bet, and *never* criticize or humiliate them.

Specific changes: Bet or raise with questionable hands. Don't bluff. Don't call with marginal or even OK hands. If they raise, run.

Loose-passive games: Easiest to beat, but frustrating and sometimes boring.

Accept that the rules are different. You will lose many hands that you would usually win. The increased size of your winning pots will more than compensate you for your unexpected losses. Many pots quickly become so large that loose calls become correct or nearly so. You have to show down the best hand to win. You will usually need a better hand to win. High cards and pairs go down in value, while drawing hands become much more valuable.

Adjusting to these different rules. Make winning the pot your first priority. Be nice, even when someone beats you with a miracle card. Play more hands than usual, especially draws. Put less value on unsuited high cards. Bet or raise with weaker hands than usual to increase your chances of winning the pot. Raise with strong draws. Resist the temptation to make certain raises that will make the pot so big that promiscuous calling becomes a nearly correct strategy. Finally, to make sure you've gotten the message, I'll repeat it: *Make winning the pot, not increasing its size, your first priority.*

If You are Loose-Passive

Consequences: Lose lots of money because you give action, but don't get it. Welcome everywhere. Can relax and socialize. Many people are secretly or even openly contemptuous.

Strengths: Competitively, you have no strengths. You give action, but do not get it. From a social and recreational perspective, you can relax, pass the time, and enjoy socializing.

Weaknesses: Competitively, your style is all weaknesses. You lose too much on your weak hands, and do not win enough on your good hands. Most importantly, you lose many pots by giving free cards that beat you.

Your motives: Since your style is hopeless, you don't play to win. You play to relax, pass time, socialize, and express your need to please other people, plus, perhaps, get the kick of taking a risk.

Stylistic changes: You don't have a chance without getting tighter and more aggressive.

Specific changes needed:

- *Study* some basic books.
- *Tighten up.* You *must* play fewer hands and stop chasing so much.
- *Play more aggressively* without trying to change your basic self. Specifically, check less, and bet, raise, and bluff more.
- *Sit to the left of aggressive players.* Let them act before you do, then fold if necessary.
- *Develop card reading skill* by taking an observer's role.
- *Exploit your image*, especially by bluffing.

Right games: Lowest limits you can stand. Many LPPs. Friendly, relaxed atmosphere.

Tight-Passive Opponents

Beware: They are hard to beat and frustrating. If your frustrations and impatience make you gamble with them, they will beat you.

Play with them? Probably not, unless the rest of the game is easy.

Where to sit? To their right because they rarely raise, and you can steal their blinds and bring-ins.

Read their cards: Very easy. They don't call without good cards, raise without excellent ones, or reraise without at least a near-lock.

Strategic objective: Win modestly by keeping your head. Don't expect or try for a big win.

Strategic adjustments: Don't yield to your boredom and desire for action. Don't give them any more action than they give you. Bluff and semi-bluff frequently, but selectively.

Specific changes: Don't call without a good hand or raise without a great one. On the end, don't bet marginal or even OK hands, even after they check. Don't check-raise or slow-play. Bluff or semi-bluff often, but selectively. Steal their blinds or antes.

Tight-passive games: Don't expect much action or profit. Control your impatience and frustration.

Accept that the rules are different. Fewer people will be in each pot; more hands will end before showdown; and weaker hands than usual will win most pots. Pairs and high cards go up in value, and draws go way down.

Adjust to these different rules. Call early round bets *less* frequently. Become much less aggressive except bluff, semi-bluff, and steal blinds and antes more often. Avoid pure drawing hands.

If You are Tight-Passive

Consequences: Win a little in the right games; lose a little in the wrong ones. Boredom and frustration. Often bluffed. Can relax and socialize. Not welcome. Others are hostile or contemptuous.

Strengths: Extreme patience, the single most important quality. It will make you a winner in most small games. Your style also lets you relax and enjoy a steady stream of small wins with infrequent, small losses.

Weaknesses. You will probably lose to fairly skilled players, but you should not lose much. You do not get enough value from your winners, are very vulnerable to bluffs, and do not steal enough pots. You also give too many free cards that beat you. You may also be bored or frustrated by the poor action and negative attitudes about you.

Your motives: Conservative, prefer small steady wins, low risks, with small and infrequent losses, to larger profits and greater risks. Socialize, pass time, relax.

Stylistic change: Stay tight, but get more aggressive.

Specific changes needed:

- *Avoid* playing "weak-tight."
- *Create* a looser image.
- *Sit to left* of aggressive players.
- *Don't* give so many free cards.
- *Develop* card reading skill after folding.
- *Slow-play* big hands.
- *Check-raise* selectively.
- *Invite* people to bluff.

- *Call* more often on the river.
- *Exploit your image,* especially by bluffing and stealing blinds or antes.

Right games: Lowest limits you can tolerate. Smallest antes or blinds. Many LPPs. No more than one aggressive player, especially not an LAP. Large pool of players. A full table.

Tight-Aggressive Opponents

Avoid and Beware: They are the hardest to beat. Your wins will be small; your losses could be huge.

Play with them? Not unless the game is otherwise soft; you want to test yourself, or you want to learn from them.

Where to sit? On their left or as far away as possible.

Reading their cards is difficult because they are so deceptive and analytic, and they bet or raise for varied purposes. Try to learn their purposes and their opinions of the opposing players and hands.

Strategic adjustments: Don't play unless you are at your best. Avoid confrontations.

Specific changes: Mix up your game. Bluff less often, but be willing to semi-bluff. Don't bet marginal hands for value. Don't raise without a great hand. Check-raise less often. Don't steal their blinds.

Tight-aggressive games: The toughest games of all; *beware and avoid.*

The rules are not *different.* Most good poker writers play in and write about these games.

Adjusting to these tough games. Don't play unless you have a *strong* desire to test yourself or learn from them. Even then, don't play unless you are at your very best, and the game is *not* short-handed. Decide how much you will risk, and don't rebuy. Tighten up, especially on early streets. Pick your seat very carefully. Follow the rules for playing against TAPs, even after they fold.

If You are Tight-Aggressive

Consequences: Win if play within your limitations; go broke if you ignore them. May damage health. Not welcome in most games. Respect, especially from good players. Many players will envy and/or dislike you.

Your motives: Make money, test yourself, get a sense of accomplishment from winning.

Stylistic changes: None needed for these motives. If you also want to relax and socialize, soften style *slightly.* Generally, stay right where you are.

Specific changes:
- *Soften* your image.
- *Let* people enjoy playing with you.
- *Don't* try to win every last dollar (you'll get more of them in the long run).

Right games: The biggest you can handle. Experiment until you find your level. Move up slowly, and don't move further until you prove yourself at that level. Don't risk your whole bankroll in the bigger game. If necessary, move down to the level where you are most comfortable and effective. It's better to win consistently at $20-$40 than to struggle to survive at $50-$100.

Appendix D

Suggested Reading

Alvarez, A., *The Biggest Game in Town,* Boston, MA, Houghtin Mifflin, 1983.

If you like anecdotes about great players and big money, you'll love this book. Ignore his rather pretentious sociological observations, and don't expect it to help your game. It will also give professionals a glimpse of the life they can anticipate if they make it big. It's a bit dated, but things don't change that much.

Brunson, Doyle, (with many collaborators) *Super/System: A Course in Power Poker.* Second edition, B and G Publishing Co., Inc., 1994

He and his collaborators are champions, and they offer advice about all of the major games. The book is a little dated, but very worthwhile. However, people without great intuition could get into lots of trouble trying to imitate his style, especially in no-limit hold 'em.

Caro, Mike, *The Body Language of Poker: Mike Caro's Book of Tells,* Van Nuys, CA, Gambling Times, Inc, 1994, distributed by Carol Publishing Group, 120 Enterprise Ave, Seacaucus, NJ 07094.

By far the best book on this subject. I recommend it without any reservations. However, his statements about how much money you will make from learning this or that tell are utter nonsense. Also, many advanced players have read it and know how to send confusing signals.

Caro, Mike, *Fundamental Secrets of Poker,* Las Vegas, Nevada, Mad Genius Info, 1991.

A short, easy to read book with lots of ideas on strategy and psychology. For beginners only.

Ciaffone, Bob, *Omaha Poker, The Action Game, Millenium Edition,* (self published), 1999

Ciaffone, Bob, *Improve Your Poker,* (self published), 1997

Cooke, Roy with Bond, John, *Real Poker: The Cooke Collection,* Hollywood Park, CA, Mike Caro University, 1999

Some excellent columns on a wide variety of subjects. His refreshing criticism of his mistakes helps us to admit and correct our own mistakes.

Feeney, John, *Inside the Poker Mind; Essays on Hold 'em and General Poker Concepts,* Henderson, NV, Two Plus Two Publishing LLC, 2000

This collection of essays for intermediate and advanced players emphasizes the thought processes of poker — particularly hold 'em — and suggests strategies for moving to higher limits. The author, a clinical psychologist, addresses or presents new insights into topics — particularly "emotion and poker" — which other writers have barely discussed.

Hayano, David, *Poker Faces: The Life and Work of Professional Poker Players,* Berkeley, CA: The University of California Press, 1982.

The most thorough and scholarly book on this subject, but it is somewhat dated. Anyone considering turning professional should definitely read it.

Malmuth, Mason, *Poker Essays, Poker Essays: Volume II*, and *Gambling Theory and Other Topics,* Henderson, NV, Two Plus Two Publishing LLC, 1996 and 1999.

Some of his best columns on a wide variety of subjects. On many of these subjects — especially choosing a game — he offers the best advice you can get.

Oliver, Gary, *Low Limit 7-card Stud, Casino Strategy,* Phoenix, Arizona, Poker Tips, 1991.

A simple book on basic strategy. It is useful only for beginners.

Othmer, Konstantin with Ekkehard Othmer, *Elements of Seven Card Stud,* 1992, Cupertino, CA Strategy One Publishing

An outstanding book. It is extremely well organized and provides more solid evidence than you will find in nearly all books. However, in places it is hard to read. Use it to learn basic strategy, then refer to it repeatedly as a reference.

Percy, George, *Seven Card Stud: The Waiting Game,* 1979, (self published)

The title says it all. It could be titled, *How To Be A Rock.* Since the most common and destructive mistake in poker is being too loose, his advice is well worth taking. However, he takes it too far, and his charts are boring and confusing.

Silberstang, Edwin, *Winning Poker for the Serious Player: The Ultimate Money Making Guide*, New York, Cardoza Publishing, 1992.

A good book for near beginners. The title is misleading; it is much too basic for serious players.

Sklansky, David, *The Theory of Poker,* Henderson, NV, Two Plus Two Publishing LLC, 1994 and 1999

This book established his justified reputation as poker's foremost theorist. Instead of focusing on one game, he considers theoretical issues that apply to all games, such as pot and implied odds, semi-bluffing, and adjusting to short-handed games. His "Fundamental Theorem of Poker" is probably the most original and useful idea I have ever read on poker. An excellent book for serious players, but too advanced and abstract for casual players.

Sklansky, David, *Hold 'em Poker,* Henderson, NV, Two Plus Two Publishing LLC, 1976, 1989, and 1997.

The first book on the game. A worthwhile primer, but not as good as its sequels, *Hold 'em Poker for Advanced Players* and *Hold 'em Poker for Advanced Players: 21st Century Edition.*

Sklansky, David and Malmuth, Mason, *Hold 'em Poker for Advanced Players: 21st Century Edition,* Henderson, NV, Two Plus Two Publishing LLC, 1999

The best book on hold 'em. In addition, this new edition includes extended discussions of general strategy and playing in loose and short-handed games that apply to nearly all poker games, not just hold 'em.

Sklansky, David; Malmuth, Mason; and Zee, Ray, *Seven Card Stud for Advanced Players: 21st Century Edition*, Henderson, NV, Two Plus Two Publishing LLC, 1999

Sklansky, David, *Getting The Best of It*, Henderson, NV, Two Plus Two Publishing LLC, 1997.

Zee, Ray, *High-Low Split Poker for Advanced Players*, Henderson, NV, Two Plus Two Publishing, 1994.

Index

NOTES

NOTES

NOTES